THE CHALLENGE IN KASHMIR

THE CHALLENGE IN KASHMIR

Democracy, Self-Determination and a Just Peace

Sumantra Bose

Sage Publications
New Delhi/Thousand Oaks/London
in association with
The Book Review Literary Trust
New Delhi

First published in 1997 by

Sage Publications India Pvt Ltd
M–32 Greater Kailash Market–I
New Delhi 110 048

Sage Publications Inc
2455 Teller Road
Thousand Oaks, California 91320

Sage Publications Ltd
6 Bonhill Street
London EC2A 4PU

Published by Tejeshwar Singh for Sage Publications India Pvt Ltd, typeset by Line Arts Phototypesetters, Pondicherry and printed at Chaman Enterprises, Delhi.

Library of Congress Cataloging-in-Publication Data

Bose, Sumantra, 1968–
    The challenge in Kashmir: democracy, self-determination, and a just peace / Sumantra Bose.
        p. cm.
    Includes bibliographical references and index.
    I. Title.
DS485.K27B67   1996b   320.954′6—dc20   96–36651

ISBN: 0–8039–9350-1 (US–HB)   81–7036–592-9 (India–HB)

Sage Production Editors: Malathi Ramamoorthy and
                       Pramod Kumar Singh

To the memory of Subhas Chandra Bose
who united the subcontinent then
and continues to inspire all its peoples today
in the centenary year of his birth

and

To the people of Jammu & Kashmir

Contents

Preface

Why another book on the conflict in and over Kashmir? Hasn't that vexed topic been flogged to death already?

This book is an initially unintended by-product of research towards my doctoral dissertation at Columbia University. That study, when it is published a couple of years from now, is likely to be rather different from this one. Titled 'Democracy and National Self-Determination: A Comparative Inquiry', it is a theoretically-structured, strictly 'academic' study which goes to the heart of some of the currently salient issues and debates among scholars of comparative politics. As such, it is intended to make a contribution to democratic theory (of both empirical and normative varieties), and to comparative scholarship on nationalism, especially the problem of 'self-determination' in the contemporary world.

The link of this book to that research is that that study uses the question of 'self-determination' in Kashmir (in relation to Indian democracy) as one of several cases analysed in a cross-national, cross-regional theoretical framework—Kashmir's hapless companions in this daunting yet superbly challenging intellectual enterprise being the Tamil problem in Sri Lanka (which has already had the misfortune of being exposed to my close attention and scrutiny), the breakdown of Yugoslavia's one-party socialist federation and its aftermath, the Quebec issue in Canada and the Basque and Catalan questions in post-Franco democratic Spain. Yet as my work progressed, I became increasingly convinced that a subject of the topicality and importance (in manifold ways) of the struggle in Kashmir merited a book-length study in its own right. The question that remained was whether I would be able to make a contribution that was sufficiently original and distinctive from the existing literature, so as to make the venture worthwhile—for me and for everybody else.

While that judgment is ultimately for the discerning and thoughtful reader to make, I am now personally satisfied that I have been at least reasonably successful in that objective. I was not so confident, however, when I drafted the first version of this manuscript in April 1994. But as I presented the (constantly evolving) manuscript at seminars and conferences on three continents during 1994 and 1995, I was immensely heartened by the (somewhat unexpectedly) positive response I received from quite diverse audiences, consisting of a cross-section of scholars, policy specialists and practitioners, and undergraduate and graduate students, among others. But that in itself was not sufficient to induce me to take the plunge into writing a book on a subject which is, virtually by definition, a veritable whirlpool of contention and controversy.

What decided me was my experience during the summer months of 1995, which I spent in intensive field research throughout the violence-wracked zones of Indian-administered Jammu & Kashmir (J&K). That experience, more productive, and instructive, than I had ever imagined possible, owed much to the unbelievable courtesy, generosity and helpfulness of my dear friends there, old and new. What made it so instructive? That is more difficult to convey, but in a nutshell I can say this. Though I have in the past few years had plenty of first-hand experience of devastated, war-ravaged societies in Sri Lanka and the former Yugoslavia, and plenty of opportunity to admire and marvel at the courage and grace of people compelled to live in such environments, I have never before witnessed the suffering and oppression, and the resilience and fortitude of the human spirit that I have encountered in Kashmir.

In this volume, I have tried to combine multiple (if organically interrelated) goals and synthesise several ingredients—an incisive if complex and nuanced set of central arguments with a sense of flowing narrative; a substantial critical discussion of the various empirical aspects and attributes of a highly complicated and multidimensional problem; and an informed contribution to the compelling practical imperative of finding ways of alleviating and eventually resolving that problem. While I have consciously attempted to keep the account readable and the analysis lucid (thereby making this work accessible and interesting, I hope, to a wide cross-section of the non-academic reading public as well), I have also tried to take special care not to compromise intellectual rigour in the process. The one chapter in which I *have* allowed my vocation, that of a comparative political scientist, somewhat free rein is Chapter 5, which is by far the most theoretically-oriented of all the chapters. It is also, however, an essential complement to the more empirically-oriented chapters: a problem such as Kashmir fairly cries out to be situated and analysed in an explicitly comparative framework and perspective.

A few more *caveats* may be warranted. As I stress in the introduction and in other parts of this study, my focus is squarely on the Kashmir question in its *contemporary* dynamics and manifestation. The 'historical review' chapter is thus intentionally short and concise. Though this is partly because there already are a number of competent and informative studies of the genesis and historical and legal aspects of the Kashmir question (practically all published in the 1950s and 1960s), this approach is primarily motivated by my concern that an emphasis on historical background should not become burdensome and irrelevant baggage, as it has an insidious tendency of becoming when the subject of analysis is the Kashmir question. For, while developing this study, I concurrently developed a firm conviction that the historical roots of the crisis have little to do with the pressing political problem in Jammu & Kashmir today.

Second, in the course of research, I became conscious of the quite astounding amount of 'disinformation' (a euphemistic expression for lies, distortions and myths) that has accumulated over the past fifty years, but with noticeably renewed vigour since 1990, on the Kashmir conflict. It is partly for this reason that I have been reluctantly compelled to expend not inconsiderable time, space and energy on those dimensions and issues of the Kashmir conflict on which the accumulation of such irritating but nonetheless profoundly dangerous nonsense has been most prolific (for example, the circumstances surrounding the unfortunate exodus of the majority of the Kashmiri Hindu population from the Valley in 1990, or the ideological and mobilisational role a shared Muslim identity has played in the *azaadi* uprising). I felt it was necessary to address such questions head-on, and not simply because 'disinformation' on these and other issues enjoys widespread currency, especially in India and Pakistan. My more basic reason is that these issues are intrinsically important to understanding the Kashmir question today, and, I believe, in confronting the challenge it poses—the challenge of realising the inseparably interconnected objectives of democracy, self-determination and a just peace—in which the future of the entire South Asian subcontinent is fundamentally at stake.

Finally, some might find it useful to note in advance that I do not *necessarily* make any *a priori* claims to 'impartiality' or 'objectivity'. There are profound moral and ethical questions involved in this conflict, and only the idiot or the scoundrel would claim that she/he has discovered a way of transcending those in a perfectly detached and 'dispassionate' analysis of the problem. As I have occasion to discuss at some length in Chapter 4, the pretence of 'objectivity' is just that—a pretence. There is simply no social or political science that is entirely uninfluenced by the scholar's own normative orientation and values—this is simply not possible, and even if it were, it would not be desirable. Those who propagate the absurd fiction of an unbiased scholarly truth are thus either desperately deluded or disgracefully dishonest, or some peculiar combination of both. In any case, I happen to be proud of my own normative orientation and values, and I strongly believe that they can only enhance and enrich, never undermine, the credentials of my professional work.

That said, I should also mention that when, for example, I give significant attention to the scale of human rights violations in Indian-administered Kashmir since 1990, I do so not principally to 'foul-mouth' anyone (though I do believe that such abuses should be publicised as widely as possible), but because comprehending the magnitude and nature of such abuses, and their political implications, is essential to an informed understanding of the Kashmir conflict in its present phase. The careful reader will also find that in this book I do not advocate any particular solution as a panacea to the challenge in Kashmir. While I am markedly more sympathetic to some points of view than others (and more harshly critical of some positions than others), I emphasise throughout this study, especially in Chapters 5 and 6, that there are no obvious or readymade solutions that can miraculously resolve this conflict. My investigation has in fact led to the somewhat depressing inference that even with the utmost sincerity, goodwill and a spirit of cooperation and compromise on all sides (which, needless to say, does not exist), a workable solution that does justice to the (often conflicting) aspirations of the various social groups and political tendencies that exist today in what was, in 1947, the princely state of Jammu & Kashmir, would be extremely difficult to devise in theory, let alone implement in practice. But I have argued even more strongly that this reality does not at all obviate the need for searching for ways to meet the equally real challenge of democracy, 'self-determination' and a just peace in Kashmir and in South Asia.

While working on this book, I have sometimes felt like a tight-rope walker or trapeze artist. I have constantly struggled to reconcile a perspective characterised by at least a degree of vision (which I think it is indispensable to retain, for without it any work of this nature becomes stunted in ideas and impoverished in substance), with an approach which is sensitive to the unavoidable exigencies and constraints imposed on the problem in Kashmir by considerations of realpolitik. I have done my best to combine and harmonise these sometimes competing but by no means incompatible sets of imperatives, and I trust I have been reasonably successful in doing so.

Research for this work commenced in late 1993, and culminated in an extended field trip to Indian-administered Jammu & Kashmir during the summer of 1995. During this trip, I visited (in addition to my base, Srinagar) virtually every town in the Kashmir Valley, including Baramulla, Sopore, Kupwara and Handwara in northern Kashmir and Anantnag/Islamabad, Bijbehera, Awantipora and Pampore in the southern part of the Valley. I also travelled to many remote villages in the rural areas of the Valley. In addition, I extensively toured the Jammu region, including Jammu city, camps in Jammu district housing Kashmiri Hindus (Pandits) who have migrated from the Valley since 1990, and the towns and rural interior of the highly mountainous, insurgency-wracked district of Doda, which borders the southern areas of the Valley. I had in-depth conversations with most leading political figures (of wildly diverse persuasions) in Indian-administered Jammu & Kashmir, with prominent members of the academic and professional intelligentsia, and with numerous political activists and many hundreds of ordinary people at the grass-roots level in towns and villages throughout Jammu & Kashmir.

I am particularly grateful to the following persons for sharing their thoughts, views and experiences with me (sites of interviews are given in parentheses): Mohammad Yasin Malik, chairman of

Jammu & Kashmir Liberation Front or JKLF (Srinagar and Calcutta); Shabbir Ahmed Shah, leader of People's League (Srinagar); Shakeel Ahmed Bakshi, general secretary of JKLF (Srinagar); Abdul Ghani Lone, leader of People's Conference or PC and a senior figure in the All-Party Hurriyat Conference or APHC (Srinagar); Syed Ali Shah Geelani, chief of Jama'at-i-Islami in Indian-administered Jammu & Kashmir (Srinagar); Ghulam Mohammed Butt, deputy chief of Jama'at-i-Islami in Indian-administered Jammu & Kashmir (New York); Altaf Ahmad Khan *alias* Azam Inquillabi, leader of Mahaz-e-Azaadi (Srinagar); Abdul Ghani Butt, head of Muslim Conference or MC (Srinagar); Abdul Qayyoom, leader of the Jammu & Kashmir Janata Dal (Srinagar); Chaman Lal Gupta, general secretary of the Bharatiya Janata Party (BJP) for Jammu & Kashmir (Jammu city); Manmohan Gupta, Doda district president of BJP (Kishtwar town, district Doda); Mehmooda Andrabi, organiser of *Dukhtaran-i-Islam* or Daughters of Islam (Doda town); Mohammad Qasim Khokhar, JKLF leader in Mirpur, a major town in Pakistan-controlled ('Azad') Kashmir (New York); Haleem Khan, JKLF organiser in rural Poonch, 'Azad Kashmir' (New York); Zafar Khan, JKLF (Amanullah Khan group) general secretary for diplomatic and international affairs (London); Afzal Khan Tahir, secretary for international affairs of the Jammu & Kashmir People's National Party (JKPNP), based in 'Azad Kashmir' (New York); Ved Bhasin, editor-in-chief of *Kashmir Times*, the most respected and influential daily newspaper in Indian-administered Jammu & Kashmir (Jammu and Calcutta); Dr Mirajuddin Munshi, eminent medical specialist of Srinagar and prominent JKLF sympathiser (New York); Jalil Andrabi, senior human rights lawyer in Srinagar and JKLF supporter (Calcutta and New York); Ghulam Nabi Hagroo, leading lawyer of Srinagar and APHC functionary (New York); several senior members of the departments of history, political science and sociology at Kashmir University (Srinagar); Professor A.C. Bose, former head of the Department of History at Jammu University (Jammu city); and a sizeable number of guerrilla fighters (so-called militants or mujahideen) and spokesmen of various insurgent groups active in Indian-administered Jammu & Kashmir (Kashmir Valley and Doda).

Heartfelt thanks, warm affection and gratitude go to Imtiaz Ahmed Sofi, Abdul Ghani Khan and Ved Bhasin for making my stay in Jammu & Kashmir as productive (and enjoyable, in the circumstances) as it turned out to be. Raju Kerni, Khursheed-ul Islam and

Shujaat Bukhari also took out time to help me with my field research. A special note of appreciation must go to Qasim Khokhar for his friendship. Thanks are also due to the Rangrez family of Srinagar, especially to Nissar.

I am very grateful to the Institute for the Study of World Politics (Washington, D.C.) for providing financial support which enabled travel to and fieldwork in Jammu & Kashmir. The Social Science Research Council–MacArthur Foundation Program in International Peace and Security helped boost morale by awarding me a Dissertation Fellowship.

At Sage Publications India (Delhi), I would like to thank Harsh Sethi, Acquisitions Editor, for his efficient assistance and enthusiastic support.

I have given conference presentations and seminars based on material from various parts of this manuscript at King's College, University of Cambridge (June 1994), the Delhi School of Economics (January 1995) and Columbia University (October 1995).

All responsibility for the contents of and views expressed in this book, however, rests with me alone. A couple of minor additional points should also be noted: quotations in the text, without footnotes, are from personal interviews I had with the person(s) quoted; and in some cases (especially conversations with ordinary citizens in Jammu & Kashmir) I have changed names and/or addresses for reasons of security.

Finally, some thanks of a more personal nature. To Amrita Basu, whose role as an anchor and source of good and caring counsel in my life and work has, happily (for me), increased in the years since I graduated from Amherst College. To Lisa Anderson, whose quiet yet steadfast support, and confidence in my abilities, at Columbia University means more to me than she probably realises.

To Shahzad and Nancy, for their affection and support as we toiled away in very different fields of graduate study on the East Coast of the United States. To Rajesh, for his jokes and ready help in times of computer crises. To Shi, for sharing in the irreverent humour that is so crucial to dealing with our common predicament as political scientists. To Joydeep and Sophie, for being such good friends—their wonderful presence has made New York a much better place for me in the past year. To Ananjan, who claims to have discovered the real reason for my fascination with Kashmir—and wishes this claim to be recorded in the preface to my book.

To my brother, sister, brother-in-law and little nephew.

Lastly, to my father and mother, Sisir K. Bose and Krishna Bose, for not just tolerating but encouraging the interests and opinions of their son that less versatile parents might just have found, well, a bit intimidating.

Calcutta and New York
April 1996

Sumantra Bose

1

Introduction

The question or need for...plebiscite in any part of India, including Jammu & Kashmir, simply does not arise. The people of Jammu & Kashmir have exercised their democratic rights repeatedly, as [have] people in other parts of India.

— Foreign Ministry, Government of India, January 1994

Kashmir is the jugular vein of Pakistan and the day is not far when it will be a part of this country.

— Benazir Bhutto, prime minister of Pakistan, January 1994

About 7–8 per cent of them [Kashmiri Muslims] want to stay with us [India]. About 10 per cent want to join Pakistan. The rest want independence.

— A top Indian politician and high-ranking Cabinet Minister in the Government of India, February 1992 (in private conversation)

Freedom is our birthright. We will all die, but we will never give it up. We refuse to remain in India as subjugated slaves. But neither do we wish to exchange one gulami [slavery] for another. We say no to India and Pakistan with equal vehemence. Our struggle is for one thing only: Azaadi *[independence].*

— 'Shahbaz', military commander of Jammu & Kashmir Liberation Front (JKLF) for Srinagar city, capital of Indian-administered Jammu & Kashmir (personal interview with author, early 1994)

'Kashmir', wrote Kalhana, the twelfth-century Kashmiri historian and chronicler, 'can be conquered by the power of spiritual merit, but never by the force of soldiers'.[1] As the popular Kashmiri uprising against Indian Army, paramilitary and police troops continues in its seventh year, at least the latter part of that wise observation seems to bear considerable plausibility. Alienation from the Indian state (synonymous, in Kashmiri eyes, with a regime of occupation), and mass sentiment in favour of independence (not incorporation into Pakistan) is still quite strong in the Kashmir Valley, and has caught on in at least one district of the Jammu region as well. Pro-*azaadi* and pro-unification feelings have also been growing, especially since the late 1980s, among the inhabitants of Pakistani-controlled 'Azad' ('Liberated') Kashmir.

Yet in the constant cacophony of competing Indian and Pakistani claims to Jammu & Kashmir, the conflict usually gets presented as simply a long-running, intractable 'territorial dispute' between belligerent rival states. In the process, the aspirations and interests of the *peoples* who populate this benighted territory are frequently obscured, or mentioned merely as a marginal afterthought. This is so despite the penchant of both regional powers to pay lip-service to 'the people of Jammu & Kashmir'. One normative goal of this study is to challenge this wholly unwarranted imbalance and omission, which is common to scholars and policy-makers alike. More particularly, I seek to illuminate the linkages between the uprising in Indian-administered Kashmir and the two most powerful collective urges of our times: the struggle for democratic government, and the quest for 'national self-determination'.

One position on this conflict, reflected most frequently in the pronouncements of what might broadly be termed the Indian 'establishment', rests crucially on the claim that Jammu & Kashmir has, since 1947, been an integral and functional part of a 'democracy', and a 'federal' one, at that. Hence, the current uprising is both illegitimate and anti-democratic. It simply cannot be regarded in any sense as a struggle for democratic rights and freedoms; and, of course, as the product of an externally engineered conspiracy, masterminded by Pakistan, it cannot claim the mantle of an indigenously born emancipatory movement either.[2] In any case, the notion of Kashmiris constituting a social formation that might, conceivably, lay claim to the title of a people in its own right is precluded by the Indian state's legitimising ideology, which holds, explicitly or implicitly, that the only bonafide 'nation', to which citizens owe the duty of allegiance, is the pan-Indian one.[3] On the contrary, Indian military forces combating 'Pakistan-sponsored' terrorists, fundamentalists and secessionists are the true defenders of democracy, of the 'nation' and its territorial integrity, and, of course, of 'secularism', that other pillar of the post-colonial Indian state.

This book will argue, among many other things, that the position just described is bereft of almost any vestige of logic or accuracy. The mass base and dogged determination of the 'secessionist' urge in Kashmir today can be explained, I will argue, by one factor alone: the Indian state's consistent policy of denying democracy, *even* in the minimalistic sense of what the democratic theorist Robert Dahl (1971)[4] has called 'polyarchy', to its citizens in Jammu & Kashmir. This denial of democracy has historically taken two major forms. First, the reduction of representative government to a travesty through repression, fraud and manipulation of ostensibly multiparty electoral processes; second, the systematic subversion and destruction of the federal autonomy which was a *condition* of Jammu & Kashmir's accession in 1947 to the Indian Union.

There are other causal elements involved as well—for example, rampant official corruption and biased and inequitable patterns of recruitment into government service. But these are merely subsidiary problems that have arisen because of the deeper malaise. Similarly, while there is the problem of continuing urban and especially, rural poverty, as well as widespread unemployment of educated youth in the Kashmir Valley, economic factors do not seem to be the *primary cause* of rebellion. Poverty, corruption and unemployment in the subcontinent are not unique to Kashmir, though these problems have assumed *some* (though still secondary) significance, when taken in conjunction with the two basic causes outlined in the preceding paragraph, which *are* unique to Kashmir. And, of course, the policy of massive and largely indiscriminate repression, which has, so far, been the Indian state's *sole* substantive response to the Kashmiri insurrection, is antithetical to any known principle or practice of democracy.

This, according to the vast majority of Kashmiris (who happen to be Muslims), constitutes intolerable injustice and oppression, and they are apparently prepared to make considerable sacrifices in order to resist this oppression. And the reason why they seem so insistent on 'freedom' (which means, above all, freedom from Indian rule), is the conviction, born of their experiences, that their collective will for democratic, responsible and accountable government is incompatible with their presently *coerced* (as opposed to voluntary and freely consenting) status as 'an integral part of India'.

Democracy and 'self-determination' have thus become convergent, even if in practice often inchoate, focal points of their political aspirations, for popularly endorsed government, in any context, necessarily presupposes at least a measure of self-rule. This is neither an arbitrary coincidence nor a sudden development. As I will show, the political history of Kashmir in the twentieth century is that of an almost continuous, though largely futile, struggle for these interrelated goals: popularly mandated, accountable government, which necessarily presupposes that the body of citizens thus governed is not subject to domination that may be perceived by them (or even gradually comes to be perceived by them) as externally imposed and coercive. Indeed, the Kashmiri popular movement by and large favoured some form of *honourable* association with India in 1947 precisely because these aspirations seemed consistent with the founding principles of a 'democratic' and 'federal' Indian Republic. Today, however, Kashmiris stand sadly disillusioned, and it is the false promises and broken hopes that explain, more than anything else, the rage of a younger generation that has risen in armed revolt.

This work critically explores a number of aspects and issues central to an informed understanding of the contemporary configuration and dynamics of the Kashmir question, which, everyone agrees, is extraordinarily complex. Of course, one should also reiterate that the challenge is not simply one of a workable, durable and democratic resolution to the Kashmir conflict, but also involves the future of the subcontinent as a whole. As is well-known, two of the three Indo-Pakistani wars since 1947 have resulted directly from conflict over Kashmir, and the Damoclean sword of another, infinitely more devastating exchange will continue to threaten the subcontinent until a lasting solution to the Kashmir question has been found. But, as I will argue, the Kashmir problem, precisely because of its centrality to Indo-Pakistani relations (which makes a just and permanent solution so very difficult to visualise, leave alone achieve, at one level), also, perhaps paradoxically, presents an exceptional opportunity to inaugurate a new era in the history of the subcontinent.

Looking Ahead: A Brief Outline of the Study

This book draws upon a considerable range of primary as well as secondary research, and a brief outline of the conceptual and logistical organisation of the study is an appropriate conclusion to these introductory remarks. Conceptually, the book is structured around the twin themes of democracy and self-determination, as both relate in theory and practice to the Kashmir question; logistically, it is organised into seven chapters.

Chapter 2 sets the stage for the main thrust of the analysis through a brief background and review of the historical genesis and evolution of the Kashmir question, from the mid-nineteenth century to the immediate aftermath of decolonisation in the subcontinent.

Chapter 3 closely analyses, in an empirical framework, the fate of democracy and federalism in Jammu & Kashmir under India's democratic regime, and posits a key causal connection between this and the uprising for 'self-determination' that erupted in the 1990s.

Chapter 4 is devoted to a critical appraisal of issues central to the contemporary struggle for self-determination—the role and consequences of Indian state violence against the Kashmiri people since 1990; the continuing massive support for the idea of independence (and its significance) in the Valley and other areas populated predominantly by Kashmiri Muslims (as distinguished from pro-Pakistan sentiment, to which only a relatively small minority subscribe); the predicament of Pakistan-controlled Kashmir and its contemporary relevance to the Kashmir question in its totality; the question of 'communalisation' of Kashmiri identity (*Kashmiriyat*) following the 'exodus' of the bulk of the Kashmiri Hindu minority from the Valley in 1990; the ideological and mobilisational role of Islam in the movement for independence; the territorial and demographic complexities of 'self-determination' in the context of the political and social variations within and between the territory's distinct constituent regions, with a focus on Jammu (its internal heterogeneity as a region as well as its distinctiveness from the Valley).

In Chapter 5, I situate my analysis of the problems and prospects of democracy and self-determination with regard to Kashmir in an explicitly theoretical and comparative perspective, and within the context of a wide range of relevant scholarly literature on the (interrelated) topics of nationalism, 'ethnic conflict', the modern state and state power, and ideas as well as practical applications of democracy.

By way of a conclusion and epilogue, Chapter 6 comments on the longer-term implications of the emerging military and political situation in India-administered Jammu & Kashmir as of April 1996, and advances some general principles and broad suggestions pertaining to how progress towards an eventual just and lasting peace might be made.

Chapter 7, specially written for this volume in October 1996 after another field trip to Kashmir by the author in August 1996, critically analyses the implications of the revival of the electoral processes and institutions in Indian-administered Jammu & Kashmir for prospects of democracy and a lasting resolution to the struggle for 'self-determination'. This discussion of the most current developments and trends in Kashmir's politics is placed in the context of, and meaningfully related to, the broader themes and arguments of the book.

Notes

1. An English translation of his famous Sanskrit epic *Rajatarangini* (composed *ca.* 1150) is available in Stein (1991).
2. It remains unclear, though, how the Pakistani regime has suddenly succeeded in brainwashing several million people, after a remarkable absence of success for four decades.
3. The ideology of the 'Hindu nationalist' movement and of its political wing, the Bharatiya Janata Party (BJP), is but a variant of this officially sanctioned and promoted construct of Indian nationalism.
4. Dahl's delineation of the essential procedures and institutions of political democracy follows directly from Joseph Schumpeter's famous definition of 'realist democracy': 'The democratic method is that institutional arrangement for arriving at political decisions in which individuals acquire the power to decide by means of a competitive struggle for the people's vote' (Schumpeter: 269). The concept of polyarchy thus emphasises the free, competitive election of public officials through popular balloting. This, together with such associated norms as rule of law and civil rights, constitutes the minimal basis for any functioning democracy.

2

History and the Roots of Conflict

Colonialism and Kashmir

In 1846, a commercial transaction was concluded between the British, then preoccupied with bringing the entire subcontinent under their direct or indirect rule, and Gulab Singh, the Dogra king of Jammu. By the Treaty of Amritsar, the imperial authorities transferred, 'for ever', the Kashmir Valley and its adjoining territories to 'Maharaja Gulab Singh and the heirs male of his body', in exchange for the payment of a large sum of money. The British themselves had come into possession of this territory because of the gradual collapse, under sustained imperialist pressure, of the Sikh empire established by the Lahore-based ruler Ranjit Singh in northern and north-western India in the early nineteenth century, and which, at its height, included Kashmir. Indeed, the reason Gulab Singh was chosen as the beneficiary was that despite formally being a leading member of the Lahore court, he had been conniving with the British against Ranjit Singh's successors.

In return, Gulab Singh promised the British military support in their expeditions against the yet unsubordinated and recalcitrant peoples of the subcontinent. He also 'acknowledge[d] the supremacy of the British Government', and agreed to an annual token tribute to that government of 'one horse, twelve pairs of shawl goats of approved breed (six male and six female), and three pairs of Kashmir shawls' (Dasgupta 1968: 387–88). Gulab Singh had already taken over the remote and sparsely-populated mountainous regions of Ladakh and Baltistan, so with the acquisition of the Valley, he became the master of practically all the distinct regions that came to comprise the historical territory of the princely state of Jammu & Kashmir. He and his dynasty remained British vassals nonetheless. Indeed, by the time the end of empire came, Jammu & Kashmir was the largest of the system of 562 such princely states that the British had created throughout the subcontinent (covering 45 per cent of its land area), undoubtedly the most marvellous achievement of their famed construct, 'Indirect Rule'.

'For ever' lasted exactly a century, till the moment of decolonisation. For the peoples of Jammu & Kashmir, and especially the 77 per cent of state subjects who according to the Census of 1941 were Muslims (Hindus were the second-largest religious community, with 20 per cent), it was not a moment too soon. A Kashmiri Hindu writer, G.N. Kaul, paints a Dickensian picture of Srinagar in the early 1920s—prostitution, thievery, beggary, disease, illiteracy and unemployment were apparently rife, while '90 per cent of Muslim houses [were] ... mortgaged to Hindu moneylenders'. The 'plight of Sikhs was equally frightful', according to Kaul, while Pandits (Kashmiri Brahmins) seemed 'a little better-off' (Kaul 1968, cited in Akbar 1985: 221–22). As for the countryside, celebrated worldwide for its fabulous natural beauty, another Pandit writer and political activist, Premnath Bazaz (1987: 252–53), wrote thus in 1941:

> The poverty of the Muslim masses is appalling. Dressed in rags and barefoot, a Muslim peasant presents the appearance of a starving beggar ... most are landless labourers, working as serfs for absentee landlords ... almost the whole brunt of official corruption has been borne by the Muslim masses ... rural indebtedness is staggering.[1]

Indeed, by the 1920s, the absence of a mass uprising against this oppressive regime was being attributed to 'the exceptionally docile nature of the peasantry in the Vale' (Lamb 1966: 28). As a British official (Walter Lawrence) observed after touring the Valley at the turn of the century, 'the sight of blood is abhorrent to them [Kashmiris]' (quoted in Akbar 1985).[2]

Organised resistance commenced in 1931, led by a new generation of university-educated Kashmiri Muslim youth fresh from
Aligarh, the renowned centre of Muslim learning in north India.
On 13 July 1931, dozens of demonstrators were gunned down by
the Maharaja's police in Srinagar. A political organisation, the All
Jammu & Kashmir Muslim Conference, was formed in 1932 to
coordinate the popular movement for democratic government and
social justice. However, a split developed in the Muslim Conference in 1938 when almost its entire organisation in the Kashmir
Valley, led by the dynamic Sheikh Mohammad Abdullah, recon-
stituted itself as the National Conference (NC). This new force
declared its intent to 'end communalism by ceasing to think in
terms of Muslims and non-Muslims', and invited 'all Hindus and
Sikhs who like ourselves believe in the freedom of their country
from the shackles of an irresponsible rule' to participate as equals
in the democratic struggle (Lamb 1966: 31). At least a few Hindu
and Sikh members of the small urbanised intelligentsia responded
enthusiastically; by the 1940s, the NC leadership cadre included
religious minorities as well as Muslims.

The NC also swiftly consolidated its mass following in the
Valley. This was partly due to Abdullah's compelling personality
and charismatic leadership, but a much more important factor was
the party's adoption in 1944 of the social manifesto, 'Naya [New]
Kashmir', promising radical land reform once the monarchy had been
abolished. The socially conservative Muslim Conference, which
increasingly leaned towards Mohammed Ali Jinnah's All-India
Muslim League and its campaign for Pakistan, continued to be
strong in the Jammu region, especially the western Jammu districts
that later became part of 'Azad Kashmir'. It had deep roots among
the *biradaris* (extended kinship networks of landed oligarchies) in
Jammu. But in the Kashmiri heartland, the mantle of leadership
had passed to Abdullah, and his party went from strength to
strength, despite severe repression. In May 1946, the NC launched
a mass agitation which it called 'Quit Kashmir', (clearly modelled
on the Indian National Congress' 'Quit India' Movement of 1942)
against the last Maharaja, Hari Singh. Abdullah declared that 'the
time has come to tear up the Treaty of Amritsar ... sovereignty is
not the birthright of Maharaja Hari Singh. "Quit Kashmir" is not
a question of revolt. It is a matter of right' (Akbar 1985: 227–28).

Decolonisation and Kashmir

The circumstances of Jammu & Kashmir's accession to India have been recounted innumerable times, and from a variety of perspectives. Given my agenda in this volume, it is neither necessary nor desirable for me to dredge up that complicated and contentious story once again, and risk becoming mired in the facile polemics that have, to a large degree, come to dominate the increasingly irrelevant and tiresome debate over the legality and finality of accession. Therefore, I will only note a few crucial points, which are especially relevant to my broader arguments and to the analysis in the coming chapters.

As the British withdrawal approached, the beleaguered Maharaja, challenged by the popular movement for democratic change within his domain and buffeted by the cataclysmic events sweeping the subcontinent, was desperately trying to find a way to preserve his autocratic power. He even briefly toyed with the idea of working out an association with Pakistan once imperial paramountcy over Jammu & Kashmir lapsed on 15 August 1947, if Pakistan would agree to leave his throne intact. In July 1947 the Muslim Conference urged him to accede to Pakistan, which would then guarantee his privileges. By August, a limited 'standstill agreement' had indeed been concluded between the Maharaja and Pakistan, and the latter had formally been given charge of running the state's post and telegraph services and supplying the population with various essential commodities.[3]

However, things started to go awry from this point. Between August and October, a major local revolt against the Maharaja's authority developed among Muslims in the north-western Poonch area of Jammu. Hari Singh claimed, quite plausibly, that elements in the Pakistani government were actively aiding this revolt,[4] to which his forces responded with reprisals against the area's Muslim population at large. Meanwhile, the communal situation rapidly worsened. Hindu refugees fleeing systematic atrocities in western Punjab and the Frontier Province arrived in Jammu, and the Rashtriya Swayamsevak Sangh or RSS (the group which forms the ideological and organisational core of India's 'Hindu nationalist' movement), in connivance with the Maharaja's police, seized this opportunity to massacre and expel tens of thousands of Muslims from Jammu's eastern districts.

The climax to the growing crisis came in the fourth week of October, when several thousand bellicose Pathan tribesmen from the North-West Frontier Province (NWFP), led by a few former Indian National Army (INA) officers and supported with logistics and transport by the chief minister of that province, invaded the Kashmir Valley, ostensibly to liberate their coreligionists from the 'Hindu' yoke. The Maharaja's forces proved no match for them; within a week, the tribesmen had taken Baramulla, the town that is the north-western gateway to the Valley, and advanced to within 20 miles of Srinagar. During this offensive, as well as their subsequent retreat, they engaged in a campaign of indiscriminate murder, rape, arson and looting against the overwhelmingly Muslim population of the Valley. Memories of this carnage were to imbue an entire generation of Kashmiri Muslims with deep scepticism towards subsequent Pakistani rhetoric demanding Kashmiri 'self-determination'.

In this context of confusion and chaos, the panic-stricken Maharaja acceded to India on 26 October on condition that New Delhi immediately send its army to repel the invaders. Sheikh Abdullah, who had been freed from prison a few weeks earlier, quickly assumed control of the collapsing administration. By January 1949, when a United Nations-brokered ceasefire terminated the first Indo-Pakistani war, Indian troops, aided by well-organised NC workers, had largely expelled the tribesmen and Pakistani regulars (who joined the fray from early 1948) from the Valley, as well as from some contested areas in Jammu. The ceasefire left India in control of almost two-thirds of Jammu & Kashmir, including almost the entire Valley, most of Ladakh (excluding Skardu), and most of Jammu. A large chunk of western Jammu and Poonch (the MC's strongholds), as well as Gilgit and Baltistan, fell under Pakistan's control.[5]

It was however made clear from the outset that the *finality* of Hari Singh's accession to India was strictly conditional on 'a reference to the people' of Jammu & Kashmir, as Mountbatten, governor-general of the Indian Dominion, put it while accepting the Instrument of Accession. On 2 November, the Indian prime minister, Jawaharlal Nehru, declared his government's 'pledge' to 'hold a referendum under international auspices such as the United Nations' to determine whether the people wished to join India or Pakistan (Lamb 1966: 46–48). Nehru reiterated this pledge numerous times over the next several years at press conferences, public meetings and international fora. In August 1952, for example, he told the Indian Parliament that he wanted 'no ... forced unions', and that if the people of Jammu & Kashmir decided 'to part company from us, they can go their way and we shall go our way' (Noorani 1964: 61). Pakistan, after Jinnah's initial reluctance, also soon accepted in principle the idea of a referendum or plebiscite. Accordingly, the United Nations (UN) resolutions that led to the ceasefire visualised the establishment of a UN-appointed Plebiscite Administration (Dasgupta 1968: 395–403).

That 'reference to the people' has, of course, never been held. Three arguments are usually cited by Indian officialdom for this. The first, that Pakistani forces failed to vacate those parts of Jammu & Kashmir under their control (a pre-condition, under the United Nations resolutions, for the plebiscite), is arguably sound. The second, that the territory's 'lawful' ruler had acceded to India, thereby automatically confirming the validity of such accession, is also acceptable but more problematic. The fact remains that Nehru's government had committed itself to a plebiscite *despite* the legality of Hari Singh's accession. Besides, this argument implicitly vests absolute sovereignty in the person of a corrupt and despised autocrat, a stand which sharply contradicts the ethos of the democratic struggle in Kashmir, and presumably, that of the Indian national movement as well.

But it is the third contention which is most frequently invoked by those who support the case that Kashmir is 'an integral part of India'. This argument holds that the people of Jammu & Kashmir, acting through their democratically-elected representatives, have repeatedly and freely ratified the moral and legal validity of accession to India in free, competitive elections, and that India has, in return, honoured its part of the 1947 bargain by conferring on Jammu & Kashmir the privilege of regional autonomy, to an extent not enjoyed by any other constituent unit of the Indian Union, and formally enshrining it in the Indian Constitution. It is to an analysis of this claim that we now turn.

Notes

1. A quaint narrative of Kashmir's topography and society in the early twentieth century can be found in a travelogue, written by the wife of a British military officer (Bruce 1911). It focuses on the positive: 'The charm of Srinagar lies in

its variety. There are Hindu temples, Mahomedan mosques ... ' (p. 32). But it also touches on the exploitation of the peasantry: 'There is one very bad system in the administration of Kashmir. The people of the city are ... of first importance. The peasants must provide for them ... in hard years the peasants suffer ... ' (pp. 39–40).

2. Lawrence also commented that 'the Brahmins, known as Kashmiri Pandits, have seized all power and authority, and the Moslem cultivators [are] forced to work to keep the idle Brahmins in comfort. In 1889 [the year of his visit] Kashmir State was bankrupt', thanks to official mismanagement and corruption.

3. The princely state had traditionally had very close commercial and trade links with the geographically contiguous areas of western Punjab and the Frontier Province.

4. Like several neighbouring districts of western Punjab (Rawalpindi, Jhelum, Campbellpur) and the Frontier (Mardan and Kohat), Poonch was a major source of recruits for the British–Indian Army, a connection that reinforced economic, ethnic and religious ties. Military command of the rebel forces in Poonch was entrusted to Mohammed Zaman Kiani, formerly a top officer in the Indian National Army (INA), formed by the Indian nationalist leader Subhas Chandra Bose in South-East Asia during World War II.

5. It thus appears in retrospect that the Pakistanis miscalculated badly in trying to strike a deal with the hated Maharaja. In contrast to the Muslim League, Gandhi and Nehru had both solidly supported the NC-led democratic movement. This gave Indian military involvement a certain credibility among the population. The veteran Jammu-based writer and activist, Balraj Puri, says that Kashmiri opinion was 'outraged by the policy of the Pakistani government to recognise the Maharaja's sovereignty on the one hand, and on the other to decide the issue of the State's accession by force' (Puri 1995: 57).

3

Democracy of Denial:
Kashmir in India

Liberty is to faction what air is to fire, an aliment without which it instantly expires. But it cannot be a less folly to abolish liberty, which is essential to political life, because it nourishes faction, than it would be to wish the annihilation of air, which is essential to animal life, because it imparts to fire its destructive agency.
— James Madison, *The Federalist Papers*, No. 10.

It is important to note that this claim does not emanate solely from the corridors of power in New Delhi. It resounds throughout India's political and social spectrum, and even permeates what purports to be academic discourse on this question. To cite one among many possible examples, T.N. Madan (1993: 692–94), a well-known Indian scholar who publishes frequently in scholarly journals in the West, writes in apparently incredulous incomprehension that

> the way to hell ... is paved with good intentions, and so it has been in Kashmir. Although the state has been ruled since 1947 by a succession of governments, headed by Muslim chief ministers, and the representation of Muslims in the bureaucracy and professions has very considerably improved, yet a secessionist movement has erupted there which has turned violent ... what the turbulent elements are asking for is, in effect, another partition....

One might have imagined that Madan, who typifies a certain genre of writing on the Kashmir question, is entirely clueless as to the possible causes of such inexplicably irrational behaviour on part of the 'Muslims'. Except that he also notes, with apparent disapproval, that

> a special status was needed for retaining the state within the union. Article 370 is said to protect 'Kashmiriyat' or Kashmiri identity. Why Kashmiri identity needs special protection any more than, say, Bengali or Tamil identity is difficult to understand, unless it is taken to mean Kashmiri *Muslim* identity and brought under the rubric of minority rights and privileges.

This, coupled with the assertion that 'the notion of minority status as privilege is not slander in today's India, but a social and political fact' (ibid.), reveals that Madan in fact has a *very* clear-cut notion of why a violent secessionist movement has erupted in Kashmir: minority (read Muslim) appeasement is the root of the trouble.[1] In short, Kashmiri Muslims have received not only their due from democratic India, but have been unduly privileged, and it is this overly (indeed, scandalously) generous treatment which has whetted the insatiable appetite of the closet secessionist.

In what follows, I argue that this is a gross distortion of what Kashmiris have in reality experienced under India's democratic regime.

The Instrument of Accession of Jammu & Kashmir to India *expressly limited* the accession to three subjects: defence, foreign affairs and communications. Accordingly, in October 1949, India's Constituent Assembly inserted a special provision in the Indian Constitution, Article 306A, extending such autonomy to Jammu & Kashmir, though it was specified that even this arrangement was an 'interim system', pending the promised plebiscite (Noorani 1964: 47). In 1951, with no plebiscite in sight, Sheikh Abdullah organised elections to form a constituent assembly for the Indian-controlled regions of Jammu & Kashmir. His NC 'won' all 75 seats uncontested, the first instance of Indian-administered Kashmir's sorry history of utterly farcical 'elections'. There was no question of anyone opposing NC in the Valley, where Abdullah was running a virtual party–state.[2] But no contest was permitted even in Jammu, where the Praja Parishad, a 'Hindu nationalist' group, was arbitrarily prevented from participating in the polls. Subsequently, in

July 1952, Prime Ministers Abdullah and Nehru negotiated the 'Delhi Agreement', which essentially ratified Kashmir's autonomy and enshrined Article 306A as Article 370 of the Indian Constitution.[3]

However, in 1952–53, Abdullah, apparently provoked by a Praja Parishad agitation in Jammu for total elimination of Jammu & Kashmir's autonomy, publicly resurrected the idea of full independence as *one possible option*, among several, for the future of Jammu & Kashmir. The Parishad's supporters consisted primarily of ex-officials in the Maharaja's administration,[4] and of landlords dispossessed by a major land reform programme carried out by the NC in 1950 (the BJP's hysterical opposition to Article 370 thus has a long lineage, and Hindutva communalists have played a destructive, divisive and characteristically reactionary role in the state's politics for decades).

Abdullah cannot strictly speaking be faulted for reviving the notion of an independent Kashmir; the issue was still widely considered unresolved (certainly in international fora such as the UN), and hence the question of the territory's future status was at least theoretically open. But even the mention of the independence option was apparently intolerable to the Indian authorities. Accordingly, a rift was engineered in the NC leadership, the first instance of yet another ugly and abiding pattern. In August 1953, Abdullah was arrested, formally by Karan Singh, 'functioning in the interests of the people of the State', and one of the Sheikh's top lieutenants, Bakshi Ghulam Mohammed, was installed as the new prime minister of Kashmir. The people of the state were however not too enthused by this sordid coup d'état. Syed Mir Qasim, a senior NC leader who sided with Bakshi, has recorded in his memoirs (1992: 68–70) the massive protests that swept Kashmir after the Sheikh's arrest, and the brutal force employed to put them down.

Bakshi's government lasted till 1963, and is remembered largely for two salient attributes, both of which became his lasting legacy to Kashmir politics: pervasive corruption, with ministers and bureaucrats looting the public exchequer with impunity, and crude, Mafia-style authoritarianism, with the slightest political dissent forcibly stifled by police and gangs of organised thugs. Indeed, such was the extent of popular discontent that in 1958, two of Bakshi's closest colleagues, Ghulam Mohammed Sadiq and Mir Qasim, temporarily quit the ruling clique and floated their own party, tellingly named the Democratic National Conference. But Bakshi's position was for the time being unassailable, for his keepers in New Delhi had discovered in him a compliant instrument for their designs.

In 1954, a Constitutional (Application to Jammu & Kashmir) Order was promulgated by the President of India, which empowered the Indian government to legislate on *all* matters on the union list, not just defence, foreign affairs and communications. Bakshi's government was only too eager to give its 'concurrence', legally necessary to validate this law. This was the beginning of the end of Article 370, which has, therefore, *never* been truly implemented in Jammu & Kashmir (thus, the claim that Article 370 has fostered 'separatism' in Kashmir is patently absurd; something that has never really existed except on paper could not possibly have led to anything). This Order practically annulled the 1952 Nehru–Abdullah accord, which had confirmed that all powers except the three specified in the Instrument of Accession would remain vested in the Jammu & Kashmir government.

The Order also put drastic curbs on fundamental liberties: freedom of speech, assembly and association in the state could now be suspended at any time on 'grounds of security'. No judicial reviews of such suspensions would be allowed. As an Indian civil liberties activist observes, 'what we in India experienced for a brief period after 26 June 1975 [during Indira Gandhi's Emergency regime], Jammu & Kashmir has suffered for … years … we cannot deny a people rights that flow out of citizenship and then expect their allegiance' (Kannabiran 1991). It is thus very ironic that the Indian state consistently proclaims that the Instrument of Accession is sacrosanct and inviolable and that any settlement to the present uprising must be 'within the framework of the Indian Constitution'. For it is the ruling elite in Delhi that has, for the last four decades, been wantonly violating and subverting *both* the terms of the Accession and the provisions of its own Constitution with regard to Kashmir.

Other 'integrative' measures followed: on 26 January 1957, India's Republic Day, a new Constitution was adopted by the 'duly constituted' Kashmir government. This document took as its premise that 'the State of Jammu & Kashmir is and shall be an integral part of the Union of India' (Noorani 1964: 73). In 1958, a constitutional amendment was effected, whereby Jammu & Kashmir was brought under the purview of central administrative services. The eventual result of this move was that central administrative agencies, economic enterprises and banks based in Kashmir came to be mostly staffed not just by non-Muslims, but more critically, by non-Muslims from *outside* Jammu & Kashmir. Thus, while Kashmir's political arena was monopolised by corrupt, despised puppets installed at Delhi's behest through the calculated destruction of representative democracy, its day-to-day administration too gradually came to be dominated by people with no roots among the population.[5]

In subsequent 'elections', meanwhile to the Kashmir assembly in 1957 and 1962, the official National Conference, headed by Bakshi, 'won' between 95 and 97 per cent of seats. The ruling party's candidates were returned unopposed in almost all seats in the Valley (there was no contest at all in 43 and 34 seats, respectively, of the total of 75); nominal contests were mostly confined to Jammu. Riled by adverse reports in the international press, Nehru even wrote to Bakshi after the 1962 polls, advising him to lose 'a few seats' in the future, so that the image of the world's largest democracy would not be unnecessarily tarnished (Akbar 1985: 258).[6]

Bakshi was finally removed from office in 1963, and G.M. Sadiq eventually installed in his place. However, a problem arose because the majority of members of the bogus assembly remained loyal to Bakshi, who started organising a no-confidence motion against the Sadiq government. To thwart this motion, Bakshi was forthwith arrested under the Defence of India Rules in 1964, and consigned to the same prison in Jammu where Abdullah had been incarcerated eleven years earlier.

Under Sadiq, the process of coercive homogenisation and assimmilation reached its peak. In 1964–65, Articles 356 and 357 of the Indian Constitution, which respectively empower the central government to dismiss elected provincial governments and to assume all the legislative functions of the latter, were made applicable to Jammu & Kashmir. This provision was to be misused by the Indira and Rajiv regimes in the state, with ultimately catastrophic consequences, some twenty years later. Article 249, which empowers the central government to legislate even on subjects on the *provincial* list (not just the union and concurrent lists) was similarly made applicable to Jammu & Kashmir. Some twenty pieces of central economic legislation were extended to Jammu & Kashmir, and the designations of head of state and premier were formally changed to governor and chief minister, as in any Indian state. Further, from then on, the governor was to be an appointee of Delhi, rather than (as agreed before) a nominee of the (elected) Kashmir legislature; this, too, would have fateful repercussions for Jammu & Kashmir in the 1980s and 1990s.

Thus, any trace of substantive autonomy had been systematically eradicated from Kashmir by the mid-1960s, and without even the pretence of a reference to the wishes of its people. As one author has wryly commented, 'even in defeat' the extreme–centralist Hindutva communalists 'had emerged victorious' (Tremblay 1992: 164). Their agenda had been accomplished for them by the champions of democracy and secularism. It was not that the population acquiesced passively in this grotesque charade. On the contrary, the 'people of the Valley reacted with unprecedented anger', but their massive 'protests were again suppressed with brute force and large-scale arrests' (Puri 1993: 31–32). As an Indian politician, one of the very few who opposed these policies, wrote despairingly in 1966:

> We profess democracy, but rule by force in Kashmir ... we profess secularism, but let Hindu nationalism stampede us into ... establish[ing] it by repression ... Kashmir has distorted India's image in the world as nothing else has done ... the problem exists not because Pakistan wants to grab Kashmir, but because there is deep and widespread discontent among the people.[7]

Remarkably, however, this rampant discontent did not translate into pro-Pakistan sentiment. Thousands of armed Pakistani infiltrators, sent into the Valley to foment a general uprising on the eve of the 1965 Indo-Pakistan war under a strategic plan known as 'Operation Gibraltar', encountered an indifferent if not outrightly hostile population. Clearly, Kashmiris simply wanted basic democratic rights, including representative, accountable government and a voice in determining the destiny of their homeland. Unfortunately, the Indian state appeared to interpret popular opposition to Pakistan as further licence to continue trampling on those very rights.

The charade of elections also continued. In 1965, the ruling National Conference of Sadiq was instantly and miraculously metamorphosed into the Jammu & Kashmir wing of the Congress Party. In 'elections' in 1967, 39 of 75 seats went uncontested; in the Valley, Congress candidates were elected unopposed in 22 of 42 seats.

However, a problem arose in 1972, when the Plebiscite Front, a semi-illegal organisation of Abdullah's supporters founded in 1958, decided, for the first time, to contest the assembly polls. Mir Qasim, the Congress chief minister, panicked. The Front had massive popular support in Kashmir; indeed, as Qasim himself attests, since its emergence it had 'reduced the [official] National Conference to ... a nonentity in Kashmir's politics'. 'If the elections were free and fair', writes Qasim, 'the victory of the Front was a foregone conclusion' (Qasim 1992: 106, 132).

Qasim was probably quite right. Most Kashmiris I have spoken to have said that their families avidly supported Sheikh Abdullah throughout his years in captivity and political wilderness (1953–75), *if only because the Sheikh was a living symbol of Kashmiri pride and unrelenting defiance against Delhi's machinations.* The Kashmiri peasantry had an additional, very important reason to adulate Abdullah. In the early 1950s, the Sheikh, perhaps partly because he anticipated an imminent plebiscite, had implemented, without compensation to the owners, a land reform programme that had greatly benefited the vast mass of land-starved poor, mainly Kashmiri Muslims but also lower-caste Hindu cultivators in Jammu. As an impressed Daniel Thorner found in the mid-1950s, despite 'defects in implementation ... many tillers have become landowners and some land has even gone to the landless. The peasantry of the Valley ... were not long ago fearful and submissive ... None who has spent time with Kashmiri villagers will say the same today' (Thorner 1976: 50). Comparing the objectives and implementation of land reform in Kashmir with other parts of the subcontinent, Wolf Ladjensky (1977: 179–80) observed that

whereas virtually all land reforms in India lay stress on the elimination of the *zamindari* tenure system with compensation, or rent reduction and security of tenure, the Kashmir reforms call for distribution of land among tenants without compensation to the erstwhile proprietors; whereas land reform enforcement in most of India is not so effective, in Kashmir enforcement is unmistakably rigorous....

In any case, Qasim quickly resolved his dilemma with Delhi's advice and encouragement, by ordering mass arrests of Front leaders and activists, and banning its participation in the electoral process. In the 'election' that ensued, Congress 'won' 57 of 74 seats. According to some accounts, the Congress government also ensured the conservative Jama'at-i-Islami five seats in this assembly, so long as they would oppose the Front. 'It was the first occasion that the Jama'at received ... political legitimacy in Kashmir' (Puri 1993: 49), though not from its people.

Some authors have made strenuous efforts to absolve Jawaharlal Nehru, widely regarded not just as a democrat but as a visionary and statesman, of culpability in the Indian state's consistently anti-democratic Kashmir policy.[8] These efforts are entirely unconvincing. It has been claimed, for instance, by a quasi-official Nehru biographer that in August 1953, the Indian leader was on the verge of concluding a bilateral agreement with Pakistan allowing for the promised plebiscite, even if this resulted in India losing the Valley (Gopal 1979). If this claim is at all accurate, it is extraordinary that Nehru would even acquiesce in the arrest and detention of Abdullah, which also occurred in August 1953. M.J. Akbar (1985) advances the preposterous thesis that Nehru was dead against his 'old friend' Abdullah's imprisonment, but that he was baulked in attempts to secure the latter's release by a nexus of incorrigible bureaucrats and communal-minded Congress politicians. It is hardly plausible, even to the most simple-minded, that a person of Nehru's stature and authority would let his sincere wishes be defied for years by faceless, dwarfish underlings. Besides, Abdullah's removal from office necessarily implied his prolonged incarceration: it was simply impossible for the Indian-sponsored regime to continue in the Valley if he were allowed to remain free.

In mid-1954, Nehru declared that 'India still stands by her international commitments [plebiscite] on ... Kashmir' (Noorani 1964: 68). By late 1955, he was privately offering Pakistan a permanent demarcation of the ceasefire line as the interstate boundary (thus legalising the *de facto* partition of Kashmir). The offer, which was made public in mid-1956, was angrily rejected by

Pakistan. This abrupt *volte-face* was justified on the grounds that
Pakistan had joined the Baghdad and Manila Pacts (CENTO and
SEATO), the United States-sponsored security blocs against the
Soviet Union and its allies.

Apart from the questionable rationale of linking Pakistan's
broader military policy with the Kashmir issue (Pakistan being a
recognised, sovereign country with every right to decide its major
national policies in accordance with its own interests), it is also
curious that Nehru made this linkage with remarkable alacrity, and
in a tone of rather exaggerated moral outrage, *even before* Pakistan
had formally joined SEATO or CENTO. This was *despite* the fact
that Eisenhower had privately assured Nehru in March 1954 that
the United States considered India a pillar of the 'free world', did
not intend to promote Pakistan at India's expense, and cordially
offered India American military aid if Nehru so wished (Hayes
1971: 40–41).

Nonetheless, from 1954 onwards, Kashmir's plight was compounded by its becoming a pawn in the byzantine chessboard of
Cold War rivalry. In response to Pakistan's membership in SEATO
and CENTO, the Soviet Union effected a *volte-face* of its own in
its Kashmir policy. In 1948, Soviet propagandists had been hailing
NC as 'a progressive and democratic mass movement' and condemning 'Indian reactionaries'.[9] By 1953, the Soviet Union was
calling the Kashmir question an 'internal affair' of India and
decrying 'imperialist efforts to turn the ... Valley into a strategic
bridgehead [against the USSR]'. In 1955, the by now openly
uncompromising Indian stand on Kashmir received a significant
boost from Premier Khrushchev, who announced on a visit to
Srinagar that the 'people of Kashmir' only wished to 'work ... for
the welfare of their motherland, the Republic of India', and that
'the so-called Kashmir question' was a creation of 'imperialist
forces' (Jain 1979: 3–4, 15–20).

Till 1965, commensurate with this new policy, the Soviet Union
religiously vetoed every attempt to raise the Kashmir issue at the
UN. Even in 1963, with India reeling from the military rout at the
hands of China in late 1962, the most Nehru's foreign minister
was prepared to offer Pakistan was an additional 1,500 square miles
of Kashmiri territory, in return for which Pakistan would have to
consider the dispute closed. This was consistent with a by then

full-blown tendency in both Indian and Pakistani official circles to treat Kashmir and its people as objects of barter.

Nehru's attitude to the liquidation of democracy in Kashmir's domestic politics similarly smacks more of sophistry than statesmanship. During Abdullah's authoritarian tenure (1948–53), Balraj Puri, a Jammu-based writer and political activist, met Nehru and pleaded that disgruntled NC elements be allowed to form a democratic opposition in the Valley. Nehru, Puri recollects, conceded 'the theoretical soundness of my argument but maintained that India's Kashmir policy revolved around ... Abdullah and ... [that] nothing should be done to weaken him'. After Abdullah's arrest, Puri again met Nehru and repeated his request. Nehru fully agreed that Bakshi Ghulam Mohammed was a thoroughly unsavoury character, but 'argued that India's case ... now revolved around him, and that despite all shortcomings, the Bakshi government had to be strengthened'. For, according to Nehru, Kashmiri politics 'revolved around personalities', and '*there was no material for democracy there*' (emphasis mine). This statement aptly captures the profound condescension and almost imperial arrogance that defined Nehru's Kashmir policy, and subsequently, that of his successors, especially his patently less democratic daughter and grandson.

Indeed, such was Nehru's apparent aversion to democracy in Kashmir that when an attempt by the Praja Socialist Party (PSP), a left-of-centre all-India organisation, to set up a branch in Kashmir was prevented by Bakshi's hoodlums in 1954, Nehru, instead of condemning Bakshi, accused the PSP of 'joining hands with the enemies of the country'. In 1962, however, Nehru urged the PSP to contest elections in Kashmir because recurrent 'unopposed elections' were earning India 'a bad reputation'. In 1967, when Bakshi (now deposed) contested against Congress, and was elected to the Indian Parliament (what greater affirmation of India's right to Kashmir was possible?) from Srinagar despite widespread fraud, Puri was informed by central officials 'supervising' the polls that 'Bakshi had to be defeated *in the national interest*' (emphasis mine) (Puri 1993: 45–49).

It is true that Kashmir's coercive 'integration' into India accelerated following Nehru's death in 1964; however it remains a hypothetical question whether a significantly different outcome would have resulted had he lived longer. It is clear, however, that the origins of the Indian state's anti-democratic and ultimately futile and destructive Kashmir policy are to be found squarely in the Nehru period. The official *ideology* of monolithic nationalism and a unitary, zero-sum 'national interest', as inevitably reflected in the *institutional* sphere in an impetus to centralise the state-structure, was implanted by the Nehru regime,[10] and nurtured to full maturity by Indira and Rajiv Gandhi.

Kashmir's democratic aspirations were thus callously sacrificed at the altar of the 'nation' to which Kashmiris were expected to be loyal. *But the inevitable result was that when mass Kashmiri alienation from Indian 'democracy' eventually surfaced in an explosive form, as armed resistance, it was simultaneously a total and violent rejection of the Indian 'nation'.* Hence the widespread appeal of the demand for *azaadi*, or self-determination. But meanwhile, the acquiesence of unrepresentative puppets imposed from Delhi in Srinagar was passed off as the consent of the people. As Puri (1993: 89) has aptly put it, 'Nehru was undoubtedly the greatest "outside" influence on Kashmir's political history'. Tragically for Kashmir, he was 'above all a nationalist. He subordinated claims of democracy, morality and subnational aspirations to ... the claims of [a certain conceptualisation of Indian] nationalism'. In the process, Kashmiris were denied even accountable government, leave alone any right to 'self-determination'.

In 1975, an aged and weary Sheikh Abdullah finally renounced the self-determination platform. He may have calculated that after India's victory in the 1971 Bangladesh war, his bargaining power was weaker than ever: in the post-war Simla Treaty (1972), a demoralised, dismembered Pakistan had finally conceded that Kashmir was a 'bilateral' (as opposed to an 'international') dispute. In return for Abdullah's release and reinstatement as chief minister of Indian-administered Jammu & Kashmir, his deputy, Mirza Afzal Beg, signed another Delhi Agreement, which, despite its name, was more an abject capitulation to Prime Minister Indira Gandhi. The accord reaffirmed, virtually without modification, the terms of Kashmir's incorporation into the Indian Republic since 1953. In return for accepting the *status quo*, the Abdullahites were to be allowed to contest elections, and to run the provincial government if they won. A patently hypocritical clause of the agreement stipulated that 'Jammu & Kashmir ,.. a constituent unit of the Union of India, shall ... continue to be governed by Article 370'.

This was just not possible unless Kashmir's pre-1953 autonomy was comprehensively restored. Of this the agreement made no mention; it merely gave the provincial government the authority to 'review' laws on the concurrent list extended to Jammu & Kashmir after 1953, and 'decide' which of those might 'need amendment or repeal'. Even this was probably no more than a token gesture, given that no substantive action to this effect was ever taken. Instead, various restrictions were put on the jurisdiction of the provincial government, which was patronisingly permitted to legislate on 'welfare measures, cultural matters, social security, personal law'.[11]

However, the accord did pave the way for Jammu & Kashmir's first reasonably democratic election, in 1977, after thirty years of being a 'constituent unit' of a democratic Republic. The Plebiscite Front, revived under the aegis of the National Conference, obtained a decisive majority; it won an overwhelming victory in the Valley, where Congress was wiped out. Kashmiris, although disappointed with Abdullah's capitulation, obviously preferred him to the alternatives available.

Until Abdullah's death in 1982, Jammu & Kashmir was relatively stable. A year before he died, however, the Sheikh succumbed to the Indian politician's notorious predilection for nepotism by anointing his eldest son, a political novice named Farooq, as the heir-apparent. Having recovered his fiefdom after so many years, he was apparently eager to keep it in the family; after all, he was doing nothing more than emulate India's ruling dynasty.

In reasonably free and fair elections in 1983, NC, now led by Farooq Abdullah, again won a solid majority: 47 of 76 assembly seats. It swept the Valley, still mourning the elder Abdullah's death, and did surprisingly well in Jammu, with 38 per cent of the popular vote, a sign that a significant proportion of Jammu Hindus had supported NC rather than Congress or BJP.[12]

This was a major achievement, since the election had been fiercely contested against the Congress (I), the party ruling Delhi. Indira Gandhi was at this time perfecting an electoral strategy revolving around the 'national unity and integrity' theme, based on explicit appeals to India's 'Hindu' majority to defend the 'nation' against Sikh and Muslim minorities deliberately vilified as 'unpatriotic' and 'secessionist'. Both the Punjab and Kashmir tragedies have been directly precipitated by this strategy of political mobilisation. The 1983 election was an early portent of worse to come, with Mrs Gandhi launching a ferocious propaganda offensive against the allegedly anti-national and covertly pro-Pakistan NC. The campaign partly polarised Jammu & Kashmir along religious and regional lines. Congress won 21 of 32 seats in Jammu, partly at the expense of the hapless BJP, whose traditional base of urban, upper-caste Jammu Hindus responded fervently to Mrs Gandhi. Predictably, Congress was again wiped out in the Valley.

There was an additional, important reason for Mrs Gandhi's animosity towards NC. Just prior to the polls, Farooq had allied himself with Indian opposition parties trying to recreate a united political front against Congress for the impending 1984 parliamentary elections. One might have imagined that this would be a welcome development to New Delhi, for 'the emergence of Farooq as more than a regional figure, even if anti-Congress, would have automatically implied deeper political integration of Kashmir with the ... [Indian] Union' (Vanaik 1990b). But Mrs Gandhi seemingly interpreted this action as intolerable treachery. Farooq, on his part, remained defiant, and continued to associate himself with opposition unity moves.

He paid a high price for his courage. In June 1984, barely a year after the election (and the same month as the Indian Army's assault on the Golden Temple at Amritsar), a particularly vicious and sordid scheme engineered by Congress (I) culminated in twelve NC assembly members quitting the party and forming a new government supported by the Congress group in the legislature. Their leader was Ghulam Mohammed Shah, Sheikh Abdullah's son-in-law and a one-time Plebiscite Front leader, who had nursed ambitions of inheriting the Sheikh's mantle. All twelve NC defectors were rewarded with cabinet portfolios; indeed, most of them were aggrieved with Farooq because he had not included them in *his* cabinet. The entire plan was, according to Farooq, 'hatched ... in 1 Safdarjang Road, New Delhi' (the prime minister's residence) and 'directed ... by Mrs Gandhi' (Abdullah 1985:1–2).

The central role in its execution was played by Jammu & Kashmir's governor, Jagmohan, who had been appointed to that office by New Delhi merely three months earlier, after the previous governor had reportedly refused to connive in anti-democratic and unconstitutional actions. Jagmohan apparently had no such qualms. He had come into the limelight during the Emergency (1975–77), when as a senior official of Delhi's urban administration, he had been chiefly responsible for bulldozing predominantly Muslim shantytowns and brutally evicting the inhabitants in a bizarre effort to obliterate the signs of poverty from the national capital. Jagmohan readily dismissed Farooq, denied him the opportunity, required by constitutional propriety and practice, to prove his majority on the floor of the assembly, and rejected his desperate plea for fresh elections. Massive protests erupted throughout the Valley. This too had been anticipated by those who had turned the subversion of democracy in Kashmir into a fine art. The night before Farooq was ousted, large contingents of the Central Reserve Police Force (CRPF), paramilitary police under central government control, had been furtively airlifted into Srinagar.

To be sure, Jammu & Kashmir was not the only victim of the anti-democratic politics of the Congress (I) ruled centre. Before long, much the same technique would be used to depose another elected opposition government in the southern state of Andhra Pradesh. The crucial difference, however, lies in the incontrovertible fact that no other state has been even remotely subjected to the treatment meted out to Kashmir ever since 1947. Looking back, it is clear that only *two* of Indian Kashmir's 'eight democratic elections', in 1977 and 1983, have approximated conventional democratic norms. Of the two, the government elected in 1983 was not allowed to complete even a fifth of its mandated term. Even counting Sheikh Abdullah's first tenure (1948–53), which did enjoy considerable popular sanction despite its authoritarian, one-party basis, *Jammu & Kashmir has had something resembling representative government for just twelve of its forty-nine years (1948–53, 1977–84) as an 'integral part of India'.*

Kashmiris, accustomed to relieving political adversity with black humour, soon conferred an honorific title on G.M. Shah: 'Curfew' Chief Minister (for seventy-two of his first ninety days in office the Valley was under curfew to pre-empt protest demonstrations). In the December 1984 parliamentary polls, the public mood was unmistakable: while Congress swept India, all three constituencies in the Valley returned pro-Farooq candidates with huge majorities. The pathetic tenure of Gulshah (as he is popularly known) ended in March 1986, when carefully organised riots against the Valley's Pandit minority provided the pretext for his dismissal under Article

356 of the Indian Constitution. Balraj Puri, who visited the Valley immediately after the rioting, observes 'that while accusing fingers were raised against some ... secular parties, we found no evidence of the involvement of Jama'at-i-Islami' (Puri 1993: 35), while another observer has noted that 'arson and loot was most rampant in Bijbehera in Anantnag district, the constituency of Mufti Mohd. Sayeed', then Kashmir's top Congress (I) leader (Malik 1991: 77).

For the rest of 1986, Jammu & Kashmir was administered by Governor Jagmohar, who won some popularity for vigorously promoting development programmes, especially in impoverished and neglected rural areas. However, this development-oriented approach was entirely intended to serve a political purpose which it is doubtful it could ever accomplish: Jagmohan reportedly believed that 'as long as Kashmiri identity existed, Pakistan and America would ... exploit it' (Puri 1993: 36). And when not promoting development, Jagmohan was up to other, less salutary activities. He reintroduced Article 249, reduced Muslim recruitment to certain categories of government employment by a half, and, in a territory with a two-thirds Muslim majority, banned the sale of meat on the day of a Hindu religious festival.

In late 1986, Farooq Abdullah committed what must be regarded, in retrospect, as a disastrous blunder. He concluded a *rapprochement* with the centre, whereupon he was reinstalled as chief minister, pending fresh elections in March 1987. In exchange, he agreed to contest the elections in partnership with Rajiv Gandhi's Congress (I). Farooq justified his decision in terms of a 'hard political reality' he had 'come to accept': 'If I want to implement programmes to fight poverty ... and run a government, I have to stay on the right side of the centre'.[13] In other words, he had come to accept that Kashmir's right to democracy and development was conditional on its leaders' submitting to the rulers in Delhi, and serving Congress' political agenda.

However, Farooq's accommodation with a detested party and regime was interpreted as self-serving capitulation by a broad cross-section of Kashmiri opinion. George Fernandes, an Indian socialist politician, has recorded how he saw with his 'own eyes the ... adulation Farooq received [in 1984] when he fought for what ... Kashmiris called their *Kashmiriyat*' (Fernandes 1992: 287). Understandably then, when Farooq worked out an arrangement that restored his office with those who had disrespected and denied *Kashmiriyat* for forty years, he met with widespread public hostility and contempt.

With Farooq, like so many Kashmiri politicians before him, having 'betrayed' his principles for the prize of power, a broad spectrum of political groups in the Valley formed a coalition called Muslim United Front (MUF) to fight the NC–Congress alliance at the polls. MUF was a near-spontaneous vehicle for popular participation in the democratic process. As an Indian journalist observed during the campaign, it was an 'ad hoc' bloc with 'no real group ideology', consisting of 'educated youth, illiterate working-class people and farmers who express their anger at ... family rule, corruption and lack of economic development'. Its emergence meant that 'the valley is sharply divided between the ... party machine that brings out the vote for NC, and hundreds of thousands ... who have entered politics [as active participants, rather than passive objects] for the first time through the umbrella ... provided by MUF' (*IT* 1987a: 26). One of the twelve NC defectors of 1984, Khemlata Wakhloo, has written that there was a veritable MUF 'wave' in the Valley. MUF promised employment for educated youth and an end to government corruption, the latter being an especially sensitive issue with Kashmiris, who say that most of the Rs 70,000 crores given to the state as development aid by Delhi over the decades has been siphoned off by a nexus of corrupt politicians, bureaucrats and businessmen, all appointed or imposed, of course, by Delhi. But in the end it was politics and not economics that proved crucial. As Wakhloo (1992: 321) writes, 'there was only one voice on the lips of the people, that in a democracy we would bring the party of our choice to power, a party that will genuinely meet the aspirations of the people and heed their grievances'.

In an anti-climax, MUF eventually won just four seats, with the NC–Congress combine taking almost all the rest. But, once again, at the expense of democracy. An eyewitness report in a generally pro-establishment Indian magazine drew attention to 'rigging and strong-arm tactics ... all over the Valley'; to 'entire ballot-boxes [being] pre-stamped for NC'; to 'massive booth-capturing by [NC] gangs'; to numerous citizens 'simply not being allowed to vote'; and to government-nominated supervisors 'stopping the counting as soon as they saw opposition candidates taking a lead'. Meanwhile, the administration 'worked blatantly in favour of the

NC–Congress alliance', and 'the police refused to listen to any complaint' (*IT* 1987b: 40–42).

According to one remarkable school of opinion, however, this election was a contest between 'the forces of democracy and secularism and ... fundamentalists arguing for a theocratic state ... The forces of democracy and secularism won ... not by rigging, but because the people ... elected them'.[14] Given the evidence to the contrary, this seems to be a deliberate attempt at what Indians rather politely call 'disinformation'. As Qazi Nissar, a MUF leader, put it: 'I believe in the Indian Constitution. How long can people like us keep getting votes by exploiting Islam? We have to prove we can do something concrete. But this kind of thing simply makes people lose faith in the Constitution'. Another 'defeated' MUF candidate (and former Congress leader) Abdul Ghani Lone queried in despair: 'If people are not allowed to vote, where will their venom go but into expressions of anti-national sentiment?' And as a shocked Srinagar lawyer and MUF voter said: 'I don't even pray regularly. But ... if you take my vote away, I lose all faith in Indian democracy' (*IT* 1987b: 40–43). It is thus not surprising that an Indian correspondent discovered after the eruption of insurgency in 1990 that 'nearly all the young men on the wanted list today were guarding ballot-boxes for MUF' (as campaign volunteers) in 1987 (*IT* 1990a: 35–36).

Farooq Abdullah's second term (till January 1990, when his government was dismissed following the eruption of the mass uprising), was an unmitigated and unsurpassed disaster. His behaviour during his first term has been compared to that of 'a little boy with a toy'; the second was a 'virtual abdication of governance' (*IT* 1986a: 43, 1990c: 10). The promise of 'development' proved to be a cruel joke, and corruption among politicians and administrators reached levels extraordinary even by Kashmir's standards, while the chief minister amused himself in discotheques, playing golf and vacationing in exotic foreign locations. But the most oppressive aspect of the regime was the indiscriminate repression employed in a vain effort to stifle near-universal popular discontent.

Mass arrests of MUF activists had immediately followed the spurious election. *In fact, it was in prison during 1987 that the five young men who formed the Jammu & Kashmir Liberation Front (JKLF)[15] nucleus in the Valley in 1989–90 met, and, on their*

*release, took a collective decision to go to Pakistan-controlled
Kashmir in search of military training and weapons.*[16] Yasin Malik,
one of the five and currently chairman of JKLF in Indian-administered
Kashmir, has spoken of how he was beaten and abused while
imprisoned in 1987: 'They called me a Pakistani bastard. I told
them I wanted my rights, my vote was stolen. I was not pro-
Pakistan but had lost faith in India' (*IT* 1989). Ashfaq Wani, a
brilliant student and athlete who had been denied admission to
medical college because his parents could not afford the required
bribe (a Maruti car), was detained on 23 March, 1987 and subsequently charged with a crime allegedly committed on 4 April,
on which date he was in police custody. Kept in solitary confine-
ment, he was released nine months later, with cigarette-burns all
over his body.[17] Peer Mohammed Yusuf alias Sheikh Salahuddin,
presently military commander of Hizbul Mujahideen,[18] (and a
veteran Jama'at activist) was actually a MUF candidate in a Srinagar constituency (his *third* foray into electoral politics) in 1987.
He was arrested from the counting-hall for the crime of taking a
lead, and put away for nine months without charge or trial. Convinced that 'slaves have no vote in the so-called democratic set-up
of India', he picked up the Kalashnikov in 1990.[19]

Even perfectly peaceful agitations were suppressed with lethal
force. For example, public demonstrations against a steep increase
in the electricity tariff in June 1988 resulted in numerous deaths
from police firing. Hatred of the government and its patron and
sponsor, 'India', steadily mounted among the population. The first
JKLF bombings in Srinagar in late-July 1988[20] signalled the arrival
of insurgency. Every conceivable occasion: India's Independence
and Republic Days (15 August and 26 January, respectively), the
anniversary of JKLF founder Maqbool Butt's execution by the
Indira Gandhi regime in 1984 (11 February), or the death in police
custody of the elderly father of Shabbir Shah, a leading pro-
Pakistan activist, in April 1989, set off strikes and protest rallies.
The 'democratic' and 'secular' chief minister retaliated by threatening to send hundreds of thousands to prison ('I have the backing
of the Indian government', he declaimed), raze particularly rebellious districts in his capital, break strikes by forcing shops open,
and break the legs of protestors before burying them alive (Puri
1993: 56–57; *IT* 1989).

In the context of this spiralling unrest, India's parliamentary election was formally held in Jammu & Kashmir in November 1989, amidst a boycott call given by the JKLF and other opposition groups. The NC won 'unopposed' from Srinagar, while in the two other Valley constituencies, Baramulla and Anantnag, its candidates were elected with 94 and 98 per cent, respectively, of the popular vote. The catch lay in the voter turnout: despite stuffing of ballot-boxes at selected sites, the turnout was less than 5 per cent.[21] Jammu & Kashmir's major daily newspaper, the *Kashmir Times*, pleaded after this election: 'Let the image of Indian democracy not be tarnished further in Kashmir'.[22] It was a vain hope: the Indian state was not prepared to listen.

Conclusion and Theoretical Implications: A Dialectic of Democracy and Nationalism

Building on the earlier work of Robert Dahl, Philippe Schmitter and Terry Karl (1993: 39–52) have recently delineated certain minimal criteria of democracy.[23] They argue that

> what distinguishes democratic rulers from non-democratic ones are the norms that condition how the former came to power and the practices that hold them accountable for their actions.... Democracy ... may give rise to a considerable variety of institutions and subtypes ... for democracy to thrive, however, specific procedural norms must be followed and civic rights respected. Any polity that ... fails to follow the 'rule of law' with regard to its own procedures should not be considered democratic. These procedures alone do not define democracy, but their presence is indispensable to its persistence ... [moreover] the polity must be self-governing; it must be able to act independently of constraints imposed by some overarching political system. Dahl and other ... democratic theorists probably took this condition for granted ... however ... the question of autonomy has been a salient one. Is a system really democratic if its elected officials are unable to make binding decisions without the approval of actors outside their territorial domain? This is significant even if the outsiders are themselves democratically constituted....

The political history of Indian-administered Jammu & Kashmir clearly does not satisfy these minimal conditions and requirements of democratic governance. Moreover, there are other basic, indispensable components of a democratic framework that have, to a large extent, not been permitted in the state either. For example, there is virtual consensus among comparative political scientists (Dahl, Barrington Moore, Jr. and Juan Linz, to mention a few leading scholars of different ideological predilections) that 'a functioning political opposition is essential to democracy.... Democratic systems rely on *institutionalised* oppositions [emphasis mine], and it is doubtful that any regime could long survive as minimally democratic without them'.

The presence of active, organised and *institutionally sanctioned* opposition is critically important for several interrelated reasons. First, peaceful handing over of office following elections is the '*sine qua non* of democratic politics', and that in turn requires 'both the permissive freedoms of speech and association, and the presence of institutions and practices that makes it possible for counter-elites to organise and inform themselves so as to be able to contest for power'. Second, institutionalised opposition is crucial to 'the legitimacy of the democratic political order'. That is,

> providing the institutional space for opposition is essential to ensuring that discontent and dissatisfaction can be directed at particular governments rather than at the ... regime itself ... unless there are such institutional outlets for dissent within the regime's institutions, those discontented [for whatever reason] with the *status quo* may not distinguish [a particular] government [from the political system as a whole in expressing their anger and frustration].

This, obviously, is precisely what has happened in Jammu & Kashmir, especially after 1987 with all institutional channels of protest and dissent effectively blocked. Finally, 'institutional arrangements that facilitate loyal opposition ... ensure the presence of healthy political debate', which is essential to generating both democratic values among the citizenry and their allegiance to the established framework of authority.[24] Otherwise, in Juan Linz's terminology, there is every likelihood that a political opposition which would otherwise be 'loyal' (to the system), will gradually be transformed into a 'disloyal opposition', i.e., one that rejects the entire institutional framework as illegitimate and seeks to undermine or overthrow it (Linz 1978: 28–33). This is exactly what has happened in Indian-administered Jammu & Kashmir. While political opposition has, by and large, had the institutional space to operate in India's democratic framework, it is clear from the foregoing account that Jammu & Kashmir has almost consistently since 1947 been a glaring exception to the general rule. For Kashmiris, Indian democracy and its institutions is truly the god that failed, and failed disastrously.

A colossal and persistent failure of Indian democracy, justified and rationalised through invocations of the 'interest' and 'integrity' of the Indian 'nation' by power-hungry and self-aggrandising elites, has, thus, engendered the struggle for 'self-determination' in Kashmir today. As for why it took so long for Kashmiris to rise in revolt, perhaps Lenin (1970: 73) has provided an explanation that avoids the shallow determinism of 'national character' (for example, 'docility') theories: 'From their daily experience the masses know perfectly well the value of geographical and economic ties and the advantages of a big market and big state. They will, therefore, opt for secession only when national oppression ... make[s] ... life absolutely intolerable'. But if, as Walker Connor (1990: 92–103) claims, the crucial question is not 'what is a nation?' but rather 'when is a nation?' (i.e., at what juncture does collective conscious-ness crystallise and generate political action in a coordinated move-ment), that moment had definitely arrived in Kashmir by 1989.

Schmitter and Karl (1993: 39–52) have also argued that 'unlike authoritarian regimes, democracies have the capacity to modify their rules and institutions consensually in response to changing circumstances'. If this is indeed the case, the Indian state's mailed-fist, militarist response to 'fundamentalism' and 'terrorism' (as it usually chooses to characterise the contemporary Kashmir crisis) in Jammu & Kashmir, reinforced by officially-sponsored ideological dogma and inflexibility based on a purported 'consen-sus' that Kashmir is 'an integral part of India' (implying thereby that the issue is basically non-negotiable), does not speak well of Indian democracy, nor does it bode well for its future.

To borrow from Edward Said, writing in the context of the Israeli-Palestinian conflict in the Middle East, 'the terrorism craze is dangerous because it consolidates the immense, unrestrained pseudopatriotic narcissism' over Kashmir that is being routinely disseminated in India by a variety of sources (in politics, the media and even in scholarly circles), with the parliamentary Left, unfortunately, acting as willing accomplices.[25] This 'terrorism craze' has 'spawned uses of language, rhetoric and argument that are frightening in their capacity for mobilising opinion [for] ... murderous action' by those in control of state power and large machineries of coercion. But this officially-sponsored rhetoric also 'serves the purpose of institutionalising the avoidance and denial of history', and of 'deflect[ing] ... scrutiny of the government's domestic and foreign policies' (Said 1988). The crisis of 'national integration' in Kashmir today is perhaps above all a crisis of Indian democracy.

As for Pakistan's indisputable role in supporting the Kashmir insurgency, George Fernandes put it well when he was India's minister of Kashmir affairs in 1990: 'I do not believe any foreign hand created the Kashmir problem. The problem was created by us ... others decided to take advantage of it' (Fernandes 1992: 286). Mir Qasim, with a half-century of experience in Kashmir politics, concurs: 'If I dump petrol in my house ... and my opponent sets a match to it, it is largely my fault ... wherever the entire people rise up in one voice, you cannot suppress it by force' (Qasim 1992: 302–3). Farooq Abdullah has said it best: 'It is India that is responsible for what has happened in Kashmir ... they betrayed my father in '53 ... they betrayed me in '84 ... as for golf, I will never stop playing it, whether you like it or not' (*IT* 1994: 44).

But perhaps the most eloquent statement about the cause of Kashmir's agony came from one Afzal, a 22-year-old tailor in Baramulla. Asked in 1989 why he had joined the JKLF, he quietly replied: '[Because] they don't want democracy to survive here'(*IT* 1989). According to Newberg (1995: 73), 'Kashmiris came to insurgency when all politics seemed to fail; the politics of Kashmir's traditional politicians, politics between Srinagar and Delhi, and politics between India and Pakistan. They view themselves as victims of profound corruptions that sully the meaning of politics'. Indeed, most Kashmiris who developed a renewed commitment to the idea of 'self-determination' by the late 1980s sincerely believe that they have given India's democracy more than its fair share of chances. They also steadfastly believe that it has tragically failed them. The evidence of history supports their belief.

Notes

1. It is obvious that this view is virtually identical to that normally associated with Hindu nationalist politics. It is, therefore, a trifle puzzling that Madan also feels compelled to append a few apparently critical remarks about the Hindu nationalist political movement to his main arguments.

2. The NC slogan was 'One Leader (Abdullah), One Party (NC) and One Programme (Naya Kashmir)'.

3. Though the agreement did affirm the supremacy of India's flag over Kashmir's, and extended India's fundamental rights as well as the jurisdiction of its Supreme Court to Jammu & Kashmir.

4. The king had by this time abdicated and his son Karan Singh became the titular head (*Sadr-e-Riyasat*) of Jammu & Kashmir.

5. Thus, in 1989, while Muslims comprised 65 per cent of the population in Indian-administered Jammu & Kashmir (and Hindus 32 per cent), Hindus, mostly from outside the state, made up 84 per cent of high-level officers, 79 per cent of clerical employees and 73 per cent of low-level employees in the centrally-operated services. A minuscule 1.5 per cent of high-ranking officers in centrally-owned banks in the state were Kashmiri Muslims. Only 25 per cent of Indian Administrative Service (IAS) officials posted in the state in 1989 were natives of the province, and of 22 secretaries, the highest rank, a mere five were Kashmiri Muslims. The problem of inequitable representation extended to provincial-level administrative organs and economic enterprises. Here, Hindus comprised 51 per cent of senior administrators and 47 per cent of top officers in economic enterprises, the tiny Pandit minority being disproportionately overrepresented (see Bose et al. 1991: 262–67). Meanwhile, in 1987, the number of educated unemployed in the state was officially estimated at 100,000 (Malik 1991: 79).

6. Bakshi's tactics at election time have become part of Kashmir's almost surreal political lore. To this day, Kashmiris tell hilarious stories about Abdul Khaleq Malik, the Bakshi henchman in charge of summarily rejecting opposition candidates' nomination papers. The nominees approved by him became popularly known as 'Khaleq-made MLAs'.

7. Jayaprakash Narayan, in a private communication to Prime Minister Indira Gandhi (cited in Akbar 1985: 267).

8. M.J. Akbar (1985) makes a particularly blatant attempt to do this. See also Gowher Rizvi's otherwise insightful work (1993, chapter 2).

9. During this time, of course, Stalin's foreign policy was going through a 'radical' phase, and the Soviets were, among other things, backing the agrarian uprising organised by their client, the Communist Party of India (CPI), in the Telengana region of southern India.

10. Recall that in the early 1950s, Nehru initially opposed linguistic reorganisation of India's provinces (a longstanding promise of the Congress to the people of India), favouring, instead, the continuation of the 'administrative zones' of colonialism.

11. For the full text of this agreement, see Qasim (1992: 138–40). Abdul Qayoom Zargar, then a senior NC official and secretary to Afzal Beg, narrated to me

that 'we were faced with a very piquant situation after the 1975 accord. The people wanted to go on strike, to protest what they saw as an unjust and inequitable agreement. But we could not let that happen, because the prestige of none other than Sheikh Abdullah was at stake'. Personal interview in Doda town (Jammu & Kashmir), July 1995.

12. Muslims constitute only a third of Jammu's population, and they are mostly (with the exception of Doda district) Rajputs, Gujjars and Pahadis, not ethnic or linguistic Kashmiris.

13. Interview in *IT* (1986b).

14. M.J. Akbar, quoted in Engineer (1991: 291).

15. The JKLF pioneered the insurrection that erupted in Indian-administered Jammu & Kashmir in 1989–90. It is still widely regarded as the most popular political movement in the Kashmir Valley, and its ideology is said to have significant support in 'Azad Kashmir' as well. Ideologically, it is committed to an independent, democratic, secular and reunified state of Jammu & Kashmir, with the borders of the princely state in 1947 restored. The organisation is banned by the Indian regime, and has also faced considerable harassment and persecution at the hands of the Pakistani regime.

16. Of the five, Ashfaq Majid Wani, Abdul Hamid Sheikh and Ejaz Ahmed Dar have since died fighting. Mohammad Yasin Malik, the top surviving JKLF leader, was unexpectedly released from Indian custody towards the end of May 1994. He had been imprisoned without trial for almost four years, during which time he was tortured, denied medical attention for urgent health problems for prolonged periods, and frequently kept in subhuman conditions. In an interesting indication of how the Indian authorities regard rebellious Kashmiris demanding independence, Malik was confined for some time in the lunatic ward of Agra prison. Javed Ahmed Mir, who had headed JKLF in the Valley since August 1990, was also arrested in March 1994, and released a year later.

17. See his obituary in *TOI* (1990b).

18. Hizbul Mujahideen (or HM) is militarily the strongest force among the guerrilla groups presently operating in Indian-administered Jammu & Kashmir. Politically, it is closely linked to the Jama'at-i-Islami.

19. Interview in IWI (1992: 4).

20. Planned by Mohammad Rauf Kashmiri, an activist from Poonch in Azad Kashmir.

21. The voter turnout was also unusually low (a mere 38 per cent) in Udhampur, one of the two parliamentary seats from the Jammu region, which suggests a partial boycott by segments of the Jammu electorate as well. For the figures, see Singh (1994: 99–100).

22. Editorial on 30 November 1989; see the edition of 29 November for the dismal statistics of voter participation.

23. See Dahl (1982, 1989) for his recent work.

24. See the theoretical analysis of the vital role of political oppositions in democratic systems in Jung and Shapiro (1995: 271–73).

25. The rhetoric of the Indian Left on Kashmir is often indistinguishable from that of BJP, except that the Left opposes formal abrogation of Article 370, which is, as we have seen, a non-issue. In March 1990, Harkishan Singh

Surjeet, a senior leader of Communist Party of India–Marxist (CPI–M), the largest leftist group, responded to the mass uprising by appealing to 'every patriotic-minded Indian' to fight against 'separatism and terrorism'. 'The ... line has to be drawn between those who stand for national unity and those who oppose it', he announced (*HT* 1990). Satyapal Dang, representing the smaller Communist Party of India (CPI), declared that 'terrorism has to be opposed tooth and nail', and that 'the matter is entirely an internal affair of India' (Engineer: 175). In April 1990, Chitta Basu, who heads Forward Bloc, an even smaller leftist faction, declaimed that 'the need of the hour is granite-like unity ... to protect the sovereignty of the nation. Political and ideological differences need to be sunk' (*TOI* 1990a). There is no hint of condemnation or even censure of the reign of terror unleashed by Indian forces on the Kashmiri population in any of these articles, though all were published at a time of especially horrific repression. All the groups take a belligerent stand against Pakistan, however. In early 1994, a senior CPI–M leader told me that her party was opposed to raising the Kashmir issue at all, since this provided an opportunity for BJP propaganda. I pointed out that if the issue were allowed to fester unresolved, the BJP would always have a tailor-made plank to capitalise on and exploit to its electoral advantage; besides, wasn't it strange for India's 'communists' to have their agenda virtually dictated to them by BJP? (personal conversation in Calcutta).

4

The Struggle for 'Self-Determination': Kashmir in the Nineties

State Violence and Popular Resistance: The Radicalisation of Mass Opinion

The extent and nature of state violence in Indian-administered Jammu & Kashmir since January 1990 has been ably and amply documented by a variety of Indian, Kashmiri and Western human rights and civil liberties organisations, as well as by numerous eyewitness or on-the-spot reports in the Indian, West European and North American press. The reader is thus best advised to consult some of these accounts for detailed and meticulous information.[1]

The overall picture that emerges from these diverse sources is both macabre and heartbreaking. The forms of state violence appear to have included recurrent massacres of civilians; widespread torture, often involving almost unbelievably cruel and sadistic methods;[2] rape, including numerous instances of reported gang and mass rape; summary executions of hundreds, perhaps thousands of detained youths suspected of being 'militants' (as the guerrillas are known in South Asian parlance); random killings of bystanders and pedestrians, and defenceless people inside their homes, often in 'revenge' for armed actions by guerrilla groups; repeated incidents of large-scale arson of entire localities, involving, in some cases, razing of scores of civilian homes, properties and public institutions in major towns, also usually as a form of 'collective punishment' to a 'disloyal' population; obstruction and harassment of, and attacks on, (sometimes resulting in murder) medical and fire-fighting personnel trying to carry out their duties; arbitrary detention of thousands without recourse to any procedure of law whatsoever, not even notorious anti-democratic legislation such as Terrorism and Disruptive Activities (Prevention) Act (TADA) and Jammu & Kashmir Public Safety Act[3]; extended periods of blanket curfew in major towns and cities including Srinagar, sometimes lasting weeks; a persistent pattern of soldiers looting civilians of money and valuables; and cordon-and-search operations and road-block checks frequently involving beatings, intimidation and verbal abuse.

It is important to note that these practices are *not aberrations*. They are simply too patterned and widespread to merit that con-clusion. Rather, all these forms of abuse are integral components, or at least inevitable extensions, of a *systematic policy*. This policy was begun by Governor Jagmohan in January 1990. Furthermore, the Indian army, deployed in rural and border areas, and paramili-tary forces (the CRPF and Border Security Force or BSF), respon-sible for policing major urban centres, seem to have largely enjoyed virtual immunity from control and prosecution, even in cases of egregious atrocities. Their personnel have rarely been disciplined or punished for crimes against the population, and even if punished, the nature of the punishment is almost never made public, osten-sibly for fear of 'demoralising' the guardians of democracy, na-tional integrity and secularism (in any event, the number of cases in which the Indian government occasionally claims to have taken action—a few hundred at the most since 1990—represents a drop in the ocean compared to the scale of human rights violations). And no Kashmiri has been safe from these depredations: though poor and middle-class people are more vulnerable, even 'affluence and influence [are] no longer safeguards' (Kagal 1990). Indeed, even members of the locally-recruited Jammu & Kashmir police have been tortured and murdered by the army and paramilitary forces.

Furthermore, as I can personally attest from extensive travels through the violence-torn regions, many Indian officers and soldiers seem permeated with hostility and hatred towards the entire popu-lation, and this attitude is frequently reflected in totally vicious behaviour towards civilians. Indeed, the lack of restraint and dis-crimination displayed towards even peaceful protestors, and people

demonstrably not involved in supporting guerrilla activity, is
shocking, even allowing for the fact that the security forces have
had to contend with a serious and (at least in the first several years)
popularly-backed insurgency problem.

A few concrete examples will be helpful. Questioned about
summary executions of youths under the so-called catch-and-kill
policy, one official responded: 'Yes, they're killing them. Maybe
because the jails are full—or they want to frighten the people'.
Another proudly stated in April 1993 that 'we don't have custodial
deaths here, we have alley deaths ... if we have word of a ...
militant, we will pick him up, take him to another lane and kill
him' (Noorani 1994: 44–48).[4] In a typically ghastly incident in
August 1990, a number of women in a remote village in Kupwara
district were reportedly gang-raped by army soldiers after their
convoy had been ambushed: one woman reported that the soldiers
asked her prior to the attack: *'Maar loge, ya pyaar doge?'* [Will
you take violence, or give love?]. A Kashmiri trade union activist
who has participated in numerous labour agitations in India was
tortured by the army; when he tried to tell his torturers about his
Indian friends, they retorted: *'Humme sab kuch maloom hai. Tum
sab Pakistani ho'* [We know everything. You are all Pakistanis].[5]

As for the treatment meted out to unarmed demonstrators, the
following instructive account has been supplied by Farooq Wani,
a government engineer who was accidentally drawn into one such
volatile but non-violent protest in Srinagar on 21 January 1990:

> I ... fell down on the road ... I saw small boys being shot ... I
> remained lying ... till I saw a paramilitary officer coming ... I
> saw him pumping bullets into bodies of the injured lying on the
> road ... A boy trying to hide was killed ... As I lifted my head,
> a CRPF man shouted, 'He's still alive!' I pleaded: 'I'm a
> government officer, please don't shoot'. The officer shouted
> abuses at me and said, *'Islam mangta hai?'* [You want Islam?]
> and fired at me. My back and hands were injured ... Another
> paramilitary moved up to me and shouted: *'Tum sala zinda hai,
> mara nahin hai?'* [You bastard, you're not dead yet?] ... he left
> after kicking my back ... [then] a truck was brought, and all of
> us, dead and injured, were piled into it ... they loaded about
> 30–35 dead bodies. As there was no space for more, the officer
> ordered the driver: *'Baaki ko naale mein phenk do'* [Throw the

rest into the river]. A tarpaulin was thrown over us ... after some time we stopped ... and I heard voices speaking Kashmiri. One of the injured among us cried out. The tarpaulin was lifted and we saw a Kashmiri constable, who ... said: 'My God, there are living bodies here' ... three other people were still alive ... (Bose et al. 1991: 229–30).

Mr. Wani survived with six bullet wounds. He later discovered that the constable who saved him had suffered a heart attack.[6]

The effect that such behaviour has had on Kashmiri mass opinion is similar to what was eloquently described by Frantz Fanon (1963: 72) in the context of the Algerian war of independence against the French: 'The repressions, far from calling a halt to the forward rush of national consciousness, urge it on. Mass slaughter ... increases that consciousness, for the hecatombs are an indication that between oppressors and oppressed everything can be solved by force'. Wholesale repression succeeded (till about 1994), in 'eliminating militants in arithmetical progression and generating ... militants in geometrical progression'; almost all guerrillas took to the gun only from 1990 onwards. Not only did 'militant' ranks multiply exponentially, but the mujahideen assumed almost cult-like status in the eyes of the public. Even 'children no longer dream of becoming doctors and engineers', an Indian journalist found in 1992, 'their ambition is to become mujahids' (*IWI* 1992: 6). Indeed, the main problem the Indian state has faced in tackling this insurgency is *not* that the guerrillas are extraordinarily effective militarily,[7] but that the *azaadi* movement encompasses 'workers, engineers, schoolteachers, storeowners, doctors, lawyers, former MLAs and ... Jammu & Kashmir police' (*IT* 1990c: 13), as also the peasant population, victims of severe repression in the countryside. In other words, the popular base of the *azaadi* movement encompasses practically all sectors of Kashmir's society.[8]

The ultimate denial of democracy—rule through violence and coercion—produced a situation by 1990–91 where the gunman came to be revered as the harbinger of freedom. As the father of JKLF pioneer Ashfaq Wani put it: 'I disagreed with my son and turned him out ... but he found a much larger family' (*TOI* 1990b). In April 1990, the largest political rally in Kashmir's history, surpassing even Sheikh Abdullah's funeral, took place when over

500,000 mourners turned out, defying curfew orders, to honour Ashfaq at *his* funeral (he had been killed in a shoot-out with the security forces). Five years later, mention of Ashfaq Wani or Hamid Sheikh's 'martyrdom' still brought tears to the eyes of many Kashmiris, I discovered. They and countless other *shaheed* have become part of Kashmiri lore, and Srinagar's Id Gah ground, which houses the biggest martyrs' graveyard, is practically a pilgrimage site for Kashmiris today. As a veteran police officer put it in 1990, this younger generation, which has come to believe that Kashmir and India are incompatible opposites, is 'a defiant new breed of Kashmiri' (*IT* 1990a).

State Violence and Popular Defiance: The Latest Phase

As I extensively toured Jammu & Kashmir in July and August 1995, it became clear to me that the protracted war of attrition that has been raging since 1990 is approaching a potentially crucial turning-point. The Indian state, with its enormous police and military resources, is now arguably showing greater resilience and stamina in this struggle than the ideologically divided and organisationally fragmented Kashmiri guerrilla movement. Guerrilla activity, as of the time this book goes to press (July/August 1996), is clearly on the decline and has been for some time now in many areas, both urban and rural. In retrospect, 1994 seems to have been the benchmark year, when the guerrilla resistance started losing steam and the security forces started to decisively gain the upper hand. Moreover, the faltering armed struggle is increasingly dominated by elements alien to Kashmir, especially Pakistanis and Afghans. And as the kidnapping and murder episode involving several Western tourists during the summer of 1995 (which received wide publicity in the international media) has demonstrated, these foreign elements have scant regard for Kashmiri public opinion (which, I can personally testify, is overwhelmingly opposed to such acts), and little in common with the social base they claim to represent.[9]

Yet the cost of curbing and containing armed militancy may have been the permanent loss of whatever residual faith Kashmiris may have retained in the Indian Union even after 1990. By converting the Kashmir Valley, as well as Doda district in Jammu division, into a vast prison for its people, where no rule of law exists and the most elementary humanitarian and civil norms are systematically violated by the 'security' forces, the authorities in New Delhi have managed to completely discredit India's claim, in Kashmiri eyes, of being a democratic and secular state. The acute danger is that the Indian government, encouraged by the apparent 'dividends' of its policy of sustained, merciless repression, may confuse a military edge over armed insurgents with a permanent solution to its Kashmir problem. That could be a catastrophic error of judgment.

The fact is that despite the confusion, demoralisation and factionalisation in the *azaadi* movement as a whole, a degree of popular disenchantment with internecine killings and criminalisation among some guerrilla groups,[10] and a widespread yearning for peace among a population exhausted by violence, the people continue to be very resolute in one conviction: that Indian rule over them is illegitimate and unacceptable. The mass euphoria that ignited the uprising in 1989–90 is no longer evident in that particular form, but popular defiance has congealed into a seething, smouldering cauldron of rage and resentment against the Indian government and its military forces.

It is not too difficult to discern why. For all the talk of imminent 'normalisation' in Kashmir,[11] Srinagar still resembles an occupied city. Soldiers nervously fingering their triggers are still stationed 10 yards apart on most roads, and almost every street corner is adorned with a sandbagged bunker covered with wire netting (the latter to stop grenade attacks). Grim-faced soldiers on foot-patrol are in evidence everywhere, while military vehicles with mounted machine-guns constantly drive around in intimidating style. The dreaded 'crackdowns' (cordon-and-search operations in which entire localities are sealed off) are still a regular occurrence in the old city's maze of neighbourhoods.

The situation is equally fearful and oppressive elsewhere in the Valley. Military convoys and patrols, armed to the teeth, rumble incessantly along highways and rural backroads alike. Humiliating and frequently brutal searches and interrogations at the ubiquitous checkpoints are routine. Even tiny rural hamlets have been converted into military encampments, I found. Summary executions, custodial deaths due to torture, incidents of indiscriminate shooting, rapes and sexual molestations continue. Citizens are also regularly subjected to verbal abuse (often of a rabidly communal nature), random assaults and vicious beatings, theft and looting of money and valuables, and destruction and vandalisation of property by members of the security forces. Meanwhile, the towns and villages are filled with maimed, traumatised and bereaved people, and the central squares and marketplaces of almost every major urban centre—Srinagar, Sopore, Bijbehera, Handwara, Doda, all of which I visited—remain disfigured by large-scale arson (often accompanied by massacres) committed at one time or another by the security forces.

In a remote village in the border district of Kupwara, for example, I visited Naim Ahmed Khan, a 21-year-old farmer, in his hospital bed. Khan had been picked up from his home a few days earlier by soldiers belonging to the Rashtriya Rifles (RR), a special counter-insurgency force of the Indian Army, on the basis of a false complaint lodged against him by the *sarpanch* (headman) of his village, with whom he had been engaged in a minor land dispute. When I saw him, he was just about alive, barely able to speak or move. There were clear marks of severe torture all over his body, and the sturdy youth had been reduced to a cripple.

Naim Khan, however, was fortunate to be alive at all. Around the same time in late July 1995, Mukhtar Butt, a 45-year-old officer in the government's education department, was beaten to death by RR personnel near Kupwara town in 'retaliation' for a mine blast near the town which had injured five security personnel. Four other civilians were critically hurt in course of the retaliation, and Butt's death was reported in that evening's security briefing in Srinagar as having occurred from the mine explosion.

Or consider the fate of Marouf Ahmed Hub, a 22-year-old shopkeeper in Kishtwar, a politically volatile town deep in the mountainous reaches of Jammu's Doda district, which shares a border with the Valley district of Anantnag. When he was detained by the BSF in March 1995, his uncle, the *imam* (chief preacher) of the local mosque, rushed to intercede with the BSF authorities and obtained an assurance that the young man would be released the same evening. What *was* eventually released was his mutilated corpse, the throat slit, the body and genitals disfigured by electric shock. Recalling the incident, and the massive demonstration for *azaadi* that followed in Kishtwar, the Imam told me: 'The Indian government claims we are citizens of this country. But it treats us worse than enslaved subjects'.

His sentiments were echoed by Afzal Hussain, whom I met at Drugmulla, a village on the road from Baramulla to the border town of Uri. A middle-aged schoolteacher, Hussain was detained in a 'general crackdown' (i.e., all able-bodied males in the area were indiscriminately arrested) in May 1990, and tortured with electric shocks and red-hot iron rods at various Army detention centres for forty days. 'The tragic irony', he said with a wry smile, 'is that I'm an MA in philosophy. As a realist and a secularist, I believed wholeheartedly in India'. Indeed, such ex-believers in India are legion in Kashmir today. Abdul Qayoom Zargar, a veteran political figure in Doda town and formerly a senior National Conference leader, is a totally embittered and disillusioned man today. So is Habibullah Naik, an elderly lawyer who founded the Congress party's first branch in Baramulla town in 1964.

As a group of pro-Pakistan youth in Anantnag town told me with barely concealed glee: 'This repression is strengthening us. Every atrocity increases the people's anger against India'. Their views were echoed by Abdul Ghani Butt, a pro-Pakistan politician who heads a small faction called Muslim Conference and is reputed to have close links with Sardar Abdul Qayyum Khan, till recently 'prime minister' of Pakistan-controlled 'Azad Kashmir': 'As much confusion as possible must be created in Kashmir', he told me. 'And I must say the attitude of the Indian government and the behaviour of its forces is helping us enormously in maintaining this state of confusion'. There cannot be a more succinct expression of the strategy being orchestrated from across the Line of Actual Control. The bizarre but incontrovertible fact is that this strategy has been consistently aided and abetted by the actions and policies of the Indian state.

Independence, Not Pakistan

The near-desperate imperative of pro-Pakistan elements to generate 'confusion' in Kashmir is an understandable one. Despite the coercive and manipulative efforts of both the Indian and Pakistani authorities, mass opinion in the Valley (and among the Kashmiri Muslim majority in Doda) is not only not 'confused', but by and large unambiguous and unequivocal in the belief that only independent statehood would constitute genuine emancipation. There are a few exceptions to this general rule. For example, in the northern town of Sopore, a long-standing Jama'at-i-Islami stronghold, I found public opinion vertically split between independence and merger with Pakistan. There also appeared to be a sizeable pro-Pakistan minority in the southern town of Anantnag, where the People's League, a pro-Pakistan party founded by the popular Kashmiri politician, Shabbir Shah, has long had a base of support.

But elsewhere, popular allegiance to the ideal of independence ranges from decisive to overwhelming. 'Even the soil and the rocks and boulders here want freedom, from both India and Pakistan', declared an elderly handicapped man in rather poetic terms in Sheri village, Baramulla district, as the large crowd gathered around him in the village market nodded in vigorous assent. As a senior Jama'at activist and Hizbul Mujahideen (HM) ideologue I met in Kupwara district admitted ruefully: 'I am committed to Pakistan. But the *awaam* [people] don't agree. I think 80 per cent support the notion of independence'.

Why is this so? Sada, a bright 16-year-old girl in Pampore, a town just south of Srinagar, explained briefly but eloquently: 'I don't think what we seek—the preservation of our distinct identity and way of life—can be achieved by joining Pakistan. I do think it would be best for both India and Pakistan to leave us strictly alone'. Added Nazir Ahmed, a young chemist in the same town: 'Pampore is the hometown of Sheikh Abdul Aziz [now in an Indian prison], commander-in-chief of Al-Jehad [a pro-Pakistan guerrilla force that grew out of Shabbir Shah's People's League]. He is the most prominent political personality in this area and we respect his right to his opinion'. 'But', he continued as the customers in his shop nodded assent, 'we don't want to exchange one *gulami* [slavery] for another'. Khurshid Ahmed, 35, a cloth merchant in the nearby town of Bijbehera, in Anantnag district, pointed to the plight of Mohajirs in Pakistan to justify his preference for independence: 'Can you believe it, they are still regarded as refugees there, even after fifty years'. And how about India, I asked him. 'Even if all the boys who are militants [guerrilla fighters] now are killed, I will pick up the gun and continue the fight', came the immediate response.

Indeed, the assertion of Mohammad Yasin Malik, 30-year-old leader of the JKLF, that 'it is still JKLF ... the most principled and consistent advocate of independence, that represents the wishes of the people', is not far off the mark. The JKLF's leadership structure and cadre strength was decimated by combat deaths and arrests in 1990–91, and its members have since continued to suffer grievously from attacks by both the Indian forces and pro-Pakistan (particularly HM) gunmen. But the organisation's ideology continues to resonate powerfully with both the middle class and the masses in Kashmir. Moreover, the party's organisational apparatus, although largely dormant and inactive outside Srinagar because of fear of the two sets of guns, is still intact to some extent. Yasin Malik's decision to declare an unconditional, unilateral ceasefire against the Indian forces upon his release from prison in June 1994 (a gesture not reciprocated—the Indian forces have continued to hound and kill JKLF supporters) also correctly anticipated the growing disenchantment in Kashmiri society with the atmosphere of intimidation created by the activities of myriad gun-wielding groups.[12]

Indeed, the popular appeal of the independence slogan is such that even overt and covert pro-Pakistan forces are usually compelled to adjust or defer to it. At the very least, they cannot deny its existence. Thus, Syed Ali Shah Geelani, the senior Jama'at-i-Islami leader in Indian-administered Jammu & Kashmir, who has managed to miraculously combine a lifelong commitment to Pakistan with three terms as an elected member of India's Jammu & Kashmir legislative assembly, claims that he simply wants implementation of the (obsolete and by now largely irrelevant) UN resolutions calling for a plebiscite in Kashmir, which, of course, exclude the 'third option' of independence. But why is the 'third option' so inadmissible, I asked him. 'Because', Geelani replied, faithfully echoing the recent pronouncements of, among others, Benazir Bhutto on the subject, 'in that case India might win [a hypothetical referendum], since the Muslim vote will get badly divided while the Jammu Hindus, Kashmiri Pandits and Ladakhi Buddhists vote *en masse* for India'. Such statements seem to represent an oblique yet unmistakable acknowledgement that a very significant pro-independence constituency exists in Jammu & Kashmir, and serve as a reminder that many pro-Pakistan elements, like many prejudiced and misinformed Indians, tend to view the

Kashmir conflict in terms of extremely reductive and superficial communal categories (on this subject, more later).

Similarly, covert sympathisers of merger with Pakistan often tend to hide behind the expansive and nebulous rhetoric of 'right to self-determination'. Mehmooda Andrabi, organiser of *Dukhtaran-i-Islam* ('Daughters of Islam', an Islamist women's organisation) in Doda district and a follower of Shabbir Shah, is typical of this category. 'We only want our right of self-determination to be granted', she told me. 'After that, it's up to the people to decide'. Despite repeated queries, she persistently refused to take a stand on what her own political convictions on this question might be. This kind of equivocation is highly unconvincing to many Kashmiri civilians, such as Abdul Ahad Wani, an elderly working-class resident of Ganderbal, a town on Srinagar's outskirts. Both Wani's brothers were murdered in 1993 (and he himself brutally assaulted) by HM cadres (whom he described as 'fundamentalists') for daring to rebuild a *ziyarat* (shrine cum mausoleum) to a Sufi saint that had been burned down by members of that guerrilla group.[13]

Indeed, the continuing popular appeal of the ideology of independence has been the one constant in the many twists and turns the uprising has taken since 1990. As early as April 1991, for example, large anti-Pakistan demonstrations erupted in Srinagar after a JKLF area commander was killed by HM gunmen. In February 1992, Pakistani forces shot dead at least twelve people (twenty-one, according to JKLF sources), and beat and arrested hundreds more, to break up a symbolic cross-border 'unity march' from 'Azad' Kashmir to Indian-administered Kashmir by an estimated 30,000 JKLF supporters. When this news reached Srinagar, reported an Indian newsmagazine, '60,000 people gathered' within hours at Hazratbal mosque, Kashmir's holiest Muslim shrine, 'defying [Indian] curfew', in response to a JKLF call for mass protests against the killing of Kashmiri activists by Pakistan. The episode was described as 'a major [political] victory for JKLF groups operating in the Valley over Pakistan-sponsored factions like HM' (*IT* 1992a: 15; 1992b: 31–32).

In May 1993, Javed Mir, then the top JKLF political leader in the Valley, said in an interview (*IT* 1993b: 27) that he was 'aware' that 'Pakistan has floated its own groups in the Valley', and that 'we will fight Pakistan too if the need arises'. But he reiterated that 'India is our first enemy', for 'Pakistan is at least not raping our women and setting fire to our homes'. Asked about HM's military supremacy, he replied that 'gunpower is not the only thing that matters. The public is the most powerful weapon and it is on our side'.

In May 1994, in a mammoth display of popular support, hundreds of thousands flooded the streets of Srinagar to welcome Yasin Malik back from captivity.[14] A particularly poignant moment of truth arrived in June 1994, following the assassination of the prominent political and religious leader, Qazi Nissar, by an alleged HM member. 'An unprecedented outburst of fury against pro-Pakistani insurgents' erupted at his funeral, with 'more than 100,000 Kashmiris' shouting such slogans as 'Down with HM', 'Death to Pakistan' and 'We want freedom'. A general strike called to protest the murder paralysed life throughout Kashmir, and 'houses all over the Valley turned off their lights between 7 PM and 10 PM in a show of solidarity'. It was correctly noted, however, that the Indian government had little cause to be cheered by this development, for 'the slogans in no way indicate that Kashmiris want to live within the Indian union. Rather, they send a clear signal that Kashmir wants independence from both its neighbours'.[15]

Indeed, it is increasingly clear that Pakistan's heavy-handed, self-interested meddling in the uprising has boomeranged on the civilian and military establishment of that country, and seriously damaged the latter's credentials (even as a purely strategic ally), in the eyes of most Kashmiris. Edward Desmond (1995: 11–12) writes of the long-term implications of the Pakistani policy of sowing 'confusion' in the *azaadi* movement by channelling material aid solely to favoured groups, and expediting the fragmentation of the movement by encouraging the formation of numerous splinter parties:

> It is clear that in the Valley, Pakistan's heavy influence on the movement is deeply resented, especially among JKLF supporters. India clearly hopes to exploit the sentiment, once the Kashmiris find the fight is futile. In the long run, Pakistan's powerful intervention may prove to have undermined the very uprising it sought to fortify.[16]

Another observer has gone even further; she predicts that 'in the end, Pakistan's policies may push Kashmir, however reluctantly,

more deeply into India's fold' (Newberg 1995: 73).[17] It is noteworthy, in this connection, that even HM commander Salahuddin
has emphatically stated that 'no settlement can be reached without
the active physical participation of the representatives of Kashmir.
Kashmir is the real party in the case. India and Pakistan will not
decide by themselves. It is not possible'.[18]

The Status of Pakistan-Controlled Kashmir

Indeed, Pakistan's vociferous advocacy of Kashmiri self-determination rings hollow and hypocritical when one considers that
one-third of Jammu & Kashmir which has been under Pakistani
domination since 1947–48. This consists of two distinct geographical entities: the five districts of Muzaffarabad, Bagh, Rawlakot,
Kotli and Mirpur, which constitute 'Azad Jammu & Kashmir'
(AK); and Gilgit and Baltistan, sparsely-populated and remote
mountainous territories in the upper Himalayas, constituting the
'Northern Areas' which are directly administered by Pakistan.

The concepts of rights and representation are largely unknown
in Gilgit & Baltistan. The area has been ruled directly by Pakistan's
Ministry of Kashmir Affairs (MKA) since 1947 through an executive administrator, invariably a Pakistani bureaucrat or retired
military officer. The administrator is nominally assisted by a twenty-
six-member 'council' composed of local notables, which has an
'advisory' role. The area is essentially a vast Pakistani military
base, in much the same way that Ladakh, a contiguous and similarly huge and thinly-populated mountainous territory which is part
of Indian-administered Jammu & Kashmir, is an Indian military
base.

No genuine elections have ever been held, and the judicial
system is rudimentary. When the pro-independence Jammu &
Kashmir People's National Party (JKPNP) organised a public rally
in Gilgit in 1993, it provoked much curiosity among locals, to
whom the notion of a political meeting is apparently something of
a novelty. In 1985–86, the Gilgit & Baltistan Bar Association
(which continues to be vocal today) submitted a petition to the
Pakistani government, requesting that the territory be incorporated
into Pakistan as a constituent province, with rights and duties

thereof, or at least be given local government on the AK model. The result was a fierce crackdown by the military regime of Zia -ul Haq, in which hundreds were reportedly killed. In addition, the Pakistani authorities have apparently been instigating Shia–Sunni clashes in the area to keep the population divided.[19] In 1963, Pakistan also unilaterally ceded a sizeable chunk of Gilgit & Baltistan to China, which has long had territorial claims in the area.

There is nothing particularly 'azad' (free) about Azad Kashmir either. For one thing, its constitution stipulates that 'no person or political party in Azad Jammu & Kashmir shall be permitted to propagate against or take part in activities prejudicial or detrimental to the ideology of the State's accession to Pakistan' (cited in Tahir 1993: 2). JKLF and JKPNP do not participate in elections to AK's supposedly autonomous assembly, because to be allowed to do so, they have to first sign legally-binding affidavits affirming this principle. Bureaucrats and other government employees suspected of disloyalty to the officially-sanctioned ideology are routinely dismissed from their jobs. Like Indian-administered Jammu & Kashmir, Azad Kashmir is heavily militarised, with a huge Pakistan Army presence. Outside visitors, including journalists and human rights activists, are closely watched, and their movements are strictly circumscribed. One such visitor found in 1990 that development has been grossly neglected: 'While roads are maintained … to facilitate troop movement … the villages and smaller towns are anything but prosperous' (IT 1990b).

While AK has had a series of 'autonomous' governments, it has been observed that 'from 1948 into … the early 1970s, it was … the MKA that probably had the best claim to being … head of the Azad Kashmir government' (Rose 1992: 238). Since the 1970s, authority has been divided between the AK government in Muzaffarabad, its capital, and a council based in Islamabad, Pakistan's capital, with most significant matters delegated to the latter. Both the AK police chief and chief secretary (the top administrator) are invariably Pakistanis, 'on deputation' from Islamabad, as are other high-ranking civil and police officials. AK has no fiscal autonomy worth the name, and is totally dependent on the central government for its finances. An ex-president of AK has described this situation as 'government of Azad Kashmir, by Pakistanis, for Pakistan'. He has also pointed to the striking continuity between the earlier British and present Pakistani rule: a similar viceregal system, with the MKA in the metropolitan capital as the paramount authority, and the *biradari* system, with its feudal–oligarchical connotations, continuing to be the basis of local politics (ibid.: 246, 252). Election results are crudely manipulated, and occasionally subverted, from the centre,[20] and corruption is rife in official circles.[21]

All in all, the fate of 'Azad Kashmir' at the hands of military–bureaucratic Pakistan bears a remarkable similarity to what Kashmiris in the Valley have suffered in democratic India. The former has been subjected to all the bizarre political experiments of Pakistani military dictators (spurious 'basic democracy' under Ayub Khan in the 1960s, martial law and enforced 'Islamisation' under Zia-ul Haq in the 1980s), and Pakistan's reactionary laws pertaining to the status of women and religious minorities are applicable in AK. The recent incumbent in Muzaffarabad, 'Prime Minister' Abdul Qayyum Khan, has consistently displayed an exaggerated obsequiousness towards his masters. Recently, he clearly stated:

> I look at Kashmir from Pakistan's point of view ... the Kashmiris and Kashmir are not a separate geographical or historical entity, but part and parcel of Pakistan ... JKLF stands for independent Kashmir ... I am opposed to the idea of an independent Kashmir ... I am also averse to local geographical nationalism ... I am prepared to forget about Kashmir if it comes to a ... choice between the security of Pakistan and Kashmir ... Kashmir can be sacrificed for Pakistan, but Pakistan cannot be sacrificed for Kashmir (*ISF* 1992: 175–200).[22]

The conclusion is inescapable: the leader of 'liberated' Kashmir is a stooge of the Pakistani state.[23] Perspectives on Kashmir emanating from the Pakistani political and military establishment are not grounds for optimism either. One recent anthology (Jan and Sarwar 1990) is, with few exceptions, a distillation of coarse prejudice, paranoia and sectarianism. Almost all its contributors axiomatically equate Kashmir's 'liberation' with incorporation into Pakistan, and some are deluded enough to regard the present uprising in the Valley as the unfinished business of partition (long-awaited vindication of the 'two-nation theory'). Significantly, no Pakistani government has ever admitted, even in principle, that Kashmiri self-determination might possibly take the form of independent statehood. Indeed, even though Pakistan still rhetorically demands the plebiscite, Benazir Bhutto agrees fully with her Indian counterparts that the 'third option' (that of independence) cannot be allowed under any circumstances.[24] Little wonder, then, that Dr Mirajuddin Munshi, a prominent pro-independence member of the intelligentsia of Srinagar, believes that 'if [hypothetically] we are integrated into Pakistan, there will be another uprising in ten years' time'.

It is noteworthy, however, that there has been a significant resurgence of pro-independence sentiment in AK in the last few years. According to Qasim Khokhar, a JKLF leader from Mirpur, a major town in 'Azad Kashmir', the 1980s were an especially difficult and frustrating decade for independence activists, what with the crushing burdens of martial law and Islamisation. However, by the end of the decade, the insurrection across the border had begun to have a tremendous demonstration-effect on Azad Kashmir, and attendance at JKLF meetings, for example, rose dramatically, despite the threat of harassment and victimisation.[25] Tens of thousands joined the Pakistan-based JKLF chairman Amanullah Khan's cross-border march in 1992, and following its forcible suppression, much to the discomfiture of Pakistan and its supporters, AK observed a total three-day general strike in protest. Pro-independence feelings are, according to the testimony of several AK residents I have spoken to, especially widespread among the younger generation, while older people tend to be more acquiescent.[26]

A European human rights activist who visited the area in early 1994 reported widespread 'yearning for freedom from Pakistani rule', and rising support for the notion of a reunified and independent Kashmir (*IA* 1994b: 12; 1994: 4). An American scholar has provided a similarly revealing account of his conversation, in 1989, with members of the Kashmir Liberation Cell, a body sponsored and funded by the Pakistani and AK governments. When he queried why maps of Jammu & Kashmir on Cell publications included Aksai Chin, currently under Chinese control, as well as the area of Gilgit & Baltistan ceded to China by Pakistan, the Cell's director 'asserted with some fervour that "this is what Jammu & Kashmir was before and what it will be again when we are independent"'. Obviously, it is not only India that has ... cause for concern about the future of its relationship with Kashmir' (Rose

1992: 251). As one Indian author has commented, 'obviously the majority of Kashmiri Muslims whether in India or Pakistan share a vision of independence' (Kadian 1992: 140).

The 'Communalisation' of 'Kashmiriyat'? Re-examining the 'Pandit Exodus' and its Aftermath

Some 100,000 of the approximately 140,000-strong Pandit community[27] of the Kashmir Valley have moved to Jammu, Delhi and other locations since the uprising began in January 1990. Most of this 'exodus' occurred within the space of a few weeks in February and March 1990. The ostensible catalyst was the killing of several dozen persons belonging to this group by 'militants' between September 1989 and March 1990.

A remarkable preoccupation with this 'exodus' pervades much recent writing by Indians on Kashmir, spurious scholarship and popular journalism alike. Thus, T.N. Madan claims that

in the Valley ... Hindus were a 3 per cent minority of about 180,000 [?] ... a couple of thousand of whom have been reportedly killed or critically injured, and many of whose properties have been plundered and burnt ... not only Hindus, but those Muslims, too, who do not seem in full agreement, are the targets of fundamentalists and secessionists. In fact, about three times as many Muslims as Hindus are reported to have been killed (Madan 1993: 694).

Two Pandits (one an expatriate living in the United States, the other a refugee in Jammu), in their contribution to a recent anthology on various aspects of the Kashmir question, claim that 'over 260,000 [Pandits] ... had to run for their lives', 'thousands of ... homes [were] looted or burnt', and a 'number of ... women gang-raped', especially in 'far-flung villages'. They attribute this 'terrorist violence' to 'Pan-Islamic fundamentalism in Asia'. In remarks obviously directed at JKLF, they add that 'if there are any groups involved who call themselves secular, their ... actions against religious minorities belie their self-serving pronouncements. They could have stood up for protection of Hindus right from the beginning' (Kaul and Teng 1992: 175–88). And a recent feature article in a mass-circulated Indian newsmagazine reports that 1,200 Pandits have been killed in the Valley, 1,600 houses burnt, 50 temples destroyed, and that over 350,000 Pandits have fled, all 'because they refused to embrace Islam' (*Sunday* 1994: 70–74).

These are serious charges, and their implications are grave indeed. If they are true, the centuries-long harmonious coexistence of the Valley's Pandit minority and Muslim majority, sustained by the majority's eclectic, mystical Sufi tradition, has been brutally disrupted by a mass upsurge of extreme intolerance, cruelty and hatred among Kashmiri Muslims. It also means that the Kashmiri uprising is nothing but a communal terrorist campaign which has systematically targeted the lives, property and places of worship of a tiny, vulnerable minority. The implications for the Kashmiri movement's claim to the right of self-determination are equally obvious. A people who wantonly violate the basic rights of their own minorities cannot possibly have a moral right to demand self-determination for themselves, leave alone claim any 'democratic' credentials for their struggle. Quite the opposite: such a struggle must be ruthlessly exterminated if 'secularism', the Indian state's organising principle, is to survive. Any serious discussion of the Kashmir question must therefore take these allegations of abuses into account, and clarify their veracity and significance.

A consideration of the available evidence reveals that these allegations are, largely though not entirely, a potpourri of fabrication and exaggeration. The most blatant falsehoods are obvious. It is simply impossible for a community numbering fewer than 140,000 to generate 260,000 or 350,000 refugees from Islamic terror, especially since there is *still* a sizeable Pandit population (perhaps 20,000) living in Kashmir's towns and villages, interspersed among over 3.5 million Muslims. The number of Pandits actually killed is in the dozens, not thousands. For example, the All-India Kashmiri Pandit Conference stated on 15 March 1990, with the exodus substantially complete, that a total of thirty-two Pandits had been killed by militants since September 1989 (Bose et al. 1991: 261).[28] It is difficult to determine where Madan, for example, has obtained his figure of 2,000 dead and mortally wounded; he alludes to 'newspaper reports' but provides no specific citations. But even the wildest concoctions published in the

Indian press mention around a thousand casualties (*TS* 1991; *Sunday* 1994), and even an RSS publication devoted to documenting 'genocide' of Kashmiri Hindus claims that 600 Pandits have been murdered, and thirty-six temples 'sacrileged and desecrated' (it provides about sixty specific 'cases' of killings and assaults) (RSS 1991: 28, 36).

As for temples destroyed: in February 1993, an investigative team from India's leading English-language newsmagazine visited Kashmir, armed with a list of twenty-three 'destroyed or desecrated' temples, obtained, after much effort, from BJP's Delhi office. BJP's senior leaders had been speaking out about these temples since 1990, and a few days after the December 1992 demolition of the Babri Mosque in Ayodhya, BJP president L.K. Advani had stated with much moral outrage in response to criticism: 'None raised a voice when forty-odd temples were desecrated in Kashmir. Why these double-standards?' The investigators, who visited and photographed each and every site, found that twenty-one of the twenty-three shrines were totally intact; they had never even been threatened, attested their *pujaris* (priests), some of whom willingly showed the visitors around. Indeed, the journalists found that 'even in villages which are left with only one or two Pandit homes [the rest having joined the 'exodus'], the temples are safe. The Pandit families have ... become custodians of the temples. They are encouraged by their Muslim neighbours to regularly offer prayers'. This was true even 'in villages that abound with militants' (*IT* 1993a: 22–25).

The respect that Kashmiri Muslims have customarily shown towards Hindu places of worship has, therefore, endured for the most part even in these troubled times. And there are plenty of other recent precedents that substantiate this fact. Following the destruction of a few temples in the engineered riots of 1986, for instance, Balraj Puri visited Anantnag, the worst-affected district. After he appealed for repair funds in front of a damaged temple, he writes, local Muslims donated a total of Rs 10,000 within minutes (Puri 1993: 35).

As for reports of burnt and looted homes, the Indian government's then minister of Kashmir affairs, George Fernandes (1992: 291) publicly testified after extensively touring the Valley in the autumn of 1990: 'The property, houses, orchards owned by the Pandits have not been damaged in the last one year. The apples ... from these orchards have been plucked and the money deposited. The houses are being looked after [by local Muslims] as they were earlier'.[29] A team of Indian civil libertarians visiting the Valley in March–April 1990 found that 'whenever local papers appear, there is always an appeal on behalf of the Mujahideen ... on the front page, requesting ... Pandits to return.... In this appeal, the Muslims are warned against occupying, tampering with or selling any movable or immovable property belonging to ... Pandits' (PUCL et al. 1991: 214). When in April 1992 two Pandit women were in fact raped and killed by armed men, large-scale protests, led by furious Kashmiri Muslim women, erupted in the Valley. All this is in stark contrast to the sentiments normally expressed by self-proclaimed Pandit 'spokesmen', who typically dismiss 'so-called violations of human rights of Kashmiri "civilians" by Indian security forces' as concoctions of the 'Pakistani propaganda mill' (Kaul and Teng 1992: 180).

But what of the several dozen Pandits who were murdered in the early months of the insurgency? It seems that at least some of these killings were inspired by some sort of political motive, rather than simply 'pan-Islamic fundamentalism'. For example, the first assassination, in September 1989, claimed the life of Jammu & Kashmir's BJP president; the second victim, two months later, was a (Hindu) judge who had years earlier sentenced Maqbool Butt to death. JKLF, which took responsibility on both occasions, was at some pains to emphasise that the two were not targeted because of their religion. In February 1990, the respected Pandit director of the Srinagar station of India's state-owned television was shot by JKLF gunmen for the 'offence' of implementing the government's media policy of suppression and disinformation.[30] Indeed, the first major political assassination, in August 1989, claimed a *Muslim* NC official, and over the next several months, up to a hundred (not 6,000, as Madan seems to be insinuating) Kashmiri Muslims were killed for 'collaborating' (Bose et al. 1991: 261).

Other Hindu victims included Indian intelligence officials. In fact, the relatively high proportion of Pandits among targeted 'collaborators' can to some extent be explained by the disproportionately high Pandit representation in the government services, including intelligence service. An early report on the exodus based on interviews with migrants in Jammu found that most migrant families had not been directly threatened, though many said that they had felt insecure and intimidated by the generally disturbed atmosphere, and at the sight of huge *azaadi* processions chanting distinctly Islamic slogans (*Allah-o-Akbar*, etc.). One migrant who said he *had* received death threats had been a magistrate in Sopore, responsible for issuing firing orders on protest demonstrations (*TT* 1990).

In other words, while there is evidence of selective targeting of some Pandits, especially those with connections to government, bureaucracy, or pro-India political parties, there is no evidence of a concerted murder and mass expulsion campaign directed exclusively at Kashmiri Hindus, and no evidence that points to a systematic pattern of abuse of Hindu properties and shrines. It is indeed remarkable that neither the National Front (1989–90) nor the Congress (I) (1991–96) governments in Delhi made *any* effort to challenge the blatant disinformation being put out by organisations like RSS and BJP on this score; it was left to individual journalists and human rights activists to do so. More reprehensibly, what these disoriented and uprooted Pandits (many of them well educated, and used to a life of relative affluence and privilege) have received from government and bureaucracy in India is not sympathy and succour, but indifference, neglect and even outright hostility.[31] As a result, most organised relief and rehabilitation work has fallen to the RSS and its affiliates, especially in Jammu, and the latter have preyed on the refugees' insecurity and degradation to make Hindutva recruits of many of them.

One vociferous section has even floated the concept of a 'sterilised Pandit homeland' in the Valley. The proposed homeland, to be known as 'Pannun Kashmir', would cover 55 per cent of the Valley's land area (8600 of 15853 sq km), and contain all four of its largest towns: Srinagar, Anantnag, Baramulla and Sopore (*Sunday* 1994: 70–74).[32] What would happen to the several million Kashmiri Muslims who live in this area is left unspecified.

There is also near-universal conviction among Kashmiri Muslims that the departure of such a large number of Pandits within such a short period of time was the result of instigation by, and connivance of, the administration of the then governor, Jagmohan, who took over for four particularly repressive months after Farooq's dismissal in January 1990. This view holds that a fear-psychosis was deliberately created in the community by Jagmohan's administration, in two ways. First, by conveying to Pandits that the fundamentalist hordes would make them a prime target, and second, by informing the leaders of their community organisations (in early February 1990) that the government was planning an indiscriminate military crackdown to eradicate the uprising once and for all, and that Pandits, who live interspersed among huge Muslim majorities in most places, should *temporarily* leave the Valley for their own safety. Various incentives were allegedly provided to encourage the 'exodus', including in some cases government transport, promises of free and comfortable accommodation in Jammu and of guaranteed salary-payments for those in government employment. This was allegedly done under cover of a media blackout: in late January, the Indian and foreign press was expelled from the Valley, and crippling restrictions were placed on the local press.

This view is supported by two letters written by migrant Pandits 'rotting' in Jammu camps to an Urdu newspaper in Srinagar, *Alsafa*, and published on 22 September and 18 October 1990.[33] When, in March 1990, a visiting Indian civil liberties team asked Jagmohan's chief secretary about persistent rumours of government transport being provided to the evacuees, he first denied it altogether, and then said that while this was not government *policy*, he could not rule out the possibility of some officials doing it on their own initiative. This team, and another which visited some time later, found many Pandits living quite confidently in Srinagar. One of them, a middle-aged man, told his interviewers that 'if anyone has to run away from the valley, it will be the Muslims ... the way they're being killed'. In another case, a young woman was living as a tenant with a Muslim family: the women of the family 'told us with pride that they ... looked upon Mrs Sapru as their daughter and come what may there could be no question of her leaving the family' (Bose et al. 1991: 238, 241; PUCL et al. 1991).

There is further circumstantial evidence of official complicity in the mass flight of Pandits. In mid-March 1990, for example, Balraj Puri helped set up a joint Hindu–Muslim committee in Srinagar to try and halt the 'exodus'. Within weeks, however, a senior Pandit member of this committee arrived in Jammu as a 'refugee'. He informed Puri that days after the committee was established, 'the Governor sent a DSP [Deputy Superintendent of Police] to him with an air ticket for Jammu, a jeep to take him to the airport, an offer of accommodation at Jammu and advice to leave Kashmir immediately' (Puri 1993: 65). An Indian journalist visiting Srinagar in April 1990 reported that '"Hindu or Muslim?" is the routine question at numerous BSF and CRPF barriers' (Kagal 1990). And according to another Indian journalist visiting in 1992, 'if the answer was Hindu, the reply invariably was: *'Phir tum yahan kya kar rahey ho, marna hai kya'* [then what are you doing here, want to die?] (*IWI* 1992: 10).[34]

But in the ultimate analysis, it is best to let Pandits who have experienced life in the Valley since 1990 speak for themselves. In September 1990, Som Nath's was one of only two Pandit peasant families living in Nunarr, a village in Srinagar district. With his best friend, Ghulam Mohammad Sofi, a shopowner, sitting by his side, Nath told an Indian journalist who inquired about his safety: *'Yahan par aise log hai jo hamare upar marte hain'* [There are people here ready to die for us]. He further pointed out that 'no one has touched' the fields of other Pandits who had fled the village (*Frontline* 1990). In the summer of 1992, Amitabh Mattoo, a young Pandit studying at Oxford, returned to visit his home in Srinagar. He went in trepidation, having been repeatedly warned that 'Kashmiri Muslims had undergone ... a collective Kafkaesque metamorphosis'. He found that

> our *mohalla* [neighbourhood] ... had not changed except for ... two CRPF bunkers ... I was amazed at the friendliness and warmth with which I was greeted. Muslim neighbours turned up with *mithai* [sweets] and blessed me ... as soon as word ·got around I was in town and invited me to their house to celebrate the reunion with *sevion-ki-khir* [vermicelli pudding, a delicacy]. There was not a single Muslim friend or acquaintance ... who did not greet me as he would have ... before the troubles began (*IWI* 1992: 10).

Indeed, when the unavoidable pre-dawn 'crackdown' took place in his *mohalla*, 'Hindu, Muslim and Sikh neighbours were united in their resentment against the security forces' (ibid.).

Yet another eloquent testimony comes from Khemlata Wakhloo. She and her husband were kidnapped in late 1991 by the Hizbullah, a guerrilla group. Freed after forty-five days in captivity, she writes:

> During this time we lived for varying periods ... in 57 homes. All those people showered love and hospitality on us ... we owe

them all a debt of gratitude. With their sympathy ... we were better able to cope with ... agonising moments ... We met a cross-section of people in the villages and a sizeable number of youth belonging to manifold militant organisations. We talked to all of them about education, religion, social life, political situation, *Kashmiriyat*, human emotions and above all, ways and means of building bridges and winning hearts. These interactions have reinforced our faith in the values of love and goodness which are still very deeply ingrained in the Kashmiri ethos (Wakhloo 1992: 396).

In the latter half of 1995, I also found that the spirit of amicable coexistence between individuals and communities professing different religious faiths was, although severely strained, not entirely absent in Jammu & Kashmir. In a major town in Baramulla district, for example, I met Lalit Kumar Chukku, a 45-year-old Pandit resident. A clerk by profession, Chukku has been living in this town for the past eighteen years. 'I have spent my whole life in Kashmir, as have my father and grandfather before me', he said. 'Not once, since 1990 or before that, have I ever had any problem with my Muslim brothers. They always give me full *izzat* [respect]. In fact, we are just not used to thinking in terms of Hindus and Muslims here. We consider ourselves part of the same community'. Glancing affectionately at his co-worker, Abdul Majid Dar, 30, he continued: 'I'm a bachelor, I have no family. But Abdul Majid is like a younger brother to me. When I fell seriously ill recently, it was he who took me to the hospital and arranged for my medicine and injections'. When a wedding took place recently in a Hindu family, Chukku recounted, the *baraat* (marriage party) travelled openly and safely from the town to Ganderbal, near Srinagar, escorted by local Muslims. 'Nothing has changed', he told me. 'During *Eid* [Muslim festival], I invariably visit the houses of [Muslim] neighbours and friends to offer *mubarak* [greetings], and they inevitably show up with sweets and good wishes at my door during *Shivratri* [a Hindu religious event]. In fact, during *hartals* [strikes] and curfews, local [Muslim] shopkeepers and vendors have insisted that I take their fruits and vegetables for free'.

Chukku's sentiments were echoed by another Pandit, 25-year-old Moti Lal, a minor government employee in the same town. Lal lives in the town with his young wife and three small children.

'No one has ever threatened, harassed or mistreated us here', he said. When I met the entire family in their modest two-room home, they were perfectly contented and relaxed, and visibly living in complete harmony with their Muslim neighbours.[35] Gurdial Singh Bains, 40, a third generation Sikh resident of the same town, similarly attested that 'relations between the Muslim community and Hindu and Sikh minorities are generally cordial. There are occasional exceptions, but then, there have always been exceptions'. Even in 1947, he pointed out, 'while most local people protected the Hindus and Sikhs here, some misguided elements did side with the raiders [from Pakistan]'.

These are not isolated instances. In a remote village in Baramulla district, I encountered Pyare Lal Raina, who left the Valley in fright in 1990, but returned in mid-1991. Why, I asked him. 'Because Kashmir is my homeland, and I don't feel comfortable anywhere else', he replied. 'Since coming back, the affection and sense of security I have received from the Muslims here has surpassed all my expectations. I will never be able to forget it'. His account was corroborated by Bansi Lal Bazaz, a 35-year-old Pandit and resident of the same village since 1991. 'We have always lived in complete safety and dignity here', he told me, his wife and three young children at his side. Both men stated clearly that they are totally opposed to armed insurgency, and only wished for a speedy end to the violence. But their experiences completely contradict the lie that Kashmiri Muslims have undergone a collective, Kafkaesque metamorphosis into fundamentalist fanatics.

Similarly, the residents of Doda district (which is 60 per cent Kashmiri Muslim, 40 per cent Hindu) are justly proud of their record of communal amity, which they are struggling to maintain despite severe pressures and provocations. In fact, the district, which is part of the Jammu region, has a long history of political movements transcending sectarian divisions. In 1974, for example, a major local agitation took place in the mountain town of Kishtwar, with Hindus and Muslims unitedly demanding establishment of a college in Kishtwar town and separate district status for Kishtwar *tehsil* or subdivision (Doda district is vast, encompassing 12,000 sq km). Five persons, among them both Hindu and Muslim, died then in police firing.

More recently, in August 1993, when sixteen Hindus were pulled out from a bus near Kishtwar town (which is 52 per cent Muslim,

48 per cent Hindu) and massacred by unknown assassins, Maulana Farooq Hussain Kitchloo, the *imam* of the local mosque, promptly denounced the killings and declared a general strike in protest, thus helping forestall the obvious incitement to communal violence. He did the same in July 1995, when ten members of a Hindu marriage party (including six Hindus and four Muslims) were abducted by guerrillas from a mountain village near the town. As Manmohan Gupta, Doda district president of BJP and a resident of Kishtwar town (he has survived three attempts on his life) narrated to me: 'There is still a lot of friendship and *humdardi* [solidarity] between the communities. The other day, when a Hindu girl got married, it was the Muslim boys of the *mohalla* who carried her *palki* [the bridal palanquin]. When a death occurs in a family, it is often difficult to tell whether it's a Hindu or Muslim household, since the mourning is in common'.

And Kishtwar is no solitary exception either. In July 1992, the entire market in Doda town (80 per cent Muslim, 20 per cent Hindu) was razed by the CRPF as reprisal against a guerrilla raid. Of the money collected at the town mosque for relief and reconstruction, Rs 75,000 went to a Hindu who had lost his shop in the arson.[36]

In sum, the tragic displacement of the Kashmiri Pandits has to be seen in its proper context: their tragedy is but part of the broader, continuing tragedy that has engulfed and overwhelmed the whole of Kashmir since 1990. Since the ultimate fate of the Pandit minority is inescapably and inseparably connected to how events unfold in Kashmir in the next few years, their sad plight can only change for the better if a serious, sincere effort is initiated to find a just, durable and democratic solution to the Kashmir crisis in its totality. That, in turn, can only be accomplished through a civilised process of dialogue and, eventually, negotiations.

The Role of Islam in the Kashmiri Independence Movement: An Interpretation and Assessment

The evidence of powerful grass-roots efforts at unity, harmony and cooperation notwithstanding, it seems clear that much of the political, military, diplomatic, media and 'intellectual' establishment in India continues to view the Kashmir question, explicitly or implicitly, through the jaundiced and distinctly 'communal' lens of Hindu–Muslim conflict. Madan, for example, writes that 'the silence of Muslim political leadership in India on ... Kashmir underscores the tragic fact that all is not well with Indian secularism (Madan 1993: 694). It is not clear why Indian Muslim 'leaders', whoever they may be, should feel obliged to comment on Kashmir, *unless*, of course, the uprising is regarded simply as a communal problem created by malevolent Muslim 'fundamentalists' and 'secessionists'.[37] What is thereby obscured is what the Kashmir crisis reveals above all: that all is not well with India's democracy.

And this kind of world-view can have quite deadly consequences for human lives, especially when it permeates entire institutional apparatuses of power and control, such as the Indian state. To many Indians, first and foremost the several hundred thousand heavily-armed defenders of democracy and secularism in Kashmir, 'the face of the Kashmiri' has dissolved 'into a blurred, featureless mask. He has become a secessionist-terrorist-fundamentalist traitor' (Kagal 1990). This warped image,[38] and the rhetoric of 'national unity and integrity' that buttresses it, have nothing to do either with democracy and secularism, or, one might argue, with the ideals of those who once fought oppression and injustice in the name of Indian nationalism.[39]

On 30 March 1990, for instance, several schoolchildren had gathered for private tuition in the Srinagar home of a Pandit teacher, Bhushan Lal Bazaz. CRPF men broke into the house after a fire-fight with local 'militants', and asked everyone present their names. The one Muslim pupil, Nazeer Sofi, 14, was shot dead on the spot (Kagal 1990; PUCL 1991: 215). On 31 July 1992, BSF soldiers broke into an upper middle-class home in downtown Srinagar after a similar incident, and killed two teenaged brothers watching television. According to their sister, who survived, the soldiers were yelling: *'Saale Musalmaanon, hum tumko zinda nahin chhodenge'* [Muslim bastards, we won't leave you alive] (*IWI* 1992: 6).

Indeed, Kashmiris of both sexes and all ages and social backgrounds complained to me about the coarse communal insults to which they are routinely subjected, at roadblocks and during crackdowns, and I was an eyewitness to several such incidents. A

76-year-old Muslim preacher in Sopore was forced to chant 'Ram Ram' at gunpoint by army soldiers (Asia Watch 1991: 70–71), and women in a Srinagar *mohalla* were lined up and ordered to shout *'Bharat Mata ki Jai'* [Victory to Mother India] (Kagal 1990).[40] It seems that though, much like in Bosnia–Herzegovina, many Kashmiris do feel 'they are being killed and destroyed because they are Muslims' (PUCL et al. 1991: 217), they have, on the whole, shown significant restraint and temperance in the face of extreme provocation. And to the extent their movement may have been hijacked by 'fundamentalist' elements, the culpability (or credit!) for this lies first of all with the repression practised by the Indian state, and second, with the Pakistani regime, who are the sponsors of most such elements. There are indeed several hundred *Jehad* specialists, mainly underemployed Afghan mujahideen and Pakistani religious radicals but also men from the Sudan, Lebanon and Egypt, among other countries, fighting in Kashmir. My conversations with Kashmiris indicate that by and large, these 'guests' are merely tolerated, and increasingly viewed as a nuisance and embarrassment.[41]

But even if the spectre of 'Islamic fundamentalism' looming over Kashmir is largely a scaremongering myth assiduously promoted by certain quarters in order to justify a policy of repression, the question remains: what role, precisely, *has* Islamic identity played in Kashmir's politics, historically and in the contemporary uprising? This question cannot be resolved with reference to Kashmir alone, but necessarily has to be situated in the context of a broader framework of analysis.

Since the Iranian Revolution of 1979, a particularly pernicious tendency has developed in influential segments of Western academia and media to demonise Islam as a faith, and to depict Muslim societies, with varying degrees of candour and crudity, as 'menacing, recalcitrant, corrupt ... profoundly perverse ... [and] fundamentally wicked', and their religion as having 'an essential, primordial, unchanging character' (Anderson 1991: 93).[42] A recent article primarily devoted to delineating an alleged Islamic threat to 'Western interests, values and power', with the help of such bizarre concepts as 'civilisation-rallying', by an American political scientist, Samuel Huntington, is a good example of this type of characterisation. Huntington (who, the noted philosopher George Kateb (1984: 184–86) has argued, essentially represents an 'anti-democratic authoritarianism', and not what he purports to champion, liberal democracy) locates a particularly menacing, primordial 'civilisa-tion' in 'the crescent-shaped Islamic bloc of nations, from the bulge of Africa to Central Asia'. 'Islam', he proclaims, 'has bloody borders'. And he speaks of 'the historic clash between Muslim and Hindu in the subcontinent' (Huntington 1993: 22–49); this, no doubt, would be his explanation of the Kashmir conflict.

Of course, there is nothing novel whatsoever about such hypotheses. This is the American conservative's 'order-and-stability' paradigm gone quite wild, and this particular formulation is per-haps shaped by a sour mix of 'anti-democratic authoritarianism', genuine paranoia and intellectual bankruptcy. As Edward Said (1981) would observe, this is the 'canonical hymn to the beleaguered Western ethos which appears ... periodically in the ... West'. And Said has excellently summarised its essential characteristics: 'A penchant for dividing the world into pro- and anti-American ... an unwillingness to report political processes [and, I would add, a grotesque ignorance and caricaturing of complex histories], an imposition of patterns and values ethnocentric or irrelevant or both, pure misinformation, repetition, an avoidance of detail, an absence of genuine perspective', as well as the 'redivi[sion of] the world into Orient and Occident ["West against the Rest" is Huntington's favoured phrase] ... the better to blind ourselves not only to the world but to ourselves and to what our relationship to the so-called Third World has really been' (ibid.: 35, 40). Apart from being absurd, this is hackneyed stuff.

This form of thinking, which presents 'Islam' as 'a resurgent atavism', threatening 'the destruction of what is ... referred to as the democratic order in the Western world' (Said 1981: 51), is now being extended with a vengeance to the Indian subcontinent, es-pecially as an explanation for Kashmir's bid to separate from the Indian state, although even 'the most cursory review of the his-torical record illustrates the compatibility of Islamic religious pre-cepts with varied cultural expressions and political arrangements' (L. Anderson 1991: 94).

The inherent incompatibility, stated or implied, of 'their' religion with 'our' democracy and 'our' secularism thus becomes an alibi not just for practices that make a travesty of all democratic and secular claims, but also a convenient mechanism for blinding 'ourselves' to what 'our' relationship with Kashmir really has been. This 'institutionalised ideological rhetoric' (as Said puts it) of defending

'national unity' against the encroachment of those 'bloody borders', which pervades, in varying degrees, much Indian political,
journalistic and 'academic' discourse today, serves the purpose of
producing 'the illusion, if not ... the actuality, of consensus'. It also
means that Indians are left with little opportunity to view Kashmir
'except reductively, coercively, oppositionally' (to paraphrase Said
1981: 49, 51). This naturally precludes any possibility of self-
criticism, of seriously thinking about rejuvenating and reinvigor-
ating 'our' democracy and 'our' federalism, so that those systematically deprived of democracy and federalism are not driven to
seek them through 'self-determination'.

Occasionally, this discourse parades in the garb of cultural
authenticity. 'Human rights', it is claimed, among others by India's
former Prime Minister Narasimha Rao, is a 'Western concept',
inapplicable to 'our' apparently unique nation and society. But
then, aren't the notions of multiparty democracy and universal
citizenship also of Western origin? In that case, why not be done
with those as well?

Sometimes, especially in academic and media circles, it mas-
querades under the 'mask of rational objectivity' (Said 1981: 158).
This might involve the affectation of a lofty 'academic' tone; in
the crudest instances, it might even involve scarcely-concealed
contempt for 'emotional' or 'biased' scholars who do not, or will
not, conceal their normative beliefs and democratic concerns. In
the case of the media, we have the example of a documentary film,
The Kashmir Story, screened in various parts of the world in
1994–95. Made by Indians, this film delivers a version of Indian
officialdom's interpretation of the Kashmir 'problem'. There is
nothing wrong with that, except that an exceptionally blatant
attempt is made to camouflage this fact with a self-proclaimed
'Gandhian perspective'. The film's strongest points include plen-
tiful footage from the Valley; people's trust and hospitality have
thus been exploited to essentially denigrate them and caricature
their movement. Or consider *Roja*, a hugely successful commercial
film in India, which portrays the anguish of a young Indian woman,
whose husband has been kidnapped by Kashmiri 'terrorists'. Someone who doesn't know anything about Kashmir is bound to come
away from this film with the impression that Kashmiris fighting
for *azaadi* are a bunch of misguided idiots at best and near-
pathological zealots at worst.[43]

In many of these instances, there is an implicit attempt to deny or downplay the fact that 'such unscientific nuisances as feelings, habits, conventions, associations and values', ranging from 'national feelings like patriotism or chauvinism to private emotions like fear or despair', are 'an intrinsic part of any interpretation', and that 'there is no such thing as a neutral or value-free interpretation'. As for the spurious claims to 'scientific objectivity' in academia,

> politics here seems associated with narrow partisanship, as if the real scholar is above petty squabbles, being preoccupied only with ideas, eternal values and high principles ... worse, there is a deliberate attempt to conceal the connections between scholarship and what we might call worldliness, for the sake of maintaining the fiction of nonpolitical and unpartisan scholarly truth (Said 1981: 132, 156).

No matter that

> all theories that assert their value-neutrality, for deliberate ideological purposes or not, contain a *status quo* bias. Their objectivist ethos formally denies any explicit [social or political] commitments, and [thus] ... leaves them without the normative basis needed to critique their own role, and the role of other theories ... [so-called] scientific objectivity ... masks ideology while stripping theory of the power of criticism (Reus-Smit 1992: 5).

To return to the subject of analysis, then, the central importance of a deeply-felt collective Muslim identity in the Kashmiri struggle for 'self-determination' cannot, and need not, be denied. 'It is the blending of these two tendencies, nationalism and Islamic consciousness', one well-meaning author has concluded, 'that distinguishes the new nationalists from their erstwhile democratic–secular counterparts'. This, in turn, is taken to signal 'a basic metamorphosis ... [in] the self-conception of Kashmiri Muslims', and 'a basic change in the nature of Kashmiri nationalism', reflected in the emergence of 'the mosques [as] the new centres of power' (Pasha 1992: 369–87).

This is a flawed and misleading argument, on at least two counts. First, it is wholly ahistorical. 'Islamic consciousness' has *always* been a prominent and integral component, along with other political ideals and forms of identity, of Kashmiri nationalism and its democratic struggles. The upsurge of 1931 was in many ways the revolt of the politicised elements of a subjugated *Muslim* population against a Hindu autocrat, bureaucracy and military (Bazaz 1941). And there are deep historical reasons for the enmeshing of 'Islamic consciousness' with Kashmir's nationalist and democratic movements in the modern period. As Balraj Puri (1995: 56, 60–61; *see also* Khan 1994) puts it:

> Islam in Sufi form came to Kashmir not as a destroyer of tradition ... but as its preserver, consolidator and perpetuator ... the mass conversion of the people of Kashmir to Islam owes to ... *Alamdar-i-Kashmir*, Sheikh Nooruddin Noorani, popularly called Nund Rishi (fourteenth century) who became the patron–saint of Kashmir. He translated Islam into Kashmir's spiritual and cultural idiom ... Farooq Nazki calls him a Muslim Shaivite. According to B.N. Pandit, his poetry is a mixture of Shaivism and Sufism....[44] The fact that Islam is rooted in Kashmiri tradition and that that tradition is permeated with the Islamic spirit has enabled Kashmiris to reconcile cosmopolitan affiliations with territorial nationalism. The Kashmiri Muslim has remained a Kashmiri as well as a Muslim.... Kashmiri Muslims ... do react like any other Muslim community when their religious interests are endangered. But they are unlikely to submerge their Kashmiri identity in the name of Islam.

As one noted scholar has observed, 'the cult of Buddha, the teaching of Vedanta, and the mysticism of Islam have one after another found a congenial home in Kashmir', and its society has 'imbibed the best of Buddhism, the best of Hinduism and the best of Islam' (Sufi 1974; cited in Puri 1995: 61). Indeed, the practice of relic worship in Kashmir (as in the Hazratbal shrine, where the Prophet's hair is preserved) is clearly traceable to Buddhist influence, while in the towns and villages of Kashmir, 'Muslim [Sufi] saints are worshipped like Hindu gods and godlings' (O'Molley 1941; cited in Puri 1995: 61). The implications of this heritage for the politics of modern Kashmir are readily apparent:

This identity was obviously a misfit in the monolithic structure of Pakistan, which did not recognise any identity other than that based on religion. The federal democratic and secular framework of India, on the other hand, promised [in 1947] a better guarantee for the defence and growth of Kashmiri identity. The accession of the Muslim-majority state of Jammu & Kashmir to India, in which Kashmiri leaders played a key role, revitalised and re-validated Indian secularism, which had been seriously under-mined by partition.... Leaders of Kashmir would claim ... that Indian forces had come to Kashmir to defend their *azaadi*, which Pakistan had threatened. The insurgency that started around 1990 also proclaimed *azaadi* as its objective, except that the roles were reversed. Now India is projected as the enemy of *azaadi* while support is sought from Pakistan to defend it (Puri 1995: 57, 62).[45]

It is thus hardly surprising that the political power of Sheikh Abdullah, that 'secular nationalist' *par excellence*, stemmed largely from the fact that he controlled most of the mosques in the Kashmir Valley. His political headquarters was Srinagar's Hazratbal shrine, from where he launched both the 'Quit Kashmir' movement in 1946 and directed the opposition to the Pakistan-sponsored inva-sion in 1947–48.[46] Asked once how he had managed to marginalise the mullahs from Kashmiri politics, he smilingly replied: 'By becoming a mullah myself' (Akbar 1985: 250).[47] Not all mullahs were marginalised, however—one of the greatest 'democratic–secular' figures of Kashmir, and one-time general secretary of NC, was a leading cleric, Maulana Masoodi.

This complex and multifaceted interplay and interpenetration of 'religious' and 'secular' idioms and practices is not unique to Kashmir either. For example, Anderson (1991: 94) points to 'the varied but always important role played by Islam in the nationalist movements that protested European rule' in North Africa, even those movements that, as in Algeria and Tunisia, resulted in self-consciously 'secular', 'socialist' regimes. The binary opposition between 'secular' and 'religious' nationalism is thus a tenuous one: one can plausibly argue that some strands (for example, the domi-nant Gandhian stream) of India's anti-colonial 'secular' national-ism were suffused with Hindu religious symbols, idioms and terminology (Fox 1989:Chs 11 and 12; Vanaik 1990a: 142–43).[48]

Yet the mosque *has* emerged as especially salient in the current uprising, as numerous observers have repeatedly attested. However, what has made the mosque the focal point of popular mobilisation and resistance is not a regression to atavistic obscurantism, but the total absence of any alternative channels of collective action and protest. With no legislative body enjoying popular sanction, no executive with democratic accountability, no judiciary with autonomy and credibility, no functioning parties except underground, outlawed ones, 'the only forum left for expression of popular anger was the [local] mosque, where [typically] the entire population [of the *mohalla*] collected, shouting slogans of *azaadi* through microphones' (Puri 1993: 62). The neighbourhood mosque has also provided all the 'militant' groups, secular–nationalist and Islamist, with a readymade community centre from which to organise, agitate, protest and mobilise.

This is not necessarily a reactionary development: recall the distinction made by Ali Sharia'ti (1982: 307) between 'the Islam that generates consciousness, that is progressive and in revolt, the ideology ... from its traditional aspect, which has caused decline'. It is this former vision which most of Kashmir's radicalised youth have tried to articulate, even if often in a flawed and erratic manner, and such is its appeal that it has temporarily endowed even extremely conservative Islamist groups such as the Jama'at-i-Islami with a 'revolutionary' halo. But it is crucial to remember that this specific political expression of religious solidarity and commitment is conditioned by, and contingent upon, a political *context* of oppression and denial of democracy. To borrow from Lisa Anderson's work (1991: 110–11) on North Africa, it is therefore 'the construction of tangible, material means of guaranteeing popular representation and government accountability' that will have to be the foremost priority of any democratic resolution to the Kashmiri struggle for 'self-determination'.

The Complexity of 'Self-Determination': The View from Jammu

The Jammu region (that half of Jammu & Kashmir frequently overlooked or neglected by scholars and policy analysts concerned with the Kashmir conflict) illuminates like' no other factor the difficulties and complications of achieving a comprehensive democratic settlement to the question of 'self-determination' for Jammu & Kashmir. Jammu contains 45 per cent of the Indian-administered territory's population (the Valley has 53 per cent) and its area of 26,293 sq km is considerably larger than the Valley's. As part of an administrative entity to which democracy and autonomy has been systematically denied since 1947, the region has been adversely affected in many ways, and its inhabitants have much to complain about.

Indeed, going by certain social and economic indicators, Jammu has suffered greater inequity and retardation than the Valley. For example, Jammu received only 15 per cent of New Delhi's development allocation for the state in 1986. And while Hindus were disproportionately represented (relative to proportion of population) in provincial-level government employment, most of these are reportedly Pandits, leaving only 10 per cent, according to one estimate, for Jammu residents (almost two-thirds of whom are also Hindus). Most professional and technical institutions and industrial plants established since 1947 are located in the Valley, and most state-owned corporations and banks are based there as well, with Jammuites poorly represented among their employees. Indeed, Jammu lags behind the Valley even in road construction and rural electrification (Tremblay 1992: 156–57).

The obvious solution to such regional disparities would be comprehensive, organic decentralisation and devolution *within* Indian-administered Jammu & Kashmir. This would not only help equalise Jammu's share of socioeconomic resources and revenues, but also enable its people, who are for the most part linguistically and ethnically distinct from the people of the Valley, to enjoy wide-ranging political autonomy. The combination, it can be plausibly argued, would at least substantially alleviate the sense of marginality and powerlessness that afflicts many Jammuites.

This is precisely what democratic forces in the Jammu region have been energetically campaigning for, over the last forty years (Puri 1981, 1983). But despite the establishment of two official commissions (in 1968 and 1979) to probe Jammu's grievances, and the endorsement in principle of the idea of a multi-tiered, decentralised institutional framework for the whole of Indian-administered Jammu & Kashmir (given that Jammu's population is anything but homogeneous), by practically the entire political spectrum of the Kashmir Valley, including Sheikh Abdullah, as far back as 1968, this has not materialised. Why? The absence of the requisite political will to implement this formula on the part of both Sheikh Abdullah and Farooq Abdullah after 1975 is a secondary part of the explanation, but the cause of Jammu's maladies actually runs much deeper.

The underlying reason is that both Congress and Hindutva communalists, at all-India and provincial levels, have *consistently and vehemently* opposed any suggestion of decentralised internal government in Jammu & Kashmir, and of equitable power-sharing between the regions (Jammu, Kashmir, Ladakh) that comprise it. The main reason, in my view, is that tiered, organic devolution of power leading to an autonomous Jammu necessarily presupposes that Jammu & Kashmir *as a whole* is an autonomous unit governing its own affairs, with only residual authority over 'key matters' vested in Delhi. Only a democratically-constituted, substantively autonomous Jammu & Kashmir government can possibly delegate authority to lower levels, including the constituent regions. But the Indian state, governed by the hegemonic ideology of unitary Indian nationalism and its institutional consequence, the tendency to progressively centralise power, has, as we have seen, systematically achieved precisely the opposite in Jammu & Kashmir: the subversion of democratic processes and institutions, and the total destruction, in practice, of federal autonomy.

The people of Kashmir, practically disenfranchised for extended periods lasting decades, have been the worst sufferers. But this has also meant that Jammu's claims and grievances have gone unaddressed. The culpability for this situation thus lies squarely with successive Congress governments in Delhi. It is therefore truly ironic that in 1983, Indira Gandhi capitalised on widespread discontent in Jammu to launch a blatantly communal campaign that sought to win Jammu for Congress by polarising the state along regional and communal lines. As noted earlier, she partly succeeded, mostly at the expense of the Jammu BJP, though Farooq's NC, which swept the Valley, also won 38 per cent of the Jammu vote and several seats (indeed, in one seat, a Hindu NC candidate defeated a local BJP stalwart).

In perpetuating Jammu's political disempowerment and economic underdevelopment, Congress found an enthusiastic accomplice in the various organisational incarnations of 'Hindu nationalism', first Praja Parishad, then Jan Sangh and finally BJP. This movement, of course, subscribes to an extreme vision of monolithic nationalism and a strong centralised state-structure (see Bose 1996). But it is also a movement whose success, or even survival, is dependent on the construction of communal polarisation and violence, and specifically on fomenting fear and hatred among Hindus of the menacing 'other'.

It is therefore perfectly understandable that since the late 1940s, Jammu's Hindutva communalist politicians have been rabidly hostile even to the thought of a negotiated agreement with Kashmir's leaders which would address Jammu's regional problems, and foster harmonious coexistence and cooperation between Jammu & Kashmir's religious and ethnic groups. Since the early 1950s, when they assembled a motley collection of disgruntled monarchists and dispossessed landlords under their banner, the Hindutvaites (under the slogan, *Ek Nishan, Ek Vidhan, Ek Pradhan*—One Flag, One Constitution, One Premier—for all of Mother India) have vociferously agitated for the complete abolition of the State's autonomy, and its total 'integration' with the rest of the country. In other words, they have done their utmost to communalise its politics and precipitate religious and regional conflict.[49]

As I have pointed out, these designs have been largely achieved for them by those swearing by 'secularism', but RSS and its affiliates and allies, including the Shiv Sena, continue to foment unrest in Jammu, railing at the 'special status' and 'appeasement' of Kashmiri Muslims, who, ungrateful as they are, have returned such kindnesses by supporting a Pakistan-sponsored 'covert war'. The Hindutvaites seek to heighten communal discord by blaming previous governments in Srinagar and, by extension, Kashmiri Muslims for Jammu's troubles. As I have argued, the ultimate culpability lies in Delhi, and the Valley's population can hardly be held responsible for the failures and shortcomings of the mostly unrepresentative, unaccountable ruling cliques foisted on them.

The current Hindutva programme on Kashmir, which occupies a central position in BJP's India-wide strategy to capture state power (articulated, among others, by Hindutva communalist 'intellectuals' (*TH* 1990; *TS* 1994, 1995b), demands 'abrogation' of Article 370, and, occasionally, 'trifurcation' of Jammu & Kashmir, leading ultimately to union territory status for 'Buddhist-majority'

Ladakh, and reconstitution of 'Hindu-majority' Jammu as either a separate state or as part of the neighbouring Indian state of Himachal Pradesh (where, not accidentally, BJP is strong and well organised).[50] This obviously means fragmenting and partitioning Jammu & Kashmir on essentially communal lines. The fate of the Kashmir Valley is usually left unspecified, apart from emphasising the need to crush 'secessionism' and 'fundamentalism' without mercy or quarter.

It is ludicrous, however, that the RSS–BJP cabal consistently portrays itself as the representative and spokesperson of Jammu, and its propagandists even threaten that 'Jammu ... will ... retaliate ... with full force the moment' (*TS* 1994, 1995b) any moves are made to evolve a new, democratic approach to the Kashmir question. For Hindutva communalists, despite the noise they make, represent a minority of *at most one-quarter* of the Jammu region's population. They have *never* won more than five of the region's thirty to thirty-two assembly seats, and their share of the popular vote has usually hovered between 20 and 25 per cent (Tremblay 1992: 164). The reason is that a full one-third of the Jammu region's population is Muslim, 6 per cent are Sikhs and 18 per cent low-caste Hindus, with the result that most of Jammu's 'communities and areas [are] beyond the reach' of this sectarian movement that parades in the guise of integral nationalism.[51] Thus, BJP's 'political base is confined to a section of urban caste-Hindus', and when, in the 1989 parliamentary election, the party gained dramatically in many parts of India, it was unable to muster a majority in a single assembly segment of Jammu's two parliamentary constituencies (Puri 1993: 38).[52]

Indeed, Jammu graphically illustrates the pitfalls of thinking in terms of crude, aggregated religious categories in studying the Kashmir question. Of the region's six districts, Poonch has a massive Muslim majority of close to 90 per cent, and two others, Doda and Rajouri, have substantial Muslim majorities of between 60 and 65 per cent. Of the other three districts, Udhampur has a substantial Hindu majority of 65 per cent, though Muslims constitute one-third of the population, and the other two, Jammu and Kathua, have massive Hindu majorities of between 80 and 90 per cent (GOI 1981).

But cross-cutting cleavages of ethnicity, caste and language render these religious divisions dubious, if not altogether meaningless.

While Kashmiri is the language of the overwhelming majority in the Valley, only a bare majority of Jammu's residents (mostly caste-Hindus) speak the region's main language, Dogri; there are at least a dozen other languages spoken in the Jammu region.[53] Between a quarter and a third of Jammu's Hindu population is low-caste, and Hindus also tend to be somewhat concentrated in urban areas, like Jammu and Udhampur towns. The Muslim majorities of Poonch and Rajouri consist primarily of Rajputs, Gujjars and Pahadis (though there is a Kashmiri Muslim population in parts of Poonch district), many desperately poor, who have so far given little by way of direct support to the Kashmiri struggle (*IT* 1993b: 30–31).[54]

Significantly, however, insurgency in the Valley has spread with a vengeance to Doda district, whose Muslim majority is almost entirely Kashmiri. A large number of Kashmiri youth from Doda have joined various guerrilla organisations. Doda's highly mountainous terrain, and its relatively easy accessibility from the Valley (it shares a border across rugged terrain with Anantnag district), makes it an ideal guerrilla haven, and Kashmiri insurgents with bases there have been posing a major challenge to the Indian security forces.[55]

Thus, the Hindu-majority label conventionally accorded to the Jammu region is, while true is a limited sense, also seriously simplistic and potentially misleading. Apart from the fact that three of Jammu's six districts have Muslim majorities, it is far more accurate to characterise Jammu as a patchwork or mosaic of religious (Hindu, Muslim, Sikh), ethnic (Kashmiri, Rajput, Gujjar, Dogra, Punjabi, etc.) and linguistic (Kashmiri, Dogri, Hindi, Pahadi and Punjabi among others) groups. Thus, when BJP spokespersons claim to be the defenders of the 'interests of Jammu', they conveniently forget that such a monolithic Jammu exists only in their imagination.

Indeed, this social reality of multiple forms of identity and cross-cutting cleavages is too often deliberately ignored by those in both India and Pakistan and on both sides of the Line of Control in Jammu & Kashmir, who prefer to interpret the Kashmir conflict in reductive and bigoted communal terms. The reality, however, is that religious affiliation is but *one* axis of social diversity (and of political conflict) in Jammu & Kashmir—albeit, undeniably, a very important one. But there have historically been other, overlapping axes of contestation and conflict—region, ethnicity, language, caste and political ideology, for example.

There is thus no alternative to democratic debate and discussion between representatives of various social groups and political tendencies in the different regions of Jammu & Kashmir, if progress is to be made towards a durable political settlement. This is especially because Kashmiri leaders almost always decline to countenance truncation as the price of self-determination. Thus, JKLF chairman Yasin Malik asserts that the JKLF may accept partition, 'with much regret', *only after* majorities in Jammu and Ladakh vote against unity with Kashmir in a free and fair referendum on self-determination in which all parties (including those advocating unity) are able to campaign and canvass among the electorate in all three regions. Remarkably, even HM's Salahuddin shares this perception. Rejecting proposals of 'trifurcation' as 'unacceptable' and 'part of BJP's communal politics', he has stated (*IWI* 1992: 4) that 'even if we have to give our blood for it, we want to live as the people of Jammu, Kashmir and Ladakh'.

Such an interregional, intercommunity dialogue would inevitably have to be a critically important component of any broader or bigger dialogue in the future on the Kashmir question. Such a dialogue between the regions is precisely what Kashmiri leaders like Shabbir Shah and Yasin Malik have been vigorously advocating, and they have found support from several enlightened members of the Jammu intelligentsia. Indeed, some of the most innovative and promising ideas, over the years, for tackling the Kashmir question as a whole, and for reconciling the interests and aspirations of the different regions through equitable sharing of natural resources, administrative revenues and political authority, have come from ('Hindu') intellectuals and activists based in Jammu.

The complex ramifications of 'self-determination' are mirrored in Ladakh, a vast territory with a minuscule population almost evenly divided between Buddhists and Muslims (of the region's two districts, Kargil has a Shi'ite Muslim majority, while Leh has a Buddhist majority). There have been strong signs over the years that Ladakhis feel neglected and marginalised by the Indian state as well, and there has been a fitful agitation going on for some years now in Leh and Kargil for better representation, greater autonomy and more development resources.[56]

The complexity also extends to territories under Pakistani control. The 'Azad Kashmir' districts are culturally and linguistically closer to contiguous areas of western Punjab than to the Kashmir Valley, and the Baltis of Gilgit & Baltistan have their own distinctive dialects and way of life.

To compound the confusion, the Pandits displaced from the Valley are at loggerheads with their fellow-Hindus in Jammu. Since the Pandit influx, house rents and prices of essentials in the Jammu area have risen sharply, the transportation infrastructure and educational facilities are severely overburdened, and highly-qualified Pandits are competing with locals for scarce professional employment opportunities. All this is keenly resented by natives of Jammu (*IA* 1994b).[57] The feeling is mutual; many Pandits complain that they are mistreated and exploited. As one group of embittered Pandit migrants puts it: 'We have nothing in common with the Dogras [a section of Jammu caste-Hindus]—not even religion because the Hinduism they practise is different from the Hinduism we know ... [on the other hand] we share everything with the Kashmiri Muslims. Our history, culture, traditions, customs and language are common' (*Alsafa* 1990). There could, perhaps, be no better illustration of the sheer multiplicity of identity and interest groups, and of the numerous cross-cutting sociocultural cleavages and linkages, that are the salient characteristics of the demographic and social structure of Jammu & Kashmir.

Notes

1. A sampling of the most important documentation includes: Amnesty International (1995), which documents 715 cases of summary executions and deaths under torture since 1990; Asia Watch (1991); Asia Watch–Physicians for Human Rights (1993); Amnesty International's country report on India (1992); Varadarajan (1993); Bose et al. (1990) reproduced in Engineer (1991: 224–70); Hasan et al. (1990), which is an investigation into atrocities against Kashmiri women; Committee for Initiative on Kashmir (1991); PUCL et al. (1990) reproduced in Engineer (1991: 210–23); PUCL (1993); Institute of Kashmir Studies (1993), documents 118 cases of summary executions and deaths by torture under the Indian military administration's 'catch-and-kill' policy directed against suspected insurgents and their alleged sympathisers; Kishwar (1994: 6–21); British Parliamentary Human Rights Group (1992); and United States Department of State, country reports (1992, 1993) on human rights conditions in India. For a useful compilation of many of the best journalistic reports

of 1990 in the Indian, Pakistani, Kashmiri, British, American, Canadian, West European, Middle Eastern and South-East Asian press, see Minhas and Aqil (1991).

2. According to a journalist who covered Kashmir during 1990–91, 'in interviews … members of the security forces stated that the use of torture was absolutely vital to obtain information on weapons caches, hideouts and insurgent groups' memberships, and the whereabouts of the leaders'. See Desmond (1995: 13).

3. For details on these laws and their application, see PUDR (1993) and Asia Watch (1991: 111–27).

4. Such killings continue, even though the insurgency has since 1994 been steadily losing much of its bite. An Amnesty International report published in January 1995 accuses senior Indian civilian and military officials of, at the very least, condoning a deliberate catch-and-kill policy.

5. Reported on the basis of on-the-spot investigation and interviews in *IW* (1990). It may be clarified that the mass rape incident mentioned here is not the one alleged to have occurred in Kunan Poshpora village, also in Kupwara district, in February 1991, in which an army unit was also accused by villagers. While the Kunan Poshpora incident received a great deal of media attention (partly because of the number of women, between twenty and sixty, said to have been brutally attacked), violent sexual assaults on women have hardly been an isolated occurrence in Kashmir since 1990.

6. Peaceful demonstrations continue to be effectively banned in Kashmir. For example, in December 1994, a non-violent march to the United Nations office in Srinagar on the occasion of World Human Rights Day, led by JKLF leader Yasin Malik, was broken up by paramilitary police. In the summer of 1995, Muharram processions led by prominent Kashmiri political leaders, demanding the right to self-determination and respect for human rights, were similarly dispersed by force. JKLF general secretary, Shakeel Bakshi, was severely beaten in one such incident. Several civil disobedience-type demonstrations in the autumn of 1995 protesting against Indian policy were also suppressed by police action, and leaders like Yasin Malik, Shakeel Bakshi, Javed Mir and Abdul Ghani Lone beaten up and arrested. The unfortunate trend continues unabated in 1996.

7. Indeed, despite the massive quantities of weaponry supplied from Pakistan, the military sophistication and effectiveness of the Kashmiri armed groups does not even come close to that of, say, the Tamil Tigers in Sri Lanka. Even the Naga insurgents of north-eastern India are probably more seasoned and formidable fighters than the Kashmiris, in the sense that their organisation and grasp of strategy and tactics is probably superior. This is not at all to corroborate the offensive and perverse claims sometimes made by counter-insurgency officials that Kashmiri youths are 'soft' or 'effeminate', and break down more easily under torture, than, for example, Sikh or Tamil rebels. Also, any judgment of the military effectiveness of the Kashmiri insurgency has to take account of the quite unbelievably ruthless and ferocious repression that the rebels, and the population at large, have consistently been subjected to by the state's forces.

8. In August 1995, I happened to run into a senior officer of the Jammu & Kashmir police during a visit to the Mughal Gardens in Srinagar. On hearing that I was a student of the Kashmir problem, the gentleman (who was in plainclothes)

entreated: 'Please write something so that we are given the right to self-determination'.

9. When one of the hostages, a Norwegian, was brutally killed by his captors in August 1995, Kashmir observed a total *hartal* (general strike) in protest, following the call of the Hurriyat (Freedom) Conference, the umbrella forum of Kashmiri organisations opposed to Indian rule. JKLF leader Yasin Malik publicly denounced the 'barbaric act', and threatened to hang the perpetrators if they were found to be Kashmiris. The identity of the kidnappers, a group calling itself *Al-Faran*, remains shrouded in mystery; Indian officials say it is a front-name for the Kashmir wing of Harkat-ul-Ansar, a radical Islamist organisation based in Pakistan. Most Harkat militants active in Kashmir are themselves Pakistanis.

10. Widespread extortion of money and several cases of sexual abuse of women by some militants have particularly contributed to this disillusionment. A resident of an old city neighbourhood in Srinagar described the public mood to me thus in March 1996:

> People still deeply desire *azaadi*, and almost none accept the legitimacy of Indian rule from their hearts. But the present crop of militants are not popular or respected either. Most of the really dedicated militants are either dead, in prison, or have lost heart and given up the struggle. There is a sense of hopelessness, because people can't see any way out of their miserable situation.

11. A recent report (Mojumdar 1996a) has pithily brought out the quite peculiar nature of this normalisation. In a sign of returning 'normalcy' in Baramulla town, in north-western Kashmir, the Indian army has taken the initiative to restart screenings of commercial Hindi films in the town's cinema-hall, and locals, deprived of watching these films for several years because of the *diktats* of Islamist guerrilla groups, are queuing up for tickets. On the same day, in the town of Pampore, located just 20 km from Srinagar in southern Kashmir, terror reigns. A group of government-sponsored 'renegade' militants are laying waste to an entire *mohalla* (neighbourhood), terrorising residents and burning dozens of houses as a large contingent of their protectors, the Indian army, look on benignly.

12. JKLF suffered a split between its India and Pakistan-based wings in September 1995, when Amanullah Khan, the movement's elderly chairman based in Rawalpindi, summarily disbanded almost the entire Kashmir Valley unit. This attempted purge was the culmination of long-simmering tensions between the India- and Pakistan-based organisations. Khan forced the final rupture apparently because he was unable to tolerate Yasin Malik's independent style of leadership, and the latter's tendency to take policy decisions independent of the dictates of a distant 'central' leadership in Pakistan. Following Khan's announcement, almost the entire JKLF organisation in Indian-administered Jammu & Kashmir, barring a few individuals, rallied behind Malik, and the Hurriyat Conference recognised Malik as the legitimate leader of the JKLF movement. There were signs of disapproval of Khan's arbitrary action even among Azad Kashmiris—for example, representatives of the large Mirpuri

community in Britain, once Khan's staunch loyalists, made statements supportive of Malik. The significance of the split was perhaps more generational than anything else—with it, the younger generation of Kashmir's politically mobilised youth has come decisively into its own.

13. HM is widely perceived among Kashmiris in the Valley as an instrument of Pakistan's designs on Kashmir, and the organisation has also earned a bad reputation for repeatedly attacking other guerrilla groups (including pro-Pakistan ones). However, HM still evokes grudging respect among many Kashmiris because of its relative military effectiveness against the hated Indian forces, and for the considerable human sacrifice made by HM 'martyrs' in course of the armed struggle.

14. Malik survived two assassination attempts, allegedly by pro-Pakistan groups, within a week of being freed. His life still hangs by a thread, however, especially since he refuses to have armed bodyguards and often moves about with only a few unarmed associates. This courage, however reckless, is nevertheless a refreshing contrast to the common sight of top politicians in India surrounded by phalanxes of grim-faced, gun-toting securitymen.

A similarly tumultous welcome greeted Shabbir Shah when he emerged from prison in October 1994. Since his release, Shah, perhaps partly in response to the popular mood, has dropped his earlier openly pro-Pakistan stance, and instead advocates 'self-determination'.

15. Nissar, the *mirwaiz* (high preacher) of Anantnag, in southern Kashmir, was a leading founder of MUF in 1987. 'He [had] privately accused Hizbul Mujahideen of "holding Kashmir to ransom, to hand over to Pakistan on a plate"'. See Rettie and Khayal (1994: 11). One of the slogans raised at Nissar's funeral was: '*Jo mangega Pakistan, usko milega kabristan*' (those who want Pakistan will be sent to the graveyard).

16. Pakistan did assist the JKLF in launching the uprising. However, it soon demanded a price for continued support. When JKLF by and large refused to alter its pro-independence line, Pakistani agencies (especially military intelligence, known as Inter-Services Intelligence or ISI, which runs Pakistan's 'Kashmir programme') promptly terminated all aid to it, set about engineering defections from JKLF ranks, and began building up HM with a vengeance. However, it appears that Pakistan has been reluctant to place all its eggs even in the HM basket. Since at least 1993, Pakistan has floated several new armed groups in Indian-administered Jammu & Kashmir (such as an affiliate of Harkat-ul-Ansar, a Pakistan-based group implicated in sectarian Sunni–Shia violence in Pakistan itself), which have closer ties than HM with the Pakistani military and intelligence agencies. The Harkat's fighters in the Valley and Doda, for example, are mostly Pakistani nationals who have infiltrated from across the border.

17. Since late 1992, there has also been a sinister pattern of death-squad murders of prominent Kashmiri citizens sympathetic to JKLF and the cause of independence. At least some of these killings have been blamed on gunmen from Pakistan-sponsored groups (though most seem to have been perpetrated by hitmen from within the Indian security apparatus), and this has further intensified Kashmiri disaffection with Pakistan's motives and intentions. The roster of victims includes Hriday Nath Wanchoo, a highly respected human rights

activist; Dr. Abdul Ahad Guru, a famous cardiologist who, the JKLF revealed after his death, had long been a senior JKLF member; Dr. Farooq Ahmed Ashai, a prominent orthopaedic surgeon; Dr. Abdul Ahad Wani, a law professor at Kashmir University, Srinagar; and most recently, Jalil Ahmed Andrabi, a senior human rights lawyer in Srinagar who was abducted by Rashtriya Rifles soldiers and 'renegade' militants in March 1996 and found tortured and shot to death a few weeks later. In early 1994, Dr Mirajuddin Munshi, another leading member of the intelligentsia with close links to the JKLF, was forced to leave Srinagar for exile in the West after threats to his life.

18. Interviewed in *IWI* (1992: 4). The coexistence of secularist and Islamist currents in contemporary 'national liberation' movements is not an unknown phenomenon (for example, Palestine). In any case, the Kashmiri Jama'at-i-Islami has a limited popular base. While the JKLF movement at least initially inherited practically the entire Plebiscite Front/National Conference constituency, the Jama'at's influence in the Valley has traditionally been localised and relatively insignificant (for example, it put up thirty-five candidates in the assembly elections of 1983, all of whom lost to NC). It is doubtful that this base has expanded significantly since 1990, though the party is very well organised and well funded, and runs a network of religious schools from where it recruits indoctrinated cadres. Moreover, many Kashmiris are sceptical of the Jama'at's ostensibly radical rhetoric because the party has, in the past, repeatedly contested elections to the Jammu & Kashmir legislative assembly. The JKLF, by contrast, is as yet untainted by such 'compromise'.

19. I am grateful to M. Qasim Khokhar for this information.

20. After one such episode, Benazir Bhutto, then in opposition after having been deposed as prime minister, said in an interview (*IT* 1991): 'Pakistan ... [has] arrested the prime minister of Azad Kashmir, rigged the state election ... and alienated the Kashmiris to such an extent that they want independent Kashmir'. The reason for Bhutto's chagrin was that the ousted 'prime minister', Mumtaz Rathore, belonged to her Pakistan People's Party (PPP). In 1975, after having been similarly ousted from the 'prime ministership' by the then premier Zulfiqar Ali Bhutto, Sardar Abdul Qayyum Khan, the recent incumbent in Muzaffarabad, wrote to Sheikh Abdullah in the following vein: ' ... If you do not help us ... we, the people of Azad Kashmir, will be consigned to slavery and humiliation forever ... if you do not help, the oppressed people of Azad Kashmir have no hope' (cited in Noorani 1992: 267–68).

21. On 8 July 1989, for example, the Pakistani newspaper *Jang* estimated that 35 per cent of development funds and 25 per cent of administrative revenues were 'misappropriated' in Azad Kashmir.

22. Qayyum also has a politically ambitious son, Atiq, who is allegedly notorious for corruption.

23. In a recent appearance on *Aap ki Aadaalat*, a popular programme on Indian cable television (Zee TV) in which prominent personalities answer public accusations in a mock trial scenario, one of the 'charges' levelled against Qayyum was that he is, in reality, 'the *gulam* [slave] prime minister of *gulam* Kashmir'.

24. According to some Pakistani scholars, however, the apparent unanimity in the Pakistani establishment that Kashmir is an integral part of Pakistan is not an

entirely accurate barometer of Pakistani public opinion on this issue. Yunas Samad (1995: 65–77) argues that the irredentist position on Kashmir is most deeply entrenched among those ethnic and social groups which were in the forefront of Muslim nationalist agitation prior to the formation of Pakistan, and/or which have dominated the political structures of the military–bureaucratic state since. He mentions in particular three categories: Muslim refugees from east Punjab, Urdu-speaking Muslims who migrated from the Muslim-minority provinces of India, and trading communities who migrated from Bombay or Calcutta to Karachi and were gradually transformed into a rapacious industrial bourgeoisie with official backing. The fervent Pakistani nationalism of these groups reinforced strong feelings about Kashmir already prevalent in western Punjab (especially in those areas close to the princely state), where tens of thousands of migrant Kashmiris had settled from the late nineteenth century onwards. Like Samad, Mehtab Ali Shah (1995: 103–112) argues that 'there is no unanimity among Pakistanis about the idea of accession of entire Kashmir to Pakistan'. He claims that the appeal of the irredentist position is especially weak among Sindhis and Baluchs. Among these groups, ethnic identification (as opposed to Pakistani nationalism) is strong, perceived ties of extended kinship with Kashmiris are virtually non-existent (in contrast to Punjabis of Kashmiri origin), and a sense of political marginalisation in Pakistan's governmental structures is widespread.

25. For instance, thousands attended a mass rally organised by JKLF in Mirpur, 'Azad Kashmir', to observe 'Third Option Day' on 5 January 1995.

26. There has been serious civil unrest in Azad Kashmir as recently as February 1996. On 11 February, the anniversary of JKLF founder Maqbool Butt's execution in India, major public demonstrations against the Pakistan-backed authorities broke out in several AK towns, and a large number of student activists were arrested.

27. According to the Government of India Census of 1981, there were 124,078 Hindus (most, though not all of them Pandits) living in the Valley in 1981. No census was conducted in 1991 because of disturbed conditions. Assuming a rate of 'natural increase' of 2 per cent per annum, the approximate figure for 1990 is 140,000.

28. The Government of India's Ministry of Home Affairs claims that 326 'Hindus' (civilians, presumably) died as a result of political violence in *all* of Indian-administered Jammu & Kashmir between 1990 and mid-1993. Of these, over half, 177, are said to have died during 1990. Cited in Wirsing (1994: 140).

29. Recently, however, especially following the destruction of the Babri Masjid in Ayodhya (December 1992) and the razing of Kashmir's most famous Sufi shrine and mausoleum in the Valley town of Charar-e-Sharief (May 1995), a large number of abandoned Pandit homes in the Valley have been torched or damaged by miscreant elements whose precise identity remains unclear.

30. Incidentally, several Kashmiris told me how excruciating it is to endure blatantly distorted coverage of Kashmir on state-run TV, a notorious government propaganda mouthpiece throughout India.

31. When, in July 1995, I visited a Pandit migrant settlement at Purkho, 15 km from Jammu city on the road to Akhnur and the border town of Poonch, I found several hundred migrants still surviving in squalid conditions. Their

animosity towards their erstwhile Muslim neighbours in the Valley was surpassed only by their bitterness at the callous treatment they have received from government circles. These Pandits were, however, mostly farmers from relatively poor backgrounds who lived in rural areas of the Valley. Lacking the income and connections that the sizeable class of urban professionals among the Pandits possessed, they were cast into penury once uprooted from their land. Many wealthier and better-educated Pandits are, however, living in relatively comfortable rented lodgings in the Jammu area; some have even built new houses there.

32. The Pannun Kashmir faction is reputedly patronised by certain agencies of the Indian government.

33. The first letter was signed by a person from Srinagar living in Nagrota camp, Jammu, and the second by twenty-two others, supporting him.

34. It is worth mentioning that several Kashmiri Hindus have also fallen victim to the indiscriminate violence of Indian forces. On 27 February 1990, for example, Pyarelal Fotedar, a Pandit farmer working in his fields outside Anantnag town, was randomly shot by a passing army patrol. When news of his death spread, people reportedly took to the streets in Anantnag shouting slogans hailing Hindu–Muslim brotherhood and demanding the ejection of Indian troops from Kashmir. See *KT* (1990). In April 1993, when the BSF razed Lal Chowk, the central Srinagar square, one of sixteen civilians killed was a Hindu named Chaurasia. In October 1993, over forty pro-independence processionists, including a Hindu bystander, were massacred by BSF in Bijbehera. And in an especially sinister incident in late April 1990, a prominent Pandit Urdu scholar and his son were kidnapped and murdered by masked men; the case details, meticulously compiled by Asia Watch (1991: 61–62) on the basis of interviews with surviving family members, seem to strongly suggest that this was the work of a government-sponsored hit squad.

35. Neither Chukku nor the Lals enjoy any kind of special protection given to them by the security forces; they live and work like every other citizen. I took particular care to speak with them privately and separately, and pressed them to tell me, without fear, about any negative experiences they may have had. They just didn't have any to tell me about, they assured me.

36. The efforts of ordinary Hindus and Muslims in Doda district to maintain peace and friendship are especially commendable since there are constant attempts to create communal polarisation and ignite violence. In early January 1996, for example, fifteen Hindu residents of a remote village in the district were massacred by unidentified gunmen. Two weeks later, a Muslim family of seven was slaughtered in their home by men who, according to survivors, were dressed in military uniforms (the Rashtriya Rifles is deployed in strength in the area). During my time in Doda, I heard at least one credible account of local RSS activists helping the security forces to identify Muslim 'suspects' during cordon-and-search operations.

37. Eminent Indian Muslims, like other Indians, have repeatedly expressed a remarkable diversity of opinions on the Kashmir issue and how it should be tackled. See, for example, Engineer (1991: 295–97).

38. For a recent journalistic study by an Indian author that decisively rebuts this dangerously twisted and ahistorical image, and debunks other assorted myths about Kashmir and Kashmiris, see Singh (1995).

39. Indeed, several Kashmiris I have met, including top leaders of the independence movement, have referred in moving terms to their reverence for certain Indian freedom fighters who had taken up arms against the British.

40. All Kashmiris are also made to carry mandatory identity cards emblazoned with the legend *Mera Bharat Mahaan* (My India is Great), which, incidentally, was also the campaign slogan of the Congress (I) in the 1989 parliamentary elections in India.

41. When a shadowy armed group allegedly consisting of foreign militants murdered a Norwegian tourist in August 1995, a wave of shock and revulsion swept the Valley. Kashmiri political leaders were near-unanimous in condemning the outrage, and the Valley observed an unprecedented *hartal* in protest in response to a call given by the Hurriyat Conference. In fact, it had been said by first-hand observers as early as mid-1994 that 'Kashmiris are sick of growing criminal tendencies among proliferating armed groups, many formed by Afghans and other foreigners seeking a jihad' (Rettie and Khayal 1994: 11). Indeed, the fragmentation of the Kashmiri guerrilla movement and the violent activities of otherwise inconsequential splinter groups, many consisting almost purely of 'foreign militants', is already a major liability and may well turn out to be seriously detrimental to the armed struggle's longer-term prospects.

42. This is not Anderson's own viewpoint—she is merely describing this pernicious tendency.

43. A comprehensive deconstruction of this film, which combines slick commercial techniques with a blatant political agenda, is yet to be done. For attempts in this direction, see Bharucha (1994: 1389–95) and Niranjana (1994: 79–82). One of the most striking facets of the movie, to my mind, is its affirmation of unity through exclusion. This may seem an oxymoron, but is not, at least not in terms of contemporary Indian official nationalism. The dubious inclusive claims of this nationalism (whether in its 'secular' or Hindutva variants) go hand in hand with its deliberate depiction of those who do not subscribe to this nationalism as either confused or perversely deviant. In this sense, *Roja* is a highly political statement of an unitary and intolerant construction of Indian nationalism, and a cultural exemplar of the 'terrorism craze' and 'pseudopatriotic narcissism' that I critiqued in the closing passages of Chapter 3.

44. The deep attachment of Kashmiris to this spiritual heritage was reflected in the mass anguish that swept Kashmir when Sheikh Noorani's shrine and mausoleum, located in the Valley town of Charar-e-Sharief, was destroyed by arson in May 1995. Charar was also the site of one of the largest political rallies in the history of modern Kashmir, when in March 1990, some 300,000 congregated there in response to a 'Chalo Charar' call given by JKLF, and took a collective oath to 'fight for freedom'.

45. It is probably this stubborn resilience of Kashmiri identity and its associated idea, 'azaadi', that makes one Indian author remark that 'the flight of the Pandits and the increased strength of the Hizbul Mujahideen with its Islamic fundamentalist connotations may have only a marginal long-term impact' (Kadian 1992: 140).

46. For an account of the symbolic and actual importance of Hazratbal in the social and political history of Kashmir, see Khan (1989).

47. The Sheikh excelled in holding huge crowds enraptured by reciting beautifully from the Q'uran.
48. Vanaik points out that Gandhi transformed Indian nationalism into 'a mass movement by substantially Hinduising it'.
49. RSS and its affiliates have always been obsessed with the spectre a 'Muslim-majority' province enjoying 'special status' within India. Praja Parishad was founded in Jammu in 1947 by Balraj Madhok, an RSS activist who later became the all-India president of the Bharatiya Jan Sangh (BJS), forerunner of BJP.
50. Lately, however, the Jammu & Kashmir BJP has been distancing itself from the 'trifurcation' proposal (personal interview with Chaman Lal Gupta, BJP general secretary for Jammu & Kashmir, in Jammu city, July 1995).
51. In 1983, Indira Gandhi appropriated the ideology without the liability of the limited social base.
52. Indeed, the party's performance was extremely poor—the BJP candidate won 12.6 per cent of the vote in the contest for the Udhampur parliamentary seat, and only 6.2 per cent for the Jammu parliamentary constituency (see Singh 1994: 100).
53. Thus, according to reliable local estimates, only about 150,000 of Jammu city's 700,000 residents speak Dogri at all. There is also a tradition of some mutual dislike between members of 'Hindu' groups of different ethnic backgrounds in the Jammu region: for example, between those of Dogra stock and those of Punjabi origin.
54. This has however not saved many of them, especially in sensitive border areas, from being harassed and persecuted by the Indian army, to whom any Muslim is apparently suspect. It is however important not to exaggerate this social diversity, and these intergroup differences. The character of social cleavages and linkages (as well as their political import) in Jammu & Kashmir tends to be highly complex. For instance, Mian Bashir, the Gujjar Muslim leader in Surankote, a Gujjar-populated area in Rajouri district, reportedly criticises Kashmiri Muslims as 'conceited' on the one hand, and goes on to concede that they may have a 'right to be free', if they wish, on the other (personal interview with a senior academic in Jammu city, July 1995). Similarly, the *azaadi* movement is occasionally described by some as a Sunni demand, the insinuation apparently being that Kashmir's Shia Muslim minority is either indifferent or opposed to it. If this is correct, it is difficult to see why certain predominantly Shia neighbourhoods in the old city of Srinagar have acquired a formidable reputation for militancy since 1989, or why Maulana Abbas Ansari, the leading Shia cleric of Kashmir, is a prominent figure in the Hurriyat Conference.
55. There have also been periodic bomb explosions in Jammu city and elsewhere in the region. One deadly attack in Jammu city, for which HM claimed responsibility, during the official Republic Day ceremony on 26 January 1995 killed eight persons and injured scores. The governor of Indian-administered Jammu & Kashmir (a retired general), the apparent target, narrowly escaped the blast. There were several other blasts during the summer of 1995—the deadliest one killed eighteen civilians outside a Hindu temple complex in Jammu city in July. Indeed, after dusk, Jammu (which is only 20 km from

the border with Pakistan) resembles a city under siege, with very heavy deployment of security forces on its streets. Some guerrilla groups have also been selectively assassinating RSS and BJP officials in Doda, and kidnapping and occasionally murdering Hindu civilians there.

56. In the early 1990s, BJP tried to manipulate this agitation to its own advantage, and sought to coopt the Ladakh Buddhist Association (LBA), with its strong anti-Muslim overtones, into the 'Hindu nationalist' fold. In 1995, however, the Congress (I) central government upstaged the BJP by inaugurating a Ladakh Autonomous Hill Development Council for Buddhist-majority Leh district (Muslim-majority Kargil was inexplicably excluded). The council was packed with erstwhile LBA activists, all of whom now declared allegiance to Congress (I). 'Elections' were held to this council in September 1995. Congress (I) nominees were declared 'elected unopposed' to twenty-two of the twenty-six seats for which 'elections' were held. Old habits die hard, apparently. Demonstrations broke out in Srinagar against this 'election', viewed by Kashmiris as farcical, and against the 'autonomous council', seen as a ploy by the central government to play off communal groups against one another.

57. A popular joke in Jammu runs as follows. A Kashmiri Muslim comes to Jammu to visit his Hindu friend, who is a native of Jammu. The Jammuite complains loudly and petulantly about the Pandits, whom he regards as a liability and nuisance, and entreats his friend to take them back with him to Kashmir. To which the Kashmiri responds: 'Brother, we have been tolerating these people [the Pandits] for centuries, and you can't put up with them for even a few years?'

5

Democracy, 'Self-Determination' and the Challenge of a Just Peace: Kashmir in Comparative Perspective

How and where does one situate the particular question of Kashmir within the framework of the theoretical/comparative literature on nationalism, 'ethnic conflict', the state and state power, and democracy/democratisation? In turn, what light does the Kashmir conflict, and its causation and characteristics, shed on the contributions and shortcomings of such bodies of scholarship? Finally, what ideas and implications relevant to the important concern of developing democratic approaches geared to the alleviation, and eventual resolution, of this crisis, can be derived by locating the Kashmir question within the broader, more general context of the contemporary problem of 'self-determination'?

The case of Jammu & Kashmir graphically illuminates the two faces of the issue of 'self-determination' in the contemporary world. Both have to do with the modern state and the concept of sovereignty, though at different 'levels of analysis'.

At one level, the politics (such as that of the JKLF-led movement for independence) which regards the entire territory of the former princely state of Jammu & Kashmir as a 'national' unit, entitled to 'self-determination', seems an excellent example of John Breuilly's contention that modern nationalism, far from being some inexorable manifestation of 'religious', 'cultural' or 'ethnic' identities, is above all 'a form of politics' which 'makes sense only in terms of the particular political context and objectives of nationalism'. 'Central to an understanding of that context and those objectives', argues Breuilly, 'is the modern state'. For 'politics is about power', and 'power, in the modern world, is principally about control of the state'. Thus, the 'modern state both shapes nationalist politics and provides that politics with its major objective ... possession of the state'. Indeed, nationalism is 'one particular response' to a situation of yawning hiatus between a state and a society it governs; it arises when a society (or at least, a significant segment thereof) claims that '"your" state does not represent "my" nation' (Breuilly 1993: 1, 366, 390–91).

At another level, the recrudescence of the Kashmir question in the 1990s is germane to a 'critical transformation', which according to Crawford Young (1992: 92) has been occurring during this decade in the international system of states. This transformation involves 'erosion of the normative force of "territorial integrity" doctrines in international affairs', and the end of 'the long period of state-stability'. 'The international normative order', Young observes, 'will thus once again need to redefine the scope and limits of the doctrine of self-determination'. The interactive relationship between the two levels is well-stated by Breuilly (1993: 381) who points to 'how a system of competing territorial states appealing to the idea of popular sovereignty can shape political oppositions that also think in terms of particular, territorially defined groups striving for independence'.

My discussion of the struggle for Kashmiri self-determination has highlighted its intimate connection with the question of democracy, its meaning and content. I now argue that the key to mitigating this quest for self-government, and simultaneously contributing to renewal of democracy in India and the subcontinent, lies in a skilful renegotiation and complex redefinition of the concept and practice of state-sovereignty in South Asia. Such a process of re-evaluation would necessarily have to be based on the pragmatic recognition that 'constructs based on absolute sovereignty and rigid borders cannot provide the vision for settling difficult problems of self-determination' (Gottlieb 1993: 15). And Jammu & Kashmir is among the *most* difficult of such problems, both because of the territory's inherent regional, ethnic, linguistic and religious heterogeneity, and because the sovereignty (and, by extension, elite vested interests) of *two* states, not one, is directly at stake in this conflict.

Indeed, the complexity and apparent 'intractability' of the Kashmir conflict is almost enough to make one give up in despair, especially because of the inadequacy, even impoverishment, of the body of knowledge relevant to this sort of problem. At the level of 'domestic' politics, modern democratic theory, whether in its liberal or communitarian variants, has remarkably little to say about the meaning of a collective's right to 'self-determination' and its relationship to the theory and practice of democratic politics. This glaring omission stems partly from an exclusive preoccupation among many scholars with individual rights (particularly in versions of liberal theory), but also because 'since the late eighteenth century, advocates of democracy have ... assumed that the natural locus of democracy is the nation-state' (Dahl 1989: 4). While there is increasing recognition that this assumption is no longer universally valid (was it ever?), there is as yet relatively scant evidence of serious, systematic scholarly efforts to grapple with the theoretical and practical dilemmas this recognition poses.

At the level of suprastate analysis or 'international politics', meanwhile, we are saddled with the obsolete residue of the profoundly unrealistic 'realist theory of international relations', whose leading post-World War II text seeks to explain 'the instability of peace and order in relations among states, [and] ... their relative stability within states', based on the premise that 'protection of the nation against destruction from without and disruption from within is the overriding concern of all citizens' (Morgenthau 1985: 525, 528). In the first instance, the authority and legitimacy of the 'nation-state' is taken for granted; in the second, it is virtually fetishised. International law and legal thought, which are largely by-products of this type of thinking, are not of much assistance either.

'Power structures', write Bachrach and Botwinick (1992: 59), 'are composed of long-term, relatively persistent sets of values, doctrines, rituals, institutions, organisations, procedures and processes'. Slightly modifying their categorisation, I postulate that there are, broadly, two types of power structures which form the basis of state authority: institutional structures (i.e., institutions of the state and regime, with their formal rules, compliance procedures and standard operating practices); and ideological structures (i.e., the normative ideology that underpins and validates the established social and political order, and is reflected in mobilising slogans such as 'nationalism', 'patriotism', 'secularism', 'democracy', etc.). Institutional and ideological structures are mutually reinforcing; all institutional frameworks are dependent, in one way or another, on particular legitimising ideologies. In Iris Marion Young's (1990: 74) words, 'ideas function ideologically ... when they represent the institutional context in which they arise as natural or necessary. They forestall criticism of relations of domination and oppression, and obscure possibly more emancipatory social arrangements'. In Foucaultian terms, the 'relations of power which permeate, characterise and constitute' modern society 'cannot themselves be established, consolidated or implemented without the production, accumulation, circulation and functioning of a discourse' of power (Foucault 1986: 229).

In India, it is the rhetoric of 'national unity and integrity', 'patriotism', 'secularism' and 'democracy' (not to mention 'fighting fundamentalism and terrorism' etc.) that constitute the discourse of power, and the legitimating ideology, of the state. This rhetoric, which Benedict Anderson (1991: 160) has termed 'official nationalism' and Charles Tilly (1994: 133, 137, 142–43) 'state-led nationalism', serves the purpose of presenting the institutional context in which it is produced and circulated as natural and necessary, indeed as sacrosanct, universally beneficial and hence inviolable. We have already seen what these claims amount to in practice vis-à-vis Kashmir, and what kinds of coercive, inhuman and undemocratic practices they are frequently used to rationalise and justify.

In Pakistan, the capacity of the legitimating ideology (essentially regurgitations of the 'two-nation' thesis) to generate consent, as well as the institutional structures of representative government, are even weaker. Hence the frequent recourse to overt coercion, and military–bureaucratic authoritarianism.

Anthony Giddens (1985) has suggested that the modern state exercises control by means of a legitimising ideology and an army of administrative specialists using sophisticated surveillance techniques, while military power is focused outwards, towards other states. This has certainly been substantially true of the domestic politics of both India and Pakistan, and of their policies towards each other, since 1947. With the coming of the independence uprising in Kashmir, however, Mary Kaldor's (1990) modification of Giddens' thesis has assumed particular descriptive and explanatory power. Kaldor posits an organic link between internal pacification and external violence. In her formulation, ideologies based predominantly on external threats are used to rationalise internal pacification, surveillance and repression. The more successful this strategy, the more civil society is eroded, and the more the values and institutions that form the basis of democratic politics are undermined.

This argument is, of course, especially applicable to the Indian state's present policy in Kashmir, and has unflattering implications for its increasingly beleaguered and repressive democratic framework. But it must be remembered that the 'external threat' has also been the major pretext for the denial of democracy in Pakistan since the 1950s. The hollowness of Pakistan's concern for the democratic aspirations of Jammu & Kashmir is revealed not just by its own sorry record in Azad Kashmir and Gilgit & Baltistan, but by the fact that at least a part of Pakistan's political and military establishment has been systematically waging as much of a 'covert war' against the Kashmiri independentist forces as against the Indian state.

In other words, continuous rivalry over Kashmir, brought into sharp focus by the uprising against Indian domination, has produced deleterious consequences for democracy and development in both India and Pakistan. The major bone of contention, literally and figuratively, in bilateral relations, whose abysmal condition has propelled a wasteful and economically ruinous conventional and now a nuclear weapons race, is the property dispute over Kashmir. And there is no reason to believe that more damage will not be done. As for Jammu & Kashmir, the cumulative effect of all this has been a total eclipse of democracy in any meaningful and substantive sense, in both Indian-administered and Pakistani-controlled regions. This, in turn, has gradually fostered a firm belief among a large mass of Kashmiris, most visibly and dramatically in Indian-administered Kashmir but also in Pakistan-controlled Kashmir, that the route to popular, democratic government must first traverse the steep and treacherous pass of 'national self-determination'.

Institutional and ideological power-structures also form the foundations of a state's claim to 'sovereignty'. Since the major obstacle to initiating a democratic resolution to the Kashmir question lies in assertions of absolute, indivisible and inalienable (i.e., totally non-negotiable) sovereignty, especially in India, it will be useful to enquire further into the genesis and evolution of this concept.

The idea of sovereignty initially developed parallel to state-formation in medieval Western Europe (from where it was gradually extended to the 'Third World' during the nineteenth and twentieth centuries, principally through colonial conquest), 'not by means of fiat from above but through negotiations between monarchs and the political community within which their rule operated. This meant that the concept of sovereignty ... was always related to notions of rights and liberties', and 'only on the basis of some consent from that community ... was the monarch able to establish and enforce some kind of sovereign power' (Breuilly 1993: 373). Thus, sovereignty in this form was relatively diffuse, and power divided and shared between the monarch (the 'central' authority) and such institutions as cities, manors, guilds and monasteries (see also Spruyt 1994).

The history of the pre-colonial 'Third World', whether Africa, the Middle East or South Asia, similarly provides a rich background of conceptions and practices of multiple, layered sovereignties. Given these origins, it is indeed ironic that a 'simplistic and primitive' notion of sovereignty (Gottlieb 1993: 45), built on indivisible, non-negotiable and frequently highly unitary state authority, was the eventual legacy of Western colonial domination to much of the 'Third World'. Yet it is important to emphasise that this is very much a twentieth-century development, and that in its philosophical roots and historical moorings, sovereignty is by definition negotiated and hence (re)negotiable, and its moral legitimacy contingent and conditional on the respect shown by the state towards the rights and liberties of its citizens.

In the absence of such respect, some scholars hold, sovereignty reverts to the social base of the political community, which conferred sovereignty on the state, at least in theory, *through a process of negotiation*, in the first place. At the least, then, sovereignty is not and cannot be a cast-in-iron concept; it is inherently contestable and any particular formulation of what it means cannot be held eternally valid, binding and sacrosanct.

Indeed, shrill claims of absolute, indivisible sovereignty usually camouflage highly undemocratic patterns of exercising power and domination, as in the case of Kashmir. In such situations, a revitalisation of democracy presupposes a renegotiation of sovereignty, and that in turn entails rethinking and reformulating the ideological structures that legitimise such domination, and, of course, reconfiguring the institutional structures that give it concrete manifestation. For the scholar, it is thus essential to view the state, even the 'democratic' state, through a critical lens. One of the most provocative examples of this kind of scholarship is Charles Tilly's (1985: 169, 171), who has called state-apparatuses 'our largest examples of organised crime':

> A portrait of war-makers and state-makers as coercive and self-seeking entrepreneurs bears a far greater resemblance to the facts than do its chief alternatives.... Apologists for particular governments ... call people who complain about the price of protection 'anarchists', 'subversives' [etc.].... But to the extent that the threats against which a given government protects its citizens are imaginary, or the consequences of its own activities, the government has organised a protection racket. Since governments themselves simulate, stimulate or even fabricate threats of external war, and since the repressive and extractive activities of governments often constitute the largest current threats to ... their own citizens, many governments operate in essentially the same way as racketeers. There is, of course, a difference: racketeers, by conventional definition, operate without the sanctity of governments.

This thesis is undeniably relevant to democracy, self-determination and the struggle in Kashmir.

This discussion of sovereignty, in turn, sheds light on 'territorial integrity' doctrines frequently invoked by elites entrenched in power. But as Allen Buchanan (1991: 113) has noted, 'territorial sovereignty is an agency/trusteeship function carried out by the state on behalf of the people ... it consists of control over borders and administration of justice ... and is not strictly speaking state ownership of [that] land'. Sovereignty in this sense of an agency–trusteeship function,. given on trust by the citizenry to the state authority, is thus conditional and contingent, cannot *in itself* constitute plausible grounds for the arbitrary repudiation of a claim to self-determination, and *certainly* cannot be used to justify violation and denial of basic democratic rights and liberties. Indeed, Buchanan argues that in cases of grave and persistent injustice and oppression, including 'serious discriminatory redistribution ... violations of civil or political rights or equality of opportunity' (he does not explicitly mention massive and systematic violence), the state's claim to sovereignty over the territory inhabited by the affected group can plausibly be regarded as having been voided or forfeited (ibid.: 112–14). In Robert Jackson's (1990: 26–31) analytic scheme, 'positive sovereignty', by which a state's jurisdiction over its citizens becomes both just and meaningful, is defined by 'able and responsible rulers' and 'productive and allegiant citizens'. Whether this attribute exists today in Jammu & Kashmir is obviously questionable.

But what of the spectre of potentially uncontrollable fragmentation, perhaps even anarchy, frequently invoked by those who fetishise existing institutional arrangements and reject any and every claim to 'self-determination' *purely* on that basis? Empirically, the question can be posed in the following terms. Would not the secession of Jammu & Kashmir (I emphasise that this is a totally hypothetical and rather improbable scenario anyway), and its reconstitution as an independent state, fatally undermine the coherence and legitimacy of the Indian Union, perhaps even to the extent of setting off the 'balkanisation' of the Indian state? Furthermore, would not such an eventuality lead to a precipitous deterioration of already tense and troubled Hindu–Muslim relations in India? And would it not acutely worsen Indo-Pakistani relations, and significantly increase the likelihood of a military confrontation in the subcontinent? I believe that the answer to all of these (hypothetical) questions must, for a whole complex of solid reasons, be: No.

But let us first consider this important issue at a theoretical level. As Buchanan (1991: 102–04) has correctly observed, 'this argument [that invokes the danger of a domino-effect of snowballing disintegration] proceeds by a sleight of hand. It assumes, quite without warrant, that a right to secede must be an *unlimited* right—a right of virtually anyone to secede for virtually any reason'. But every serious student of self-determination is invariably insistent that this right, *if it is at all exercised*, be strictly qualified and conditional. Moreover, as Ernest Gellner (1983: 44–45) has pointed out, although there are 'a very large number of potential nations on earth', there have been relatively few serious secessionist movements.

Moreover, the extent and depth of secessionist sentiment in any given context is neither preordained nor immutable; on the contrary, it is volatile and malleable, and has highs and lows, flows and ebbs. This is equally true of South Asia, where despite the presence of a veritable multitude of potential 'nations', the actual number of serious secessionist impulses have in fact been relatively few over the last four or five decades. Many of these movements have had dubious levels of unity, popular support, ideological coherence, military strength and longer-term strategic vision, as a result of which some have failed, while others have been coopted, at least temporarily, into the 'system' with partial concessions and inducements. But it is doubtful whether military repression and/or insubstantive 'carrots' can foster an abiding resolution to a problem as serious and complicated as the struggle in and over Kashmir.

Yet there is still a proclivity in some quarters to make the argument, at once crudely simplistic and calculatedly disingenuous, that the Kashmir conflict constitutes the crucial test-case of India's 'secular nationalism', and that if Kashmir is allowed to 'go' (thus invoking a prospect that is not just hypothetical but has a distinct scaremongering quality to it), the disintegration of the Indian Union is bound to follow: this is the domino theory or snowball syndrome hypothesis as applied to the subcontinent. While a handy tool for professional alarmists intent on scoring debating points, this logic makes for an extraordinarily weak argument. Why so?

First, we have already seen just what kind of secularism the forces and agencies of the Indian state have been practising in Kashmir since 1990. While the several hundred thousand heavily-armed guardians of 'law and order' stationed in Indian-administered Jammu & Kashmir may be upholding a particular model of Indian nationalism, that model has nothing—absolutely nothing—to do with any ideal of secularism (or, for that matter, of democracy). While fundamental precepts of democracy and secularism may be at stake in the Kashmir conflict, only the hopelessly brainwashed or perversely dishonest would delude themselves, and others, that the Indian state's agenda in Kashmir today has anything to do with the defence or promotion of the values of democracy or secularism. The manifestly anti-democratic and shamefully anti-secular nature of the policies being implemented every day in Kashmir by the forces and agencies of the Indian state give the lie to any such claim.

But it is the latter part of the proposition, that Kashmir's (notional) 'departure' would inexorably lead to the 'balkanisation' of India, that is even more dubious. In fact, this suggestion could simply be dismissed as silly were it not so mischievous (after all, West Pakistan did not break up even after the loss of the entire eastern wing of the country, containing more than half the undivided state's population, and despite the potential for further runaway fragmentation). For this position is based on the absurd presumption, to quote Jayaprakash Narayan (1964), anti-colonial nationalist and freedom fighter, that 'the States of India are held together by force and not by the sentiment of a common nationality. It is an assumption that makes a mockery of the Indian nation and a tyrant of the Indian state'. I, too, am profoundly sceptical of such doomsday prophecies, for I do not for a moment believe that the Indian Union is built on such shallow foundations.

Those who make this kind of argument are, thus, both extraordinarily insecure and astonishingly (deliberately?) oblivious to the real strengths of the Indian Union. As I trust I have shown conclusively in this book with regard to Kashmir, movements for 'self-determination', and demands for separation from an existing state, do not, ever, randomly mushroom all over the place for no apparent rhyme or reason. A 'self-determination' struggle is normally not the kind of spark that spreads uncontrollably and becomes a blazing prairie fire. For, as Lenin so presciently and aptly put it, the masses do indeed know very well the many 'advantages of a big market and big state', and rebel only in desperation, as a last resort, when 'national oppression' reaches intolerable levels. The mass revolt that erupted in Indian-administered Kashmir in 1989–90, I have demonstrated beyond reasonable doubt in this study, is *not* the continuation of, or in any sense a throwback to, the unresolved religious–political conflict that culminated in the partition of the subcontinent in 1947. In fact, it has extremely little, if anything, to do with that tragic epoch in our common history.

The popular uprising for 'self-determination' in Indian-administered Jammu & Kashmir has been caused by an entirely different political dynamic and sequence of events, which has *everything* to do, instead, with the denial of democracy by the Indian state to its Kashmiri citizens in the post-colonial period. Kashmiris rose in rebellion not because Muslims are constitutionally incapable of loyalty to a 'secular' state, but because they saw no hope of redressal within the Indian state's institutional framework to the gross, consistent and systematic pattern of abuse of their rights as citizens and as human beings. The brutal and disproportionately violent response by which their (initially largely non-violent) protests were sought to be suppressed, especially in early 1990, steeled their resolve to seek 'self-determination', through force if necessary, and it was thus that the gun became a legitimate political weapon in a society where the 'sight of blood' (as Walter Lawrence observed at the turn of the century) was once anathema. Those who peddle the spurious thesis that the contemporary Kashmir question is a 'communal' (read Muslim) problem, and would even go to the macabre extent of holding India's 120 million Muslim citizens (from Uttar Pradesh to Bengal to Hyderabad) somehow 'account-able' for Kashmir's 'misbehaviour', are therefore *themselves* in-fected with a most virulent strain of the communal disease.[1]

Nor does the disintegration and fragmentation of the Soviet Union, Czechoslovakia and Yugoslavia lend any support to an India-specific domino-theory. These multinational states collapsed and broke up as one consequence of a *total systemic breakdown* (political, economic, social, moral, ideological) that proved termi-nal for the Soviet (or Soviet-type) model of political organisation and social life (and which, more than incidentally, had a great deal to do with the destruction of democracy by and under Soviet-type regimes). The quite exceptional circumstances of the demise of countries such as the Soviet Union and Yugoslavia do support the general contention (applicable also to India's problem in Kashmir) that when 'self-determination' movements disruptive of a state's integrity arise, they are 'more likely a consequence of institutional failure rather than a cause of it' (Przeworski et al. 1995: 21). But whatever India's problems (they are certainly many, including some of potentially grave import), the country simply does not face anything like a systemic crisis of the magnitude and perva-siveness that gripped the Soviet and Soviet-type societies. So long as the Indian state does not develop an addictive habit of respond-ing to all its democratic dissidents (of whatever colouring) with the anti-democratic mailed fist it has so consistently employed in

Kashmir, there is little risk of Kashmir's cry for 'self-determination' spreading contagiously all over India.[2] In any case, much of even radicalised opposition to state power in India tends to be articulated as caste, class, gender and other forms of resistance that preclude the adoption of an agenda that demands 'self-determination' in the sense of territorial separation. And as for India–Pakistan relations, they arguably cannot get much worse than they are right now—and it is incontrovertible that they have deteriorated to the extent that they have because of the apparent *absence* of any hopes for a substantive resolution to the Kashmir crisis.

For all these reasons, it is far from certain that even the hypothetical prospect of Kashmir's 'secession' and independence would inevitably produce a 'demonstration effect' in other parts of the subcontinent. To close this part of the discussion, it is, finally, worth pointing out that much of the controversy over the possible implications of an independent Jammu & Kashmir for the subcontinent's geography and politics has a very premature, 'jumping-the-gun' and curiously unreal feel to it.[3] First of all, whatever their other differences, the state elites of India and Pakistan are united in their opposition to the emergence in the imminent future of a juridically sovereign, reunified state entity in part or whole of Jammu & Kashmir (I take up this factor in somewhat greater detail later in this chapter).

But perhaps even more important, the independentist argument claiming the 'right to self-determination' for the whole of the erstwhile princely state has one central (some might say fatal) contradiction embedded in it. Advocates of the right to self-determination for Jammu & Kashmir will, I argue, have to confront and satisfactorily resolve this key problem before the normative desirability and practical viability of such an independent state can be conclusively established. On this crucial issue, I would now elaborate at much greater length.

But let me preface that critique with a brief survey of the current state of research on the 'right to self-determination' in democratic theory. In the past several years, a number of (predominantly liberal) theorists have tried to supplement democratic theory, and remedy its exclusive preoccupation with individual rights, by expounding the basics of a group or collective right to 'self-determination'.[4] Their arguments, typically, have two main planks. First, a claim to 'self-determination' *may* be morally justified if there is a history of persecution, discrimination, oppression, etc. against a socially and territorially coherent formation. Second, the need for and utility of protecting and preserving group identities and interests against such threats lies in the value of the group identification to *individual* dignity, interest and self-respect. Thus, Margalit and Raz (1990: 449, 451, 454–55) argue that

> individual dignity and self-respect require that groups, membership in which contributes to one's sense of identity, be generally respected and not made a subject of ridicule, hatred, discrimination and persecution ... one should not have to identify with or feel loyalty to [another] group that denigrates an encompassing group to which one belongs. Indeed, one should not have to live in an environment where such attitudes are part of the common culture ... an aspect of [individual] well-being is an ability to express publicly one's identification with the group and to participate openly in its public culture ... what matters is how well people *feel* in their environment: do they feel at home or are they alienated from it? Do they feel respected or humiliated? [emphasis mine]

This is a welcome and overdue effort to bridge the chasm between theories of individual and collective rights, and to respond, from the perspective of democratic theory, to compelling real-world imperatives. Its one problem may be a continuing individualist bias. Buchanan (1991: 54), while not free of this bias himself, rightly comments that for many, 'participation in community is itself an important ingredient in the content of the good life', and thus qualifies as a 'fundamental intrinsic good' in and of itself (see also Tamir 1993). For example, to many, 'Kashmiriyat' is an intrinsically valuable *collective* good; its value cannot be reduced to its worth to individuals alone. As Marx argued 150 years ago, human beings are inherently *social* beings.

But, concretely speaking, what sort of approach can help defuse, contain and ultimately resolve conflicts as bitter as the one in and over Kashmir? Benjamin Barber (1984) has, in a well-known work, emphasised the transformative potential of open, democratic dialogue in difficult and apparently 'intractable' situations of polarised conflict. There is much to commend this view in many cases of so-called ethnic conflict, including, I strongly believe, Jammu & Kashmir. Indeed, most of the hundreds of Kashmiris I have spoken to, both civilians and 'militants', are far from being crazed, intransigient fanatics. They are not only willing but positively eager to have a dialogue.[5] During my tours of the troubled, violence-wracked regions of Jammu & Kashmir, even those initially sceptical of my intentions invariably ended up fervently shaking my hand, or even embracing me warmly.[6]

Indeed, even Kashmiris with little formal education tend to be politically highly literate and conscious, and very well-informed about the background, genesis and evolution of the Kashmir question.[7] Nor do they all think that all 'Indians' are deceitful manipulators or habitual brutes. Too many Kashmiri intellectuals have been trained at Delhi's Jawaharlal Nehru University, too many Kashmiri doctors have graduated from teaching hospitals in Bangalore or Calcutta, too many Kashmiri shawl and carpet traders make the annual trip to Delhi or Bombay, and too many Kashmiri tourist guides and drivers have 'Indian' friends and acquaintances for that to happen. Indeed, several Kashmiris I met expressed sympathy even towards the thankless task of members of the Indian security forces, and the dreadful lives the latter are constrained to lead in the process. And Kashmiris are generally united in the pragmatic realisation that their predicament can only be mitigated, ultimately, through dialogue and negotiations—specifically, they say, a tripartite dialogue between India, Pakistan and popular representatives of Jammu & Kashmir—with the essential qualification that any such dialogue must be genuine, serious and substantive, and not the dialogue of the deaf that the Indian state, for one, seems to prefer. New Delhi's injunction that the 'problem' must the settled within the 'framework of the Indian Constitution' is not just irrelevant (the Constitution, like every other man-made document, is hardly a repository of eternally binding and inviolable Truth), but a tactical device that effectively precludes any substantive dialogue. The simple reason is that it is precisely the 'constitution' of the Indian state, in the broader sense, that is the contentious issue here.

Democratic dialogue, to be fruitful, cannot evade the substantive issues, nor can it posit moral equivalence between the powerful and the powerless. Some parties to the dialogue would likely have to give up some of their power and privilege, and those deprived of basic rights would stand to gain. For example, almost none thought the negotiated, democratic transformation of South Africa possible before 1990: it has happened, but the structure of the apartheid regime has had to be dismantled in the process. According to democratic theorist Anne Phillips (1993: 94), 'when an oppressed group is called upon to put its partial needs aside, it is being asked to legitimate its own oppression'.

But it is critically important to stress that this is *not* a zero-sum game. Thus, 'Kashmiris' might conceivably gain something, but *not at the expense of* 'Indians' and 'Pakistanis': at least, not the one billion ordinary Indians and Pakistanis. I have already pointed to the immense contribution a mutually agreed, democratic resolution to the conflict in and over Jammu & Kashmir can potentially make to the renewal of peace, democracy, federalism and development throughout the subcontinent. But then, perhaps that is what explains the antipathy of ruling elites towards everything but orchestrated jingoism, sabre-rattling and expansionist posturing. The few who would 'lose' from a democratic settlement have a lot to lose (or so they apparently think).

Nonetheless, fashioning a coherent programme for implementing a right to self-determination through democratic methods remains a daunting task in most cases, and especially, in Jammu & Kashmir. This is primarily due to the fact that Jammu & Kashmir, because of its multiple forms of internal heterogeneity, fully reflects the two key, interrelated problems typical of such situations. The first concerns the intricacies of territorial demarcations: the borders of putative autonomous or sovereign units are usually bitterly contested. This complication regarding borders is, however, usually itself a reflection of an even more fundamental problem: the *demographic* factor. Most such units contain groups, usually minorities of one kind or another within that territory, who claim, with varying degrees of justification, that self-determination for the unit as a whole will leave them as second-class citizens within the new state, force them to emigrate, or, in the worst cases, lead to mass killings and expulsions.

Such problems are of central concern to those interested in a peaceful, democratic resolution to the Kashmir question. For example, Gowher Rizvi (1993: 80–86) advocates an independent Kashmiri state on the grounds that this presents an opportunity to shed the millstone hanging around the necks of both India and Pakistan ... there is no doubt that Kashmir is a sensitive issue in both countries, but that sensitivity will be less inflamed if both sides make concessions and neither is seen as victor or vanquished.[8]

From one angle, this argument is entirely logical. But Rizvi is keenly aware of the territorial and demographic complexities involved. As a solution to the dilemma, he proposes that the new state should encompass only the Valley and the 'Azad Kashmir' districts; Jammu and Ladakh would remain in India, and Pakistan would retain the Northern Areas.

This formula does have a certain intuitive appeal and 'practical' ring to it, though it is difficult to see why Gilgit & Baltistan should be condemned in perpetuity to Pakistani domination, and Ladakh's supposed value to India as a strategic asset against China[9] would be greatly diminished if its contiguity to other Indian-controlled territories is partially interrupted, as it would under this scheme. However, on other crucial counts, this kind of proposal is seriously problematic. Some concrete problems are obvious enough: what would happen, for instance, to the Pandits, who feel like fish out of water outside the Valley yet remain steadfastly loyal to India, or to the sizeable Kashmiri Muslim population in Doda district, in the Jammu region, who share the urge for independence?

But more importantly, this type of formula runs the profound risk of perhaps inadvertently legitimising and affirming the thinking and agenda of those who see the Kashmir conflict purely in terms of communal categories. Thus, areas with large 'Muslim' majorities get independence, while the *status quo* is maintained in those populated predominantly by 'Hindus', or 'Buddhists'.[10]

But this raises precisely the disturbing possibility of 'group narrowness and group closure', and the thoroughly unhealthy prospect of 'the politics of the enclave', that has begun to worry even some firm proponents of empowering oppressed and marginalised groups. Thus, in a critique of the conception of equal, universal citizenship (which is descended from the tradition of civic republicanism associated with Rousseau's philosophy), Young (1989: 250–74) has argued that such a formal–legal equality 'suppresses but does not eliminate' substantive inequalities of status and power between groups of individuals. 'We must develop participatory democratic theory', she writes, 'not on the assumption of an undifferentiated humanity, but rather on the assumption that there are group differences and that some groups are actually ... oppressed or disadvantaged'. In other words, formally equal citizenship rights for all often masks real inequalities of power, wealth and status, as well as entrenched structures of oppression and domination. As an alternative to the false unity and chimerical equality assumed, and imposed, by universal citizenship doctrine, Young proposes the concept of a 'group-differentiated citizenship' and a model of a 'heterogeneous public'. And at a practical level, she advocates 'providing institutionalised means for the explicit recognition and representation of oppressed groups'.[11]

Young's arguments are timely and powerful. Yet they do carry the risk of an excessively idealised and uncritical celebration of group difference. Apart from not adequately coming to grips with the danger of 'ghettoisation' and insular 'enclave politics' that may arise from certain types of promotion and institutionalisation of group identities and interests (*including* those of 'oppressed and disadvantaged' collectivities), her analysis also fails to meaningfully accommodate the multiple, cross-cutting nature of the typical individual's group identifications. It is in response to such complexities and dilemmas that Anne Phillips has cautioned democrats against 'validating an exclusive and fragmented politics that leaves little space for the development of a wider solidarity', and pointed to 'the risks of freezing what are multiple and shifting identities'. For, group identities, as she observes, are not 'defined by some essential set of common attributes ... [rather] most people have multiple group identifications':

> None, I imagine, would want to flee the abstractions of an undifferentiated humanity only to end up in its opposite; none would favour the kind of politics in which people ... only ... speak for their own group identity and interests, and never ... address any wider concerns ... such a development would mean shoring up communal boundaries and tensions, which could be as oppressive as any universal norm (Phillips 1993:Chs 5 and 8).[12]

Any such outcome, needless to say, would be particularly self-defeating in the case of Kashmir, where the rationality and value of a democratic solution at least partly lies in the contribution it could make to that 'wider solidarity', to those 'wider concerns'.[13]

Nonetheless, one should remain extremely vigilant of attempts to invoke, explicitly or implicitly, the 'abstraction of an undifferentiated humanity', and to postulate 'natural' political units on the basis of such ideological constructs. In January 1994, for example, Raja Mohammad Muzaffar, a senior leader of the Azad Kashmir-based JKLF (Amanullah Khan faction), submitted a blueprint for a possible solution to the Kashmir question to a conference on Kashmir organised by the United States Institute of Peace, a policy-oriented research institution sponsored by and affiliated to the United States Congress.[14] In this document, which otherwise makes several points worthy of serious consideration, Muzaffar proposed a plebiscite throughout the territories of the former princely state with three options presented to the electorate—accession to India, to Pakistan, or an independent Jammu & Kashmir—*to be decided by a simple majority of 51 per cent of the electorate*. This formula, apart from being consistent with the majoritarian principle conventionally used in democratic decision-making processes, was perhaps also motivated by the possibility that, given the current political situation and demographic configuration, a simple majority of all people living on either side of the Line of Actual Control may, in fact, vote for the independence option. Yet this standard independentist proposal, at least in this simple form, cannot, in my opinion, provide the basis for a just and durable solution to the Kashmir question.[15]

Why is this formula (apart from the important question of whether there is any point at all in raking up the plebiscite demand any longer)[16] untenable as the blueprint for a lasting settlement? As Robert Dahl (1991: 491–96) has correctly observed, this kind of crude majority principle avoids the central 'problem of the legitimacy or propriety of the political unit within which majority rule operates'. What about those who do not 'deny the validity of majority rule within a properly constituted democratic unit but because the ... unit is itself seen as illegitimate?'[17]

A Kashmiri patriot, it can be plausibly argued, may justifiably refuse to obey India's elected government, not because she/he opposes democracy in principle, but because she/he regards the Indian state's jurisdiction over the territory of Kashmir as illegitimate. But at the same time, it does not make much sense to unilaterally declare the whole of the princely state of Jammu & Kashmir as *the* relevant democratic unit, unmindful of individuals and groups (perhaps majorities in Jammu and Ladakh, not to mention the somewhat uncertain nature of what the population of Azad Kashmir and Gilgit & Baltistan might want) which may regard *that* as an illegitimate unit for purposes of government, and disregard their concerns even if they constitute as much as 49.9 per cent of those voting in any referendum. In short, the crucial flaw in this proposal is that it is insensitive to the possible political ramifications of Jammu & Kashmir's regional, religious and other forms of social diversity.

In a sophisticated contribution whose basic argument is similar to Dahl's, Frederick Whelan (1983: 13–47) has brought out the seriousness and significance of what he calls the 'boundary problem', i.e., the problem of determining what constitutes the legitimate and appropriate boundaries of a citizen public and geographical space which is to be governed through democratic institutions and processes. The issue here is truly fundamental—the question is not 'who governs', or how, but rather—who *should* be governed? As Whelan writes, 'any democratic theory must face the *logically prior* and in some ways more fundamental question of the appropriate constitution of the people or unit within which democratic governance is to be practised'. While the boundary problem usually arises most conspicuously in the context of 'territorial disputes between sovereign states, or entities aspiring to statehood', Whelan correctly notes that at a deeper level, 'the problem is one of defining or bounding not geographical units but the *membership of the democratic body, or citizenry*' (emphasis mine).

The application of the majoritarian principle cannot solve this problem. For the question still remains: 'How do we delimit the group within which, for purposes of making a particular decision, votes are to be counted and a majority preference identified?' For the 'determination of the criteria or bounds of the citizen body ... is a matter that is logically prior to the operation of the majority principle, and cannot be solved by it'. Thus, although 'democratic theories usually focus on internal decision-making arrangements, *taking for granted* the prior existence of a well-defined group with respect to which the question of democratic governance arises', the fact remains that 'while individuals, and humanity as a whole, are entities that are naturally given, *groups of people sharing characteristics that obviously destine them for collective self-government are not*' (emphasis mine). In short, then, there are simply no natural or preordained territorial borders that are meant to be, and therefore there can be no arbitrary basis for deciding the composition, and boundaries, of a particular citizen body.

Whelan makes the provocative claim that the boundary problem 'is insoluble within the framework of democratic theory'. Whether or not that is indeed the case, this problematic is not something that advocates of 'self-determination' for Kashmir, who postulate the entire territory of the pre-1947 princely state as the logical unit for the exercise of that right, can afford to ignore or cavalierly dismiss. For, in Jammu & Kashmir, just as in most other places with comparable problems, 'it may well be the case that the appropriate boundaries, or the extent and composition of the political community, is *itself* [emphasis mine] something about which the people involved have [strong and conflicting] preferences', thereby 'rendering controversies over boundaries among the most intractable and bitter types of political conflict'.[18] And the issue of boundaries can continue to be a major problem even *after* a particular territory and body of persons has been formally designated as a unit of governance. This is because the absence of a 'fundamental consensus on the boundaries of the system' will most likely foster 'a sense of unfairness and alienation' among the aggrieved groups of citizens, and quite probably 'spur active efforts to overthrow the system, together with a repudiation of its "democracy" as a fraud'. Moreover, 'a belief among outsiders that the boundaries are illegitimate may pose an external threat to the viability of the system', thus laying the basis for revisionist claims and irredentist politics and sowing the seeds of further turmoil and instability.

Students of the Kashmir conflict will surely recognise that many of these points are relevant to the evolution of the Kashmir question since its genesis in 1947. The real significance of the boundary problem for the contemporary configuration of the crisis is, however, that this conundrum, in Dahl's words, 'cuts both ways'. It is thus imperative for votaries of self-determination for the entire territory of Jammu & Kashmir as it existed prior to 1947 to realise that there is something problematic about any one party to the conflict unilaterally predetermining the legitimate and appropriate unit (i.e., territorial space plus citizenry) for the exercise of the right to self-determination. In saying this, I do not necessarily suggest that the independentists are wrong in this regard—they may be right. My point simply is that they *cannot take this for granted.*

Yet the 'Mirpur Declaration' of JKLF, issued on the occasion of the observance of 'Third Option (right to independence) Day' on 5 January 1995, seemingly does take the matter for granted, by continuing to insist that

> Jammu–Kashmir State as it existed on 14 August 1947 (including Indian-occupied area, Azad Kashmir and Gilgit & Baltistan) is an indivisible political entity, and no solution ... not approved by a majority of the people of the entire State as a single unit will be accepted.

Apart from the limitations of the simple majoritarian–democratic formula in this context, this statement carries distinct overtones of a unitary nationalist monolithic sovereignty/inalienable territorial integrity doctrine of Kashmiri provenance. Without denying the historical fact of an international dispute over the territory of the erstwhile princely state, and the grave dangers inherent in any scheme to partition that territory along communal or sectarian lines, a valid and legitimate question can still be raised. What is so axiomatically sacrosanct about an otherwise highly disparate and heterogeneous territorial entity brought under a single sovereignty as recently as the mid-nineteenth century through the coercion and fraud practised by the Dogra dynasty, coupled with the machinations of an expanding British imperialism?

As Dahl argues, the majority principle is really of very limited usefulness here, because it 'presupposes that a proper unit already exists'. And as he remarks, 'a crisp, unimpeachable solution' to this conundrum 'would be a marvellous achievement of political theory or practice'.[19] Alas, no altogether satisfactory solution seems to exist. And proposals that seek to evade or sidestep this conundrum are non-starters, for, in the wise words of Yasin Malik, 30-year-old chairman of the JKLF movement in Indian-administered Kashmir, 'the ultimate solution shall have to be one acceptable to all citizens [of Jammu & Kashmir] regardless of their region or religion'.[20]

Finally, contemporary experience suggests that the use of plebiscite or referendum (about which different segments of society have strong and conflicting preferences) as the electoral mechanism for settling sensitive questions of self-determination may be fraught with serious practical risks of its own, and may even end up producing dangerous counter-productive consequences ultimately harmful to all concerned. In particular, the emotionally charged and unavoidably divisive campaigns which typically precede such referenda can inflame and sharply exacerbate simmering tensions between different groups of citizens who have mutually contradictory visions about the meaning and efficacy of the self-determination exercise. When such divisions coincide (as they usually do in multinational societies) with volatile ethnic, religious or linguistic cleavages, the outcome can be an explosion of violent conflict. The experience of recent referenda in two very different contexts, Bosnia–Herzegovina and Quebec, corroborates this argument.

On 29 February 1992, a referendum was held in Bosnia–Herzegovina on the subject of its secession from Yugoslavia and reconstitution as an independent state. While Bosnian Muslims and Bosnian Croats turned out in impressive numbers for this referendum and voted overwhelmingly for independence (though many Croats saw their participation as a tactical step towards the eventual merger of the Croat-majority western Herzegovina region with the neighbouring Croatian state, itself newly independent), the referendum was massively boycotted by the Bosnian Serb community (about 35 per cent of Bosnia–Herzegovina's population), who were committed to the continuation of the Yugoslav federation and wanted no part in this new state entity (i.e., they disagreed with the very rationale of the referendum). Nonetheless, since the conduct of the referendum substantially fulfilled the criteria of majoritarian democracy—64 per cent of those eligible did turn out and 99 per cent of these voters supported independence—the exercise was seen as a ratification of the independence option, and international recognition for the new state followed within weeks.

The descent into civil war in Bosnia is usually dated to the day the results of the referendum became known. In retrospect, the Bosnia referendum does seem to have been an extremely imprudent move—otherwise, the clash of conflicting claims to self-determination may not have taken such a vicious and deadly turn for the worse. Ironically, then, an exercise intended to bring an independent Bosnian state into being, through popular mandate, had the effect of actually destroying any prospects of a united, multinational Bosnia–Herzegovina.[21]

On 30 October 1995, a similar referendum was organised in Quebec, essentially to determine the popular will on separation from the Canadian federation and the declaration of an independent Quebec.[22] The referendum was eventually defeated by the narrowest of margins as per the majoritarian–democratic formula—49.6 per cent voted *Oui*, 50.4 per cent *Non* (a decisive majority of Francophone Quebecers, who comprise about 80 per cent of Quebec's population, supported independence). The campaign leading up to the referendum, and voting patterns in the referendum itself, caused unprecedented polarisation between the independentist majority among the Francophones, on the one hand, and Quebec's Anglophone, aboriginal and other minority groups (who overwhelmingly opposed independence),[23] backed by the large pro-federation minority among the Francophones, on the other. Indeed, a few days before the referendum took place, the tiny Cree and Inuit aboriginal groups (who despite their size comprise the main population in large areas of northern Quebec) organised their own parallel 'referenda', in which they affirmed their support for Canada's integrity and vowed to resist any attempts to incorporate them and their areas into an independent country. However, even if the result of the Quebec referendum had been exactly the other way around—i.e., 50.4 per cent for independence, 49.6 per cent against—the 'self-determination' conundrum would *still* not have been satisfactorily resolved. On the contrary, an even more volatile and quixotic situation would have been created, with one-half of citizens triumphantly celebrating 'freedom', the other half feeling furious about being compelled to become citizens of a new state entity against their will and nursing deep insecurities about the future.

Mercifully, in contrast to Yugoslavia, Canada's democratic discursive and institutional framework (which permits the Parti Quebecois or PQ, the independentist political party, to operate freely in the country's politics and propagate its creed and agenda through democratic means),[24] together with the democratic character of the Quebecois nationalist movement, meant that the possibility of a descent into violent conflict was virtually non-existent. However, most other places with similar problems resemble Bosnia more closely than they do Canada/Quebec. Kashmir, unfortunately, is no exception.[25]

Are those interested in the achievement of a just, democratic and durable resolution to the Kashmir question unavoidably trapped, then, in a *cul-de-sac*? Does this mean that democrats with a concern for not just theory but *praxis* should simply give up in despair? And must democracy and self-determination remain inevitably unreconciled in Jammu & Kashmir, with detrimental consequences for both and for the cause of a just peace? Is it impossible to conceive of any middle ground at all between the abyss of communal compartmentalisation and the chimera of a non-existent (or at least, highly uncertain) 'oneness'?

There are a few brave souls who, against all odds, think not. As early as 1970, JKLF co-founder Amanullah Khan (1970: 139–49) enunciated his vision of a 'united, neutralised, secular, federal republic' of Jammu & Kashmir. He wrote that the independent republic would have an extremely strong incentive to maintain strict neutrality, because it would otherwise easily become a battleground for rival powers, and be ravaged in the process. Therefore, it could simply not afford to align with one particular power against another. A 'secular set-up' was similarly essential, to ensure 'freedom of faith and communal harmony' among the 'several religious groups' in the population.

Simultaneously, Khan argued, 'justice and equity demand that the State should be a federal one to afford full opportunities to the people of its different regions to administer their own areas and to eliminate the chances of domination, economic and political, of any region over others'. To this end, Khan proposed that the reunited republic be divided into three provinces, Kashmir Valley, Jammu, and frontier regions of Gilgit, Baltistan and Ladakh (corresponding to pre-1947 administrative demarcations), with

> each enjoying maximum internal autonomy. Each Province can be subdivided into districts and these districts will have their own internal arrangements. At the centre, there should be a bicameral national parliament with the lower house having representation on the basis of population of different provinces and the upper house equal representation [for each province].

As for a socioeconomic programme, Khan strongly recommended the 'Naya Kashmir' manifesto, 'adopted by the All Jammu & Kashmir National Conference in the early forties', and premised on egalitarianism and social justice. The republic, he envisioned, would develop economic cooperation and trade links with both

India and Pakistan, and welcome tourists from all over the world, especially the two neighbouring countries. Finally, Khan declared, 'the State will be a republic since democratic values form the very basis of Kashmiris' political struggle'.

All in all, these ideas, whatever their practical relevance might or might not be today, do not appear to amount to a blueprint for 'another partition', but rather constitute a total repudiation (if that is still needed in the post-Bangladesh context, which is unlikely) of the basic premise of the 'two-nation theory'. Whatever the unresolved weaknesses or contradictions in the independentist argument may be, it is most emphatically *not* a communal or sectarian position. And it is an undeniable fact that this position resonates powerfully in the hearts and minds of a large proportion (certainly at least a plurality, and perhaps even a majority) of the inhabitants of Jammu & Kashmir, on both sides of the Line of Actual Control. That is a compelling political reality that no serious student of the contemporary Kashmir conflict, and no policy-maker who wishes to be successful and effective in the longer run, can afford to discount or ignore.

Khan's ideas bear a striking resemblance to the contents of a working paper submitted by Balraj Puri to the Jammu & Kashmir State People's Convention in 1968, led by Sheikh Abdullah, which was attended by practically all popularly-based political forces in the Valley. In this paper, Puri proposed a five-tier decentralised institutional structure for Indian-administered Jammu & Kashmir, leading to 'a [Jammu & Kashmir] federation within [an Indian] federation' (this is the crucial distinction between his ideas and Khan's: Khan's frame of reference is the entire territory of the princely state, including the Pakistan-controlled areas). The administrative tiers would be: village, block, district, region and state.

Puri suggested that each of the three constituent regions, Kashmir, Jammu and Ladakh, should have its own elected legislature and council of ministers responsible to it. He also advised that the upper house of the bicameral central assembly, formed with equal representation from each region, should be 'specifically entrusted with ... promoting inter-regional understanding [and] resolution of inter-regional disputes', and that 'any legislation intended to amend the constitution of the state, alter inter-regional relations or change the overall status of the state ... must [first] be referred to the upper house for its opinion'. He further counselled that the state bureaucracy and development planning agencies also be decentralised by region, with further devolution from the regional level downwards (Puri 1983: Annexure A).

These recommendations are in fact reminiscent of the principle of 'subsidiarity', a key part of the political architecture of the new European Community (EC). Under this principle, each level of government (Brussels, the national capitals, and substate entities like the German *Lander*) stays clear of all decisions that can be taken at a lower level.[26] In this manner, a governmental structure premised on a people-oriented bottom-up approach, responsive to the distinct needs and concerns of diverse groups of people, and optimally geared to the negotiated resolution of all disputes and conflicts, is sought to be developed.

Obviously, the development and implementation of such ideas and institutions is infinitely easier to advocate than to accomplish. Yet there is little doubt that the broad contours of a durable, democratic solution to the struggle in and over Kashmir lie in this general direction. And there is also little doubt that the route to the achievement of such a solution would lie eventually, if ever, in very difficult, even tortuous processes of democratic dialogue, debate and discussion between all three parties to this festering conflict. For a beginning to be made towards a new beginning for the subcontinent, there are certain prerequisites: the abandonment of state ideologies based on mutual hostility and rejection; a rethinking and restructuring of existing institutional frameworks and arrangements; a re-evaluation and revision of the priority given to 'national unity' and 'territorial integrity' over considerations of democracy and basic justice (not to mention a shared humanity); and a mutually agreed redefinition of the meaning and practice of sovereignty in South Asia to suit contemporary needs and realities.

Fortunately, even pillars of the Indian establishment are now openly emphasising the urgent need for a democratic approach to the Kashmir question. For example, Karan Singh, son of Maharaja Hari Singh, has called for a 'dialogue with the new forces in [Indian] J & K', and urged the inauguration of 'a process of reconciliation' (*TH* 1993: 1). General Krishnaswamy Sundarji, former chief of the Indian Army, visualises the possible emergence of 'an autonomous Jammu & Kashmir as part of a South Asian confederation within the next 20 years', and urges 'slow', 'wary', 'step-by-step cooperation' between India and Pakistan with a view to evolving a 'face-saving' formula for both powers 'that would also satisfy the Kashmiris' (*IA* 1994a).[27]

Instant fixes and cosmetic surgery are thus both precluded. As for diehard Kashmiri nationalists committed to full independence, the irony is that there can potentially be 'a range of types and degrees of self-determination', with full independence only one end of that continuum. Once this fact 'is appreciated', writes Buchanan (1992: 351), 'dissatisfied groups within existing states will not be faced with the stark choice of either remaining in a condition of total dependence within the centralised state or taking the radical step of seceding to form their own sovereign state' (see also Gottlieb 1993). It is the absence of the willingness in India, and Pakistan, to even consider exploring innovative alternatives to tackle the substance of the problem, which leaves Kashmiri independentist leaders with little option, really, but to go on defiantly projecting precisely that stark choice.[28]

'Emancipation and security', Ken Booth (1991: 319) has argued, 'are two sides of the same coin. Emancipation, not power and order, produces true security'. And John Burton (1984: 12) has claimed:

It is [a] politically realistic observation that unless there is development and fulfillment of the needs of individuals and groups, unless problems are solved and the need for coercion avoided, a social and political order may not be stable and harmonious, no matter what the levels of coercion.

Certainly, for too long have the hapless inhabitants of Jammu & Kashmir suffered as a result of being the focal point of the deep mutual hostility between India and Pakistan. *And* for too long have the teeming millions of the Indian subcontinent had *their* security and development held to ransom by the Kashmir conflict. The time is overdue to make a move towards breaking this meaningless, dangerous and destructive stalemate. The moral and pragmatic case for a just and lasting peace in Kashmir and South Asia is a compelling one. In Chapters 6 and 7 (written in October 1996), I offer some concluding observations on the longer-term implications of the military and political situation in Indian-administered Jammu & Kashmir as has unfolded in 1996, and advance a few general suggestions

I feel I can responsibly make on how progress towards the ultimate goal of a secure, just peace may be made in this context.

Notes

1. It is useful to recall that the theory that the subcontinent's Hindus and Muslims comprise separate and antagonistic 'nations', irrevocably opposed and incapable of coexistence, did *not* originate in the All-India Muslim League's campaign for Pakistan in the 1940s. This doctrine had already been elaborated at great length during the 1920s and 1930s by the early 'Hindu nationalist' ideologue Vinayak Damodar Savarkar; see for example the compilation of his writings and speeches from that period in Savarkar (1984). More recently, the same thesis has been forcefully and uncompromisingly reiterated in Madhav Sadashiv Golwalkar (1968); this engaging tract is also known as the RSS's 'Bible'.

2. This, however, does explain why the state's policy of repression and denial *vis-a-vis* Kashmir should rank as an important issue for all forms and varieties of democratic struggle in India, and with all those who care about the future of Indian democracy.

3. My purpose in the last few pages has, thus, been twofold: first, to show that even if the hypothetical and presently unlikely prospect of an independent Kashmir were to somehow materialise in the near future, it would by no means inevitably generate all manner of catastrophic implications for the subcontinent; and second, to underscore how dire warnings and exaggerated prophecies of such an (as yet fairly remote) contingency serve, in the present, to rationalise otherwise indefensible policies of state repression in Kashmir.

4. Notable examples include: Buchanan (1992: 347–65); Margalit and Raz (1990: 439–61); Kymlicka (1989, 1995a, 1995b); Lapidoth (1992: 325–46); Taylor (1991: 53–76, 1992); Gutmann (1994) which includes Taylor's original essay and critical responses by, among others, Jurgen Habermas. For an important critical perspective on this debate, consult Mostov (1994: 9–31). Discussing prospects of democratisation in several post-communist societies of Eastern Europe (including former Yugoslavia) divided by nationalities conflicts, Mostov persuasively argues that for lasting democratic development to occur, any recognition and institutionalisation of group rights must be built upon, and remain secondary to, a solid foundation of equal, individual-based civic rights (which is blind to 'ethnic' identities and differences) and a commitment to reciprocal respect and tolerance between the communities concerned. Mostov's essay is a timely warning against lapsing into overly uncritical celebrations of group identities and rights. The grim example of Yugoslavia reminds us of the dangers inherent in assertions of unqualified, untrammelled conceptions of 'national' rights, framed in zero-sum, antagonistic terms in relation to other groups.

5. In October 1993, the Socialist Group of the European Parliament organised a dialogue on Kashmir in Brussels. This dialogue included several political leaders from India and Pakistan, and constructively, brought together a number

of persons representing various strands and shades of political opinion from different regions in both Indian-administered and Pakistani-controlled Jammu & Kashmir. This forum, as well as similar meetings organised by the United States Institute of Peace in Washington, D.C., and several unofficial 'citizens' dialogues' held in India and Pakistan (including a conference in Calcutta in January 1995 which I helped organise), are the closest approximations so far to a formal tripartite dialogue, which would of course have to involve official representatives of the Indian and Pakistani governments, as well as influential political organisations and personalities of Jammu & Kashmir. For a summary report of the Brussels debate, see Brussels (1994).

6. Similar findings have been reported by several Indian journalists and numerous Indian human rights activists, among others.

7. This is in contrast to Indians in the rest of the country who have been subjected to a veritable barrage of disinformation, distortions, myths and outright lies on various aspects of the issue by the official media, with the active connivance of compliant elements of the 'free but not independent [Indian] press' (to quote the veteran Indian journalist Kuldip Nayar).

8. In keeping with this imperative of give-and-take diplomacy, A.G. Noorani, a noted Indian commentator on Kashmir, suggested the following formula at a round-table dialogue on Kashmir held in Calcutta in January 1995 as part of an international conference on peace, common security and regional cooperation in South Asia. Other participants in the dialogue included Mubashir Hasan, former finance minister of Pakistan and a prominent advocate of peaceful coexistence in South Asia, JKLF leader Yasin Malik, veteran Indian journalist and columnist Kuldip Nayar, and Ved Bhasin, editor of *Kashmir Times*, the most influential daily newspaper in Indian-administered Jammu & Kashmir. Noorani proposed that as a long-term goal and arrangement, India and Pakistan might have *joint juridical sovereignty* over the *entire* territory of Jammu & Kashmir (including Indian and Pakistani-administered areas), while *substantive authority in most fields* would be in the hands of the elected representatives of the population of Jammu & Kashmir. This, he argued, would nominally satisfy Pakistan's purpose of having a foothold (if only a juridical one) in the Valley, while conceding the same to India in what is known in India as Pakistan-Occupied Kashmir (POK). The reciprocal nature of this concession would, he suggested, help deflate domestic opposition in both India and Pakistan, while reassuring public opinion in those countries that 'territorial integrity' was not being recklessly sacrificed. At the same time, the juridical nature of Indian and Pakistani authority would allow the peoples of Jammu & Kashmir to substantively control and manage their own affairs, within an internal democratic and federal framework. Of course, any such arrangement would necessitate demilitarisation of both sides of the Line of Control currently dividing Jammu & Kashmir. For the distinction between juridical and empirical components of state-sovereignty, see Jackson and Rosberg (1982: 1–24).

9. The 'Chinese threat' is sometimes invoked by Indian official ideologues to argue that Indian military control over Jammu & Kashmir cannot be diluted under any circumstances. It would seem that this danger is exaggerated. There has been no threat of armed conflict between India and China since the brief border war of 1962, and in September 1993 Indian and Chinese leaders finally

signed an agreement in Beijing substantially resolving long-standing tensions over minor border disputes. Even more importantly, it has been convincingly demonstrated that 'China's policy towards the Indo-Pakistani deadlock over Kashmir has not been consistently and rigidly pro-Pakistan, not even after the 1962 ... war'. See Samina Yasmeen (1992: 320). Indeed, during the 1965 and 1971 Indo-Pak wars, China, to India's relief and Pakistan's dismay, strictly restricted its pro-Pakistan stance to verbal and diplomatic support.

10. Besides, Rizvi does not at all discuss the critically important issues of what kind of constitutional and institutional arrangements the putative state might have, or the acute necessity (hypothetically speaking) of demilitarising both that state and its adjoining regions in India and Pakistan.

11. For a review of the current state of research in citizenship theory, see Kymlicka and Norman (1995).

12. That said, a point needs to be made about the currently fashionable notion of 'multiple identities'. While individuals certainly have multiple foci of group loyalty, it would be an error, in my view, to assume even implicitly that all these identities are *equal in importance* in any given context and at any given time. Thus, for example, the fact that a Kashmiri living under harsh Indian military rule may have identities other than being Kashmiri does not at all detract either from the salience of his Kashmiri identity in this particular context, or from the gravity of the predicament that follows from the salience of that identity.

13. As I have already stated, both JKLF and, somewhat surprisingly, HM have declared their absolute opposition to any ideas of dividing the territory of Indian-administered Jammu & Kashmir along sectarian or communal lines.

14. The United States government has since 1990 been cultivating a lively interest in the Kashmir crisis. The policy interests of US governmental circles are reflected in Wirsing (1994). The research and writing of this book was partially supported by the State Department, including its information-gathering organs, and large parts of it could certainly serve as useful briefing for American officials. Most of the author's primary sources are establishment politicians, career diplomats and other bureaucrats, and senior military officers (some retired) in India and Pakistan.

15. The proposal (three pages) was presented to 'Conflict Resolution in the South Asian Region: The Kashmir Dialogue', a forum sponsored by the United States Institute of Peace (USIP) in Washington, D.C. See also the Institute's summary (10 pp.) of the discussions that took place, released on 31 January 1994. The formula presented by Muzaffar to this conference has been the standard pro-independence position for some time. In 1991, the Pakistan-based JKLF's leader Amanullah Khan proposed a plebiscite with the same simple-majoritarian formula. See Khan (1991: 9–10).

16. The Indian state is absolutely opposed to any suggestion of a plebiscite, and probably has the military muscle and ruthless determination to ensure that its will prevails. Pakistan rhetorically supports the demand, but is insistent that the 'third option' of independence will not be permitted under any circumstances, in which case the plebiscite loses all meaning for pro-independence Kashmiris. I noticed during my field research in the Kashmir Valley and Doda district (Jammu), when I spoke with hundreds of Kashmiris from all strata of

society, the clear majority of whom favoured independence, that very few people directly mentioned the plebiscite. Rather, most stressed the urgency of opening a tripartite dialogue on the Kashmir question between India, Pakistan and popular forces of Jammu & Kashmir (the latter especially denoting the JKLF-led independentist movement, which for obvious reasons cannot be represented in either the Indian or Pakistani delegations to such an event), preceded, of course, by a cessation of all violence.

17. Dahl uses the Soviet Union and Lithuania as his empirical examples to establish his argument.

18. Just how bitter and destructive unresolved contests over 'boundaries' can become is tragically illustrated by the fate of Bosnia–Herzegovina. There, most members of two of the three major 'national' communities, the Bosnian Muslims and to a degree, the Bosnian Croats, considered pre-1991 Yugoslavia to be an illegitimate unit of governance, and opted to create an independent state of Bosnia–Herzegovina. However, most members of the third community, the Bosnian Serbs, sharply disagreed. They wished to continue as citizens of a united Yugoslavia, and refused to recognise Bosnia–Herzegovina as a legitimate unit of governance. The result of the head-on collision is there for everyone to see, and draw lessons from.

19. A wonderfully evocative and lucid way of capturing the essence of this conundrum was suggested to me by a participant at a conference on 'What is a Nation? The Limits of Self-Determination', held near Strasbourg, France, in September 1994. This metaphor pictures two persons subscribing to different 'national' identities, and possessing contrasting views on the issue of self-determination for their territory, asking each other the simple yet potentially deadly question: 'Why should I be a minority in your state when you can be a minority in mine?'

20. Interviewed while in prison; see *KT* (1993). On being released in mid-1994, Malik immediately reiterated that any dialogue or negotiations concerning Kashmir must be tripartite, i.e., involve representatives of the peoples of Jammu & Kashmir as equal participants along with Indian and Pakistani officials. He also announced his desire to campaign politically in Jammu and Ladakh, in an effort to bridge the differences between the populations of the different regions. He further said that he would like to visit the migrant Pandits in their camps and personally appeal to them to return to the Valley, for 'we are incomplete without them'.

21. For solid scholarly accounts of the circumstances of Yugoslavia's disintegration and the ensuing civil wars in Bosnia and Croatia, see Woodward (1995) and Cohen (1995). See also Bose (1995: 87–116).

22. Though the actual referendum question was more cautiously and delicately phrased: 'Do you agree that Quebec should become sovereign, after having made a formal offer to Canada for a new economic and political partnership ... ? Yes or No'.

23. The resolute opposition of these groups to the independence idea was not without reason. The draft independence law introduced by the independentists in Quebec's parliament (known as the National Assembly) prior to the referendum stipulated that 'the new constitution shall state that Quebec is a French-speaking country' (full language rights for the English-speaking

minority have in the past 25 years been a sensitive issue in Quebec's politics), while adding that it 'shall guarantee the English-speaking community that its identity and institutions shall be preserved', and 'shall also recognise the right of the aboriginal nations to self-government ... exercised in a manner consistent with the territorial integrity of Quebec'.

24. The PQ currently runs the government of Quebec, having won the majority of seats in Quebec's National Assembly in elections held in 1994 (they first won control of the Quebec administration through elections as early as 1976, and have since alternated in office with the Quebec branch of Canada's Liberal Party, which enjoys significant support among both Francophones and non-Francophone groups in Quebec and is committed to retaining the Canadian federation in some form). The Quebec government holds and exercises autonomous decision-making authority—autonomous, that is, from the federal government in Ottawa—in a vast range of subjects. The PQ's elected representatives to the federal parliament in Ottawa—who call themselves the Bloc Quebecois—also presently constitute the largest opposition group in the Canadian parliament.

25. One conceivable method of partly offsetting the limitations of the simple majoritarian–democratic method in the case of Kashmir would be to require *concurrent majorities* in each of the constituent regions (Jammu, Kashmir and Ladakh) for any outcome to be valid. The problem with this approach is twofold. First, if, as is quite possible, majorities in different regions vote for different choices, we would be back to an impasse, which can only be broken through partition on sectarian and communal lines. More seriously, however, even such partition would be an untenable solution, for the simple reason that considerable variation in voting behaviour would be likely to occur *within* regions, and even within certain districts and towns. For example, a significant minority of voters in the Jammu region would possibly support independence, while a small pro-India vote might materialise even in the Kashmir Valley. In a town like Kishtwar, in Doda district of Jammu, where the Hindu and Kashmiri Muslim populations are roughly equal, the vote would likely be vertically split between (largely) pro-independence Kashmiri Muslims and pro-India Hindus. This would create bizarre and potentially highly inflammable situations at the local level.

26. Though it is an ironic fact that a number of key functions of the EC are in practice highly centralised in Brussels.

27. For another pro-establishment viewpoint which nonetheless advocates a gradual, negotiated solution to the Kashmir conflict synchronised with a phased normalisation of Indo-Pakistan relations, see Chopra (1994).

28. See for example the JKLF leader Yasin Malik's frontpage interview, 'No Ambiguity on Complete Independence' (*TS* 1995a).

6

Conclusion and Epilogue
(April 1996)

As Kashmir emerges from its seventh winter of war, the future of its people remains bleak and desolate, and prospects of a turn for the better seem as distant as ever. The underlying reasons for the deadlock are powerful ones:

> For India and Pakistan, Kashmir is still about their respective strengths and sovereignties and senses of security, about their titles to land and peoples, about their statures in the region and the world.... Their diplomacies seem inexorably wedded to their mutual distrust, and their domestic politics echo their fears. Neither India nor Pakistan wants to accommodate the strategic changes that would, at the very least, include Kashmiris in discussions about their future. Neither wants to revise its political philosophies, or alter the reflexive domestic opinion that supports Indian army powers on the one side, and *jihad* on the other. Neither wants to shed the light of democratic debate on the contentious subjects of nationalism and self-determination. Neither has been willing to see Kashmir in itself or for itself, or to forego the easy prospect of squeezing Kashmir as a way to torment each other.... Having marginalised Kashmir while fighting about it, both countries have allowed war to become the dominant metaphor for the subcontinent's politics. Political dialogue has been sacrificed to bellicose posturing ... (Newberg 1995: 72–74).

Yet it remains true that

[while] the Indian government may be able to wear down the insurgency, it cannot obliterate the sentiments that have propelled many Kashmiris to support the insurgency—and the rest to tolerate its effects.... Even if India wins the military battle with superior numbers and machinery, it is unlikely to win the political war (ibid.: 74).

It has become increasingly clear during 1995 and 1996 to first-hand observers of the Kashmir situation that there is indeed a growing possibility that the Indian state *may* be able to implement a *de facto* military solution to the present crisis. This turn of events is the cumulative consequence of several interactive factors: the fragmentation and demoralisation in the *azaadi* movement, and its relative lack of effective direction and leadership; the massive superiority in numbers and firepower of the Indian forces and the Indian military regime's ruthless implementation of such horrific practices as the catch-and-kill policy, which has simply wiped out large numbers of Kashmiri youth and compelled others to surrender or go on the run; and Pakistan's cynically exploitative and manipulative strategies towards the Kashmiri struggle. If this does happen, there is a related possibility: that the Kashmiri people, defeated in war by an incomparably stronger antagonist and effectively stabbed in the back by their self-proclaimed international advocate, may end up with absolutely nothing to show for years of suffering and sacrifice.

Yet for the 'victors' to anticipate triumph, even if this possible scenario does materialise, may be both premature and misplaced. For any attempt to restore the pre-uprising *status quo* will have to contend with the one reality that has been irrevocably changed by the war:

Before 1989, India and Pakistan fought over Kashmir. Since late 1989, it is Kashmiris who have done the fighting [and, one might add, the great bulk of the dying].... If the insurgency has taught anything, it is that Kashmiris are no longer willing to be considered dependent or unimportant. They have demonstrated that they mean to be taken seriously ... whatever their problems with one another ... (Newberg 1995: 74).

Robert Dahl (1991: 493) has remarked that 'in practice, as distinct from theory, the usual solution [to 'national liberation' wars and insurgencies] has been force plus time'. 'Force plus time' is precisely the linchpin of the Indian state's strategy of attrition in Kashmir. Yet the new-found political maturity and determination of the Kashmiris makes it an open question whether this strategy, however ruthless its implementation, will be able to lay the Banquo-like ghost of the Kashmir question to rest in perpetuity.

This baptism by blood and fire since 1989 is also the major reason why many Kashmiris react with hostility and derision to the Indian government's plans to revive the Jammu & Kashmir legislative assembly as a panacea to the Kashmir crisis. This response, rather than being a manifestation of irrational intransigence or surly rejectionism, is understandable when viewed in the context of the actual situation on the ground.

Kashmir's social fabric has been terribly scarred in the last seven years by continuous violence, above all the massive and systematic violence, directed against the population in general, sponsored by the state and perpetrated by its agents. And ever more anguish, suffering and indignity continues to be inflicted daily on the people, as anyone who has taken the trouble to visit the Valley and other affected areas in the recent past and interact with the citizenry well knows. In this context, the imposition of an 'election' to the assembly at gunpoint would, in popular perception, be tantamount to rubbing a lot of salt into very raw wounds, the final insult to compound many injuries:

> We know what the government's elections mean [a group of elderly men in Kupwara town told me]: we have witnessed every kind of fraud and hoax here, all in the name of democracy. This time, what they will do is pump in more forces, take us from our homes and line us up at gunpoint. Then Doordarshan [Indian state television] cameras will come and film us, and a deception about Kashmir will be played, once again, on the Indian public.[1]

A coercive and fraudulent exercise cannot, in any event, be dignified as a reintroduction of democratic processes. As one Kashmiri told me, 'the root cause of all problems here has been government of the centre [i.e., New Delhi], by the centre, for the centre'. But even though they are exhausted by incessant violence and repression, most Kashmiris are today no longer willing to passively tolerate the imposition from Delhi of unrepresentative, unaccountable and corrupt puppet cliques. Even the small potentially 'pro-India' segment of opinion in the Valley (which is fed up with violence and uncertainty, is deeply suspicious of Pakistan's intentions, remains unconvinced by the independence demand, which seems to them to be little more than a romantic slogan, and is increasingly nostalgic about the pre-insurgency days) is unequivocal on this score: the mere imposition of essentially discredited politicians like Farooq Abdullah or Congress leader Ghulam Rasool Kar would be an affront to the Kashmiris' dignity, sense of pride and self-respect, and would put the clock back even further, in the longer run, on prospects of a lasting peace.[2]

As for the Indian government's periodic announcements of plans to solve the Kashmir problem through infrastructure development and employment-generation schemes,[3] it is unlikely that the sudden emphasis on the economic well-being of Kashmir is much more than a diversionary, tactical device to avoid the substantive political issues that lie at the heart of this conflict. As such, talk of roads and bridges does not interest very many Kashmiris. As Hurriyat Conference leader Abdul Ghani Lone put it to me in Srinagar: 'Will they tell a man whose virgin daughter has been raped that they will put a paved road through his village, on condition he agrees to be loyal to India?'

Moreover, while guerrilla activity can be curbed or contained, it is folly to imagine (as Indian bureaucrats and police and military officials are frequently inclined to do) that it can be eliminated permanently and completely. Specifically, Hizbul Mujahideen, the most powerful insurgent outfit, while certainly on the defensive, is still far from being a spent force. Indeed, a senior HM spokesman confirmed to me in August 1995 that 'they [HM fighters] have received instructions from across [the border] to lie relatively low for the time being, and step up their actions at a later juncture'. Information available with pro-independence sources indicates that HM hardliners have stockpiled large quantities of weaponry in the Valley and Doda with the objective of keeping a protracted armed struggle alive at any cost. Thus, it is not possible to rule out a re-escalation of militant violence,[4] with the attendant risk of draconian reprisals on the civilian population by the security forces. If this happens, the government's hopes of 'normalisation' could rapidly evaporate.

But there are even more compelling arguments against forcing elections. Elections free of coercion will almost certainly evoke a major boycott throughout the Kashmir Valley. Partial but significant boycotts are also likely to occur in Doda district as well as in Rajouri and Poonch districts of Jammu (though the latter two districts have low levels of militant activity, there is a subtle but definite undercurrent of sympathy for the Kashmiri cause among the Rajput and Gujjar Muslim groups that dominate the population there), and perhaps also in Shia-majority Kargil district in Ladakh.[5] In this scenario, any election, which will in effect be reduced to a referendum on patriotic allegiance to the Indian Union, could well lead to greater communal polarisation, with only a cross-section of Hindus in Jammu and Buddhists in Ladakh's Leh district turning out to vote in really substantial numbers.[6]

Communal polarisation will be further aggravated if members of the Valley's Pandit minority who have migrated to Jammu and Delhi are allowed to cast absentee ballots, and if some Kashmir Valley seats are decided principally on the basis of those ballots.[7] Such a pointless exacerbation of the sectarian divide between the different communities of Jammu & Kashmir can only set the clock back even further on prospects of a just, serious and lasting solution (i.e., mutually agreed between the parties to the conflict and the different religious and regional groups of Jammu & Kashmir).[8]

How, then, might real progress be made towards a de-escalation of the conflict and the eventual goal of such a settlement?

Abdul Qayoom, 60, leader of the (largely notional) Kashmir unit of the Janata Dal party, a former education minister of Jammu & Kashmir, and a rare 'pro-India' politician to have stayed on in Srinagar since the troubles began (albeit in the city's heavily-guarded 'security zone'), is convinced that 'holding [assembly] elections will be totally counterproductive, and have disastrous consequences'. Instead, he argues passionately for 'taking the people of Kashmir into confidence', and for 'applying a healing touch to this bleeding society'. When I asked him (in July 1995) what such phrases might connote in more tangible terms, he responded that he meant, above all, 'a completely open, unconditional dialogue with all popular forces in Jammu & Kashmir, and those of the Valley in particular'.

Qayoom's prognosis and prescription found enthusiastic support from an unlikely quarter: Altaf Ahmad Khan *alias* Azam Inquillabi, a veteran Kashmiri nationalist rebel and a mastermind behind the insurrection that erupted in 1989–90.[9] While remaining fully committed to his ideal of an independent Jammu & Kashmir, Inquillabi now believes, as he himself told me in Srinagar, that dialogue and negotiations are the only route to making meaningful progress towards a lasting solution. A strong advocate of non-official discussions and consultations on the Kashmir issue between open-minded intellectual and professional leaders of India, Pakistan and various social and political groups in Jammu & Kashmir, Inquillabi also sounded a sombre note of warning in this regard: 'If this conflict is allowed to fester indefinitely, there is a real risk that the politically conscious and articulate voices of Kashmir will one by one be liquidated or marginalised. The gun has largely served its purpose—now politics must take over'.

It is therefore indeed a pity that those who rule India do not seem, as yet, to have the courage and confidence to recognise the same reality. This resistance to the notion of a substantive, open, democratic dialogue is all the more inexplicable because the ultimate guarantee of the Indian state's 'security' and 'integrity', the several hundred thousand heavily-armed police, paramilitary and military troops, are, for the present and foreseeable future at least, very much in place throughout Indian-administered Jammu & Kashmir, including its borders with neighbouring countries.

Unfortunately, however, the most recent developments in Kashmir do not provide grounds for optimism that the Indian state's policy perspective on the conflict may undergo any major revision in the immediate future. The current Indian strategy *vis-à-vis* the problem consists of three basic elements: first, continue the policy of sustained repression and further weaken the insurgents; second, arm and sponsor criminalised gangs that have broken away from the militant ranks and are now operating in the role of auxiliaries for the security forces, and use them to intimidate and demoralise the public as much as possible;[10] and third, try and undermine the Hurriyat Conference's standing by playing up allegations (some true) of corruption and ineptitude against some of its leading figures.[11] While all these are unmistakably signs of a mentality that views the Kashmir crisis purely in terms of a war that must be ruthlessly fought and won, indications of a sincere, politically-oriented, democratic and humane approach remain as feeble as ever.

In March 1996, officials of the Indian government's home ministry attracted considerable media attention when they announced
'unconditional talks' in New Delhi with several former high-ranking
leaders of avowedly pro-Pakistan guerrilla organisations. The
half-dozen Kashmiris who attended a single meeting with India's
home minister in mid-March included such former militant lumi-
naries as Imran Rahi, one-time deputy chief of Hizbul Mujahideen,
Babar Badr, one-time chief of the rather picturesquely named
Muslim Jaanbaaz Force, and Parvez Haider, former chief of
Al-Jehad.[12] However, the promised 'unconditional talks' with these
figures (none of whom enjoy any political standing in Kashmiri
society and have all been disowned, moreover, by their former
comrades-in-arms) seemed more like a photo-opportunity to com-
memorate the unconditional capitulation to the government of a
group of former gunmen who have lost heart and given up on their
cause. The propaganda value of the event for the government lay
chiefly in the fact that all these erstwhile advocates of Kashmir's
integration with Pakistan now unequivocally stated that direct talks
between Kashmiri groups and New Delhi to resolve the Kashmir
conflict should exclude Pakistan.[13] Reinforcing the impression that
the Indian authorities viewed the entire exercise as a propaganda
stunt-cum-intelligence operation, the committee set up by the government to liaise with the Kashmiri group consisted of two home
ministry bureaucrats and an intelligence official.[14]

Around the same time, meanwhile, JKLF leaders Yasin Malik
and Shakeel Bakshi were brutally assaulted by a gang of *sarkari*
militants (who were, as usual, protected by a large contingent of
security forces as they went about their business) when Malik was
addressing a mosque congregation in the southern Valley town of
Anantnag reiterating the right to self-determination and condemning the depredations of 'renegade' groups. Interestingly, the attack
on Malik was organised only a week after the JKLF leader had
held a successful rally in the northern Valley town of Sopore, and
coincided with another incident in which the popular Kashmiri
political figure Shabbir Shah (who has spent twenty of his
forty-three years in Indian prisons) was prevented by the security
forces from speaking at another scheduled public meeting in the
southern Valley district of Badgam. All this points to another

apparent component of the Indian state's current strategy in Kashmir—to prevent genuinely popular political leaders who retain credibility and a commitment to principles, and who can, therefore, keep up the sagging morale of the population, from holding even peaceful meetings and marches. This, in turn, suggests that Indian officialdom still views individuals and organisations who are genuinely representative of Kashmiri popular aspirations as threats, rather than as potential partners in a substantive, serious process of dialogue.

In late March 1996, public demonstrations erupted in Srinagar when Jalil Andrabi, a prominent Kashmiri human rights lawyer, was discovered tortured and shot to death after reportedly having been abducted by army soldiers and renegade militants a couple of weeks earlier (see Appendix). Around the same time, a stand-off between security forces and a group of armed militants near Srinagar's Hazratbal shrine ended with the killing of over thirty members of the group, a splinter-faction of the JKLF.

This latter incident seemingly revealed, once again, a disturbing proclivity on the part of the then Congress government in Delhi to use the Kashmir issue for partisan purposes—this time in the run-up to India's parliamentary elections. By finishing off a few dozen Kashmiri guerrillas who were, by all accounts, surrounded by hundreds of police-commandos and paramilitary troops (in two 'fierce gunbattles' in which the security forces suffered minimal casualties), the government demonstrated its tough stance on 'terrorism' and 'national security' to susceptible sections of the Indian electorate, thereby presumably appropriating or undercutting key planks of BJP, the main opposition. The guerrillas who were wiped out in the process represented a particularly vulnerable target, since they belonged to a splinter group with very limited popular support and military strength, and did not even enjoy the formal recognition of the Hurriyat Conference (which recognises only Yasin Malik's organisation as the legitimate JKLF). Such incidents, and what they reveal, obviously do not bode well for prospects of an end to the violence in Kashmir and the initiation of a process of dialogue aimed at developing the framework for a peaceful, honourable and workable solution.[15]

Individuals and organisations genuinely representative of a popular movement, and with at least some moral integrity and ideological

consistency, cannot be expected to summarily renounce their political platforms for the sake of uncertain 'talks' with powerful
adversaries who have a demonstrated record of deceit and ruth-
lessness. What this means is that Kashmiri leaders like Shabbir
Shah and Yasin Malik, among others, cannot be expected to simply
agree to being coopted into endorsing some 'package' of minor
concessions or piecemeal reforms drawn up on their adversaries'
terms.[16]

Gerry Adams and Martin McGuinness, the top leaders of the
Irish nationalist Sinn Fein party in northern Ireland who are both
former guerrilla commanders in the Irish Republican Army (IRA),
have not abandoned their ideological commitment to the idea of a
reunited Ireland. That did not prevent an extended ceasefire from
coming into effect in northern Ireland, nor did it in itself obstruct
a measure of tentative, halting progress towards a lasting solution
to that conflict. Even the Palestine Liberation Organisation (PLO),
which had its back to the wall (and very few cards, if any, left to
play) in the struggle against Israel by the 1990s, till recently
formally retained the clause in its founding charter which committed it to the total annihilation of the Zionist state. That, the
continuing turmoil in the West Bank and Gaza, the deadly attacks
on Israeli targets by members of the military wing of the radical
Islamist movement Hamas, and even the justified anger of Pales-
tinians living outside the Occupied Territories at having been
excluded from the ambit of the very flawed PLO–Israel agreement
struck in September 1993, have not prevented Yasser Arafat and
the Israeli government, very unequal negotiating partners indeed,
from making gradual, fitful progress in their tortuous negotiations.
The constant obstacles and problems encountered in the peace
processes in Ireland, the Middle East and elsewhere vividly demonstrate how extraordinarily difficult it is to devise and implement
equitable political solutions to complex and bitter conflicts. Yet not
even a beginning towards peace could have been made anywhere
if the 'rebels' had continued to be simply demonised, treated as
undeserving of even minimal respect, and their grievances and
aspirations dismissed out of hand as illegitimate and unacceptable.

Responsible political leaders and activists in Kashmir, whatever
their public positions and ideological commitments (which they
cannot be expected to summarily foresake), know perfectly well

that the gun alone cannot 'liberate' their people. Indeed, they fully realise that they themselves, and the political future of their people, are increasingly being held hostage by the environment of violence and fear. There are clear indications that some of these important, popularly-based forces would be willing to participate in a genuine dialogue without crippling pre-conditions of any kind on any side, that they recognise the potential efficacy of serious, substantive talks (*not* some charade masquerading as dialogue) for their people, and that they themselves have compelling pragmatic motives to respond favourably to the initiation of any such process.[17]

Yet these forces have so far been repressed, rebuffed and denied recognition as bonafide political actors representing certain deep-rooted collective aspirations. And so long as large-scale victimisation of civilians by the security forces in Indian-administered Kashmir continues, armed resistance is also likely to continue, and a climate congenial to a cessation of hostilities and commencement of dialogue, leading eventually to substantive negotiations, cannot come about.

But in the immediate future, it would be extremely myopic of the authorities in New Delhi to exploit the military edge over armed insurgents to trample wantonly on Kashmiri sentiments and aspirations yet again.[18] A peace of the graveyard will not only condemn Jammu & Kashmir to an unpromising, uncertain future, it will also freeze India–Pakistan relations in their present condition of polarised animosity, to the detriment of prospects of peace, democracy and development in the entire subcontinent.

Indeed, the international dimension to this conflict is not something that can simply be wished away. It is less than certain that any 'solution' (whatever that may be) to the struggle in and over Kashmir can be stable and final without some level of participation and acquiescence on the part of the rulers of Pakistan.[19] Similarly, at some future date, some form of international guarantee or underwriting for a permanent solution may be necessary or advisable, given that deceit and bad faith have been the one constant in the tangled, tortured history of the Kashmir question since 1947.

Perhaps the end of the twentieth century presents an opportune moment to test Kalhana's words of wisdom, and establish whether the 'power of spiritual merit', rather than the 'force of soldiers', remains the best way to conquer the contemporary challenge of democracy, self-determination and a just peace in Kashmir.

Notes

1. Indeed, in the second half of 1995, rumours were already circulating in Srinagar that the Indian government had finalised its (post-election) list of ministers for Jammu & Kashmir, and that there were plans to unleash groups of surrendered, government-sponsored ex-militants (in particular, the armed faction led by Jamshed Shirazi *alias* Koka Parray, which goes by the name Ikhwan-ul-Muslimoon) in the run-up to polls to terrorise the people.

2. The Indian government formally proposed holding assembly elections in Jammu & Kashmir in December 1995, only to have the suggestion shot down by the country's assertive Election Commission, which ruled that conditions were still not sufficiently conducive to ensure a minimally free and fair election. One apparent reason the government wished to stage an election at the height of winter in a largely Himalayan region (which would be unprecedented in Kashmir's political history) was that low rates of participation could then be partly blamed on the weather. However, even Farooq Abdullah's National Conference party (which still largely exists only in name in its earlier strongholds) has refused to take part in any such election unless New Delhi makes a binding promise to substantively and comprehensively restore Jammu & Kashmir pre-1953 autonomous status.

3. The Indian finance minister and architect of the Narasimha Rao government's liberalisation and deregulation programme, Manmohan Singh, visited Kashmir a few times in 1995 to enquire into the economic problems of the region.

4. A car-bomb blast that killed some thirteen persons (mostly Indian soldiers) in the heavily-guarded centre of Srinagar in early September 1995, and for which HM claimed responsibility, may be an early portent of worse to come.

5. After the destruction of the Charar-e-Sharief shrine in May 1995, Doda, Rajouri, Poonch and Kargil also joined the Kashmir Valley in observing protest *hartals* (general strikes).

6. Even this would partly depend on what strategy the BJP, which has some influence in the towns of Jammu, chooses to adopt. It currently says that it is opposed to any elections at this stage, till 'terrorism' is completely crushed.

As this book goes to press, elections are scheduled to be held on 23 and 30 May 1996, as part of India-wide parliamentary elections, for the six seats (three from Kashmir, two from Jammu and one from Ladakh) that constitute Jammu & Kashmir's representation in the elected lower house (Lok Sabha) of Parliament. Parliamentary elections could not be held in Indian-administered Jammu & Kashmir during the general elections of 1991 because of the violent atmosphere, so this is the first time any kind of electoral process is being attempted there since 1989. Popular participation (or the lack thereof) in this election is likely to closely approximate the patterns I have just described. In a repeat of the 1989 parliamentary poll, there will almost certainly be a major boycott in the Kashmir Valley (even Farooq's NC has declined to put up candidates), and a partial but significant boycott in one of the two parliamentary constituencies in the Jammu region. In a revealing indication of the true nature of this election, the voting in Indian-administered Jammu & Kashmir has been deliberately scheduled more than two weeks after polling will have been completed (and results known) for the rest of India, in order to enable 'redeployment' of tens of thousands of additional security forces from various parts of India to Jammu & Kashmir.

7. Some vociferous spokespersons for the Pandit community have been demanding that six of the Valley's forty-six assembly seats be 'allotted' to them.

8. Given the near-certainty of a period of instability and flux in India's national-level politics following the likely outcome of a 'hung parliament' (i.e., in which no single party or bloc commands a majority) in the elections of May 1996, there will probably not be another attempt to hold an assembly election in Jammu & Kashmir before at least autumn 1996.

9. Azam Inquillabi (literally, Azam the Revolutionary) possibly holds the record for the maximum number of violations of the Line of Control by a single individual—he has made some thirty clandestine crossings in both directions between 1969 and 1994.

10. This phenomenon of organised groups of *sarkari* or government-sponsored militants emerged during 1995, as morale, cohesion and discipline in many of the armed groups that had proliferated since 1990 steadily declined, and drop-out and defection rates rose sharply. Some members of these government-backed vigilante squads were also motivated by a particular animus towards the Hizbul Mujahideen, whom they accused of attacking and killing activists of non-HM guerrilla groups. By 1995–96, several of these 'renegade' or 'contra-guerrilla' outfits had sprouted in the Valley (the largest and most notorious being the group led by Jamshed Shirazi *alias* Koka Parray, a self-styled 'freedom fighter against Pakistan'), and further aggravated the lawless situation by engaging in acts of murder, rape, kidnapping and extortion with the active encouragement of the Indian administration and its forces. I was myself once briefly held up at gunpoint by one of these gangs near Pattan, a town in Baramulla district not far from Srinagar—the gunmen were operating virtually under the shadow of a nearby bunker manned by an Indian security force unit.

11. There is considerable anger and disillusionment among ordinary Kashmiris especially over charges of rampant corruption and self-enrichment against several senior Hurriyat leaders—the figures most frequently mentioned in this connection are Syed Ali Shah Geelani of the Jama'at-i-Islami and Abdul Ghani Butt of the Muslim Conference, a tiny pro-Pakistan faction. However, whatever the Hurriyat's problems may be, the fact remains that the Indian government still does not have a truly credible alternative to project in its place.

12. Indian officials also claimed that the talks had received the approval of Ahsan Dar, the guerrilla leader who originally founded Hizbul Mujahideen and is currently still being held in a Jammu prison.

13. The spectacle of former senior leaders of hardline pro-Pakistan groups renouncing and denouncing Pakistan may, among other things, reflect the fact that the appeal of Pakistan for most Kashmiri Muslims, if it is present at all, tends to be very superficial and skin-deep. Significantly, no leader of comparable stature of the independentist JKLF has as yet formally renounced the ideology of independence.

14. See the reports on the meeting in (*TS* 1996; *TT* 1996a). The Valley observed a total strike following the Hurriyat's call to protest these 'talks'. Significantly,

however, the Kashmiri participants at the meeting demanded an end to offensive military operations by the security forces, the release of most political prisoners, and the immediate disarming of government-sponsored armed groups as essential 'confidence-building measures' to pave the way for more substantive discussions in the future. These are all very constructive suggestions.

15. Death-squad killings continue unabated in Kashmir. In mid-April 1996, the body of Ghulam Rasool Sheikh, a newspaper editor in the Valley town of Pampore, was recovered from the Jhelum river. Sheikh had been active in documenting allegations of human rights abuses by the security forces; his family said that he had been kidnapped from his home in mid-March by army-sponsored 'renegade' militants.

16. It is hardly surprising that there were absolutely no takers in Kashmir for prime minister Narasimha Rao's offer, made on Doordarshan (government television network) in November 1995, to negotiate a solution to the Kashmir crisis on the basis of the 1975 accord between the representatives of Sheikh Abdullah and Indira Gandhi. As I have pointed out in Chapter 3, the 1975 agreement, far from being a just settlement to Kashmir's grievances, was actually an abject capitulation by an ageing and exhausted Sheikh Abdullah to the ruthless power-politics of Delhi. Given this fact, Rao's 'offer' to the Kashmiris would probably seem amusing at best and insultingly absurd at worst to anyone truly knowledgeable about the history of the Kashmir question. As already noted, even Farooq's National Conference is demanding restoration of Jammu & Kashmir's pre-1953 autonomy. The fact that even a group totally aligned with the Indian state is making such a demand is a reflection of the ground realities in Kashmir, and of the popular mood among the NC's former constituency.

17. In an interview (*IT* 1995: 38), for example, JKLF chairman Yasin Malik states that 'the [Indian] Government should come forward for negotiations on reasonable terms and without any pre-conditions. All the parties concerned—India, Pakistan and the people of Kashmir—should be involved'.

18. Former Indian Prime Minister Narasimha Rao was given to making seemingly contradictory statements on the Kashmir problem. During 1995, he predicted on the one hand that Kashmir would cease to be an issue by the time of the general elections in India (scheduled for May 1996), implying, presumably, that the problem would have been settled essentially by force by that time. He was proved wrong on the matter. On the other hand, he also explicitly stated during 1995 that the Indian government was prepared to discuss any arrangements 'short of azaadi' with the Kashmiris.

19. In the words of Yasin Malik, certainly no enthusiast of Pakistan: 'Pakistan is basically a party to this dispute. You cannot ignore or bypass that' (*IT* 1995).

7

Elections, Democracy, 'Self-Determination': A Postscript (Autumn 1996)

When Bakshi Ghulam Mohammed was Prime Minister of Kashmir [in the 1950s], he was once asked by a journalist: Bakshi saab, how many people in Kashmir are with you? Forty lakhs, he replied [the entire population of the State at that time]. Then how many people are with Sheikh Abdullah [then imprisoned], the questioner enquired in some surprise. Forty lakhs, Bakshi responded, a slight smile creeping over his face. And with G. M. Sadiq [then Bakshi's rival within the official National Conference], the reporter persisted. Forty lakhs, said Bakshi, the smile widening into a mischievous grin.

—Anecdote related by a senior officer of the Jammu & Kashmir police in Gulmarg, Kashmir, in August 1996, by way of an answer to my query as to what Kashmiris today really feel about their political predicament and which political leaders, forces and agendas they actually support.

We are desperately praying for peace and normalcy here. I will vote in elections [to the state legislative assembly in Indian-administered Jammu & Kashmir] next month, in the slender hope that the revival of a political process and the establishment of some sort of civilian government will help bring this unending cycle of violence to an end. People still want azaadi *here, but first of all we need* azaadi *from the gun culture of the security forces, the militants and the renegades [surrendered militants who operate as auxiliaries to the Indian forces]. So I will vote, and I believe the National Conference will win from this area. But if you ask me what I really want from my heart, and you wish me to be truthful, I can only reply:* Khudmukhtari *['self-rule'] for Kashmir.*

—A middle-aged shopkeeper in Badgam, a district town in the Kashmir Valley, in August 1996 (personal interview with author).

The supreme guarantee of our relationship with India is the identity of democratic and secular aspirations, which have guided the people of India as well as those of Jammu & Kashmir in their struggle for emancipation and before which all constitutional safeguards will take a secondary position.

—From the speech of Sheikh Abdullah before the Jammu & Kashmir Constituent Assembly on August 11, 1952, detailing the provisions of the informal 'Delhi Agreement', confirming the autonomous status of Jammu & Kashmir within the Indian Union, negotiated with the Government of India in July 1952.

As 1996 draws to a close, the political equations and prospects in (Indian-administered) Jammu & Kashmir are not only complex and confused, and therefore fraught with a considerable degree of uncertainty and unpredictability. They are also rife with all manner of apparent contradictions and paradoxes, and hence not just difficult to understand but easily amenable to misinterpretation.

In an effort to make sense of this complicated situation and to make an informed judgment of its implications for a democratic, durable resolution to the Kashmir crisis, I returned to Kashmir for another round of intensive travel and field research in August–September 1996,[1] even as the rest of this book went to press. I was interested, in particular, in investigating the likely longer-term implications of the revival of Indian political institutions—especially a Jammu & Kashmir provincial government and legislative assembly—for prospects of a lasting solution to the Kashmir question.

The trends I had detected a year earlier in the course of field research during July and August of 1995, had, I found, become clearer and more pronounced in the intervening year. Indeed, these trends had progressed farther and developed faster than I had anticipated in 1995. A profound exhaustion among the people with incessant violence and repression, which seemed to be leading nowhere in particular even while bleeding Kashmiri society white on a daily basis, was already evident by mid-1995. Now, however, such opinions and sentiments were both more widespread and deeply felt among the population. A yearning for peace bordering on desperation seemed to have taken hold of the public consciousness.

At the same time, armed insurgency, on the decline since 1994, seemed to have lost further ground. Large tracts of the Valley had been effectively cleared of any major guerrilla activity by the Indian army and paramilitary forces. Checkpoints had become noticeably less frequent in rural areas and the soldiers manning them visibly less tense and hostile (relatively speaking). Srinagar's ubiquitous bunkers had also declined markedly in number and many of those that remained wore a somewhat somnolent air during daylight hours—additional evidence that the war of attrition was gradually being won by the Indian state and that the armed struggle was dying a slow death. There was even a little civilian motor and pedestrian traffic in a few parts of the city after dark, a hitherto unthinkable event. Kashmir's capital still largely turns into a ghost town after dusk, a spine-chillingly eerie nocturnal urban landscape where almost every street and intersection is dominated by the silhouettes of looming figures with guns. During a half-hour drive to my hotel in central Srinagar from dinner at the suburban home of a friend one midnight, however, I was stopped and questioned by patrolling BSF units merely four times. Even a year earlier, the roadblocks and spot checks would have been much more frequent and the questioning considerably rougher.

Elections to the Indian Parliament, May 1996

In an obvious attempt to capitalise on such relative improvements in the security environment, the Government of India has conducted parliamentary and subsequently state assembly elections in Jammu & Kashmir in May and September 1996 respectively. The credibility of the elections held to fill Jammu & Kashmir's seats in the Indian parliament were severely, perhaps fatally, undermined by widespread reports of massive, systematic intimidation and coercion of the public on polling day by Indian counterinsurgency forces—particularly the regular army—throughout the Valley and the adjoining district of Doda in the Jammu region. The elections can be said to have been more or less genuine in two of the six parliamentary constituencies at stake—Ladakh and Jammu (which includes Jammu city and some other relatively peaceful areas). However, this was not at all the case in the other four constituencies: Srinagar, Baramulla and Anantnag (all in the Valley) and Udhampur (which is in the Jammu region, but includes Doda). Prior to voting, several hundred thousand police, paramilitary and army troops stationed in Jammu & Kashmir were reinforced with tens of thousands of additional forces. The polling itself was deliberately held in three phases in order to enable maximum concentration of this vast security machine in the constituencies scheduled to vote on particular days. This ensured that the Valley—a relatively small land area—was 'saturated' with armed men and that one soldier was present for every three or four eligible voters in most sectors of the four troubled constituencies. As a result, a purportedly democratic exercise degenerated into a purely military operation and resembled a massive crackdown more than anything else. The Indian army, in particular, proved utterly overzealous in carrying out its brief of 'encouraging' people to vote, thereby discrediting the entire process. Although the official turnout figures were 35 to 40 per cent in the three Valley seats and almost 50 per cent in Udhampur, a smaller—and more genuine—turnout would have been far more credible.

Despite attempts by those elements of the Indian media which seemingly accord priority to 'patriotism' and 'national interest' above such trivial considerations as democracy and human rights (not to mention truthful reporting), to whitewash what happened during these elections,[2] the vast majority of eyewitness reports appearing in the Indian and international media were strikingly consistent in their content.[3] Distressing accounts appeared of entire *mohallas* and villages being rounded up at gunpoint and herded like cattle to polling stations manned by thousands of polling personnel specially drafted from various north Indian states. Innumerable Kashmiri homes received personal visits from heavily armed and truculent soldiers 'enquiring' whether the residents had voted yet or not. Those who had not were uniformly warned of 'dire consequences if they could not' by the end of the day show 'the indelible ink mark which is placed on the finger of every citizen who votes'.[4] In some places, citizens emerging from morning prayers at the local mosque found large contingents of security forces waiting outside with transport to 'escort' the entire congregation to the nearest polling station. 'In at least a dozen villages between Srinagar and Baramulla', one correspondent reported, 'none of the hundreds of voters questioned said they had voted freely'.[5] As a leading Indian newsmagazine put it, 'the farce unfolded just when...there was a faint glimmer of hope.... Even as ordinary Kashmiris appeared to be in a mood to reject violence as the vehicle for *azaadi*, and the slogan of independence was giving way to talk of autonomy, they found themselves being ushered into another period of alienation and anger...the troops inspired not confidence but fear and loathing'.[6] Even Farooq Abdullah's National Conference (NC), which boycotted this election pending the Indian government's recognition of its demand for greater autonomy for Jammu & Kashmir,[7] was constrained to admit in a formal resolution that the elections 'were neither free nor fair' and had 'only deepened the frustration and alienation of the people'. In fact, it turned out that virtually the only Kashmiris enthused at the thought of participating in the Indian parliament were the so-called 'renegades' ('reformed militants' in official parlance)—criminalised and lumpen elements who have defected from the guerrilla ranks and now prey upon the civilian population with the active encouragement of the Indian administration and its various security agencies. Several of these gangster outfits had fielded their own candidates. At an 'election meeting' organised by one such group in support of its nominee, an embarrassed Indian journalist discovered that the several hundred villagers in attendance, 'all imported from another district', had been brought to the rally 'by a combination of inducement and threat. The promise—that of a free meal. The threat—that of a bullet'.[8]

An election held in such circumstances predictably produced some curiously anomalous results. Of the 305,000 valid votes said to have been cast for the Srinagar seat, for example, the victorious Congress candidate secured just 45,000, i.e., about 15 per cent. The rest of the vote was fragmented more or less evenly among more than a dozen other candidates, most of them completely obscure independents or persons representing hitherto unknown parties who in normal conditions would not be expected to poll more than a minuscule number of authentic ballots. There was other circumstantial evidence strongly suggestive of random or fraudulent stamping of ballot papers, either by reluctant voters as a form of protest or by security and polling officials determined to ensure a certain level of 'turnout' (or perhaps some combination of both). In the Anantnag seat, for instance, the BJP candidate managed to poll 40,000 votes, of which absentee ballots submitted by Pandit migrants[9] accounted for fewer than 7,000. In other words, over 33,000 Kashmiri Muslims living in an area known to be a hotbed of militant opposition to Indian authority had voluntarily supported the party of 'Hindu nationalism' whose declared objective is to abolish Kashmir's fictitious autonomy (as written into Article 370) even from the statute books. If this is really what happened, it goes without saying that it is strange that India has any kind of problem at all in Kashmir. The BJP performed even more astounding feats in other areas populated by Kashmiri Muslims and notorious for pro-Pakistan and pro-independence militancy. The BJP nominee's resounding victory in the Udhampur parliamentary seat owed much to an 11,000-vote lead he obtained from a remote segment of the constituency called Inderwal, located in Kishtwar division of Doda district. Inderwal's electorate is 80 per cent Kashmiri Muslim and the area is a known stronghold of the secessionist movement. When I spoke with residents of the area a couple of months after they had rendered this remarkable verdict, many complained not only that they had been forced to vote but that soldiers had specifically instructed them to stamp the lotus, BJP's party symbol. Local security and polling officials had ensured compliance simply by looking on attentively as voters did so.[10]

In other words, yet another sad chapter had been added to the ritual funerals of democracy that have defined the politics of Kashmir since 1947.

Elections to the Jammu & Kashmir State Legislative Assembly, September 1996

The Indian political establishment however insisted, against all evidence to the contrary, that the elections had been 'free and fair'. The conduct of the polling received a certificate of approval even from the country's Election Commission, whose senior officials are frequently given to indulging in self-righteous and self-congratulatory rhetoric about their mission of ensuring fair and honest elections in the country. The ostensible 'success' of these polls further provided the polyglot United Front coalition, which assumed the reins of government in New Delhi in June 1996, with the rationale for scheduling elections to the Jammu & Kashmir state legislative assembly, a body defunct since 1990, in September 1996.[11]

The advent of these elections aroused a significantly greater degree of public interest within Kashmir than the parliamentary polls had. Few people anywhere in Jammu & Kashmir have much reason to feel excited about voting to elect representatives to a distant Parliament which is largely irrelevant to their lives. Elections intended to revive the state legislature, however, are qualitatively different, especially since they offer to some a faint hope of an end to the daily bloodletting that is destroying Kashmiri society. Ghulam Qadir Lone, a 50-year-old teacher who came to vote on his own volition in Doda district, was typical of this large section of war-weary Kashmiris: 'I'm voting only for peace. I don't care who the candidate is, who wins or who forms the government'. In the same village, one of his younger compatriots, 24-year-old student Shabbir Ahmed, was typical of another large section of Kashmiris: 'I'm not voting. It makes no difference. We have seen it in the past...these elections are not going to change the situation in Kashmir'.[12]

In the course of travelling in the violence-torn regions of Kashmir in the autumn of 1996, I realised that very few people shared the celebratory view of these elections promoted by Indian officialdom, i.e., that they signal the triumphant return of democracy and the definitive defeat of 'terrorism'. Nor did ordinary citizens attach much credence to the vague talk, engaged in by several top leaders of the new Indian government (including Prime Minister H. D. Deve Gowda, Home Minister Indrajit Gupta and Defence Minister Mulayam Singh Yadav), of granting 'maximum autonomy' to the state once the elected assembly and state government was in place. These nebulous references to the possibility of autonomy gave Farooq Abdullah's NC the opportunistic pretext it needed to effectively abandon its platform of securing a binding commitment from the central government on the autonomy issue *prior* to any elections and agree to put up candidates (thereby giving the assembly elections the figleaf of respectability the parliamentary polls had lacked). Ordinary Kashmiris living in the shadow of the gun were however scarcely concerned, for the moment at least, with a few vague sentences about autonomy uttered by Indian politicians. And despite their disillusionment with armed militancy, nor were the people by and large enthusiastic about a political process that is clearly one component of the Indian state's strategy of pacification in Kashmir and is designed to restore to the formal office of chief ministership a politician whose irresponsibility and incompetence played a major role in Kashmir's descent into tragedy, and who is yet to recover any of his lost credibility with its people.

Absence of enthusiasm did not, however, signify a total lack of interest or universal hostility among the public. It became obvious to me as I toured the Valley just prior to the polls that a large body of opinion was unequivocally opposed to any electoral process intended solely to resurrect and relegitimise Indian institutions, totally deny the validity of the 'self-determination' demand, and prop up 'pro-India' politicians who have a history of corruption and misgovernance. A much smaller segment of opinion also existed—mostly among propertied and professional classes sickened by pointless violence and eager to get on with their lives and careers—which regarded the heavily rhetorical politics of 'self-determination' with disdain and was prepared to accept any leader, including such previously despised figures as Farooq Abdullah, who prioritised return to normalcy above all else. Between these two groups, however, there was a very sizeable body of opinion whose attitude was defined by a large measure of ambiguity. An elderly resident of Warapora, a remote village I visited in Badgam district, expressed the fears and hopes of this category:

I was picked up by the Army a few years ago, and spent some time in detention in their camp. As a result, I was on bed-rest for the next two years. Just when I was recovering, I was picked up by Hizbul Mujahideen militants, who tortured me again. Frankly, I am not very interested in these elections and don't plan to vote, unless of course the Army forces me to and I have to stamp a piece of paper to save my skin. But if the elections were to bring peace any closer, I would welcome them. Otherwise, they are useless. After all, elections in Kashmir are never what they seem. Last time [1987], this whole area voted for the MUF [Muslim United Front], but the National Conference candidate was declared elected by a huge margin.

In other words, the momentary political predilections of a people severely battered by violence are influenced not so much by abstract political issues as by considerations of day-to-day survival. Indeed, I am convinced that the vast bulk of even those who did not, for a variety of reasons, turn out to exercise their franchise—a category that includes, most importantly, the majority of the Valley's population—nonetheless fully share the yearning for peace and a permanent settlement to the Kashmir conflict of those who did choose to vote.

In particular, those inclined to vote (or at least, not entirely disinclined) were, I found, motivated by three factors. First, they hope that the installation of a civilian governmental apparatus, even one which is in some basic sense unrepresentative, would help dilute the absolute power of the army and other security forces, subject them to some form of restraint and accountability, and curb the wanton disregard they habitually show towards the lives and rights of the civilian population. Second, ordinary Kashmiris are desperate to escape the mounting depredations of renegade militias sponsored by the army and paramilitary forces, which have emerged as a major menace in many areas of the Valley, including Srinagar itself. The activities of these 'reformed' insurgents include murder, rape, kidnapping, extortion, robbery and smuggling. At a time when the 'gun culture' has become an object of revulsion for most Kashmiris, they are being compelled to endure a particularly vicious and criminal variant of that culture—the 'renegade culture'—courtesy of the Indian administration. As one Indian writer has aptly put it, 'the renegades...may have made "Kashmir safer for India", but they have also made Kashmir a terribly unsafe and unsavoury place for Kashmiris.... The renegades have made India a dirtier word in Kashmir than it perhaps ever was'.[13] Many Kashmiris hope against hope that a civilian administration will move to disarm these groups, or at least bring them under some semblance of control. Finally, there are thousands of Kashmiri families whose loved ones are incarcerated in Indian prisons. According to an estimate provided to me by the International

Committee of the Red Cross (ICRC), which in late 1995 received permission to monitor conditions for detainees housed in regular jails (i.e., excluding those illegally detained at any time in army and paramilitary camps), some 20,000 Kashmiri political prisoners are being held in various jails in the Valley, the Jammu region and in a number of other states like Punjab, Rajasthan and Delhi. Many of their families hope that a civilian administration staffed by Kashmiris will be more sympathetically disposed than non-Kashmiri bureaucrats and security officials to releasing their relatives.

The assembly elections however also had the instant effect of bringing the latent polarisation in Jammu & Kashmir's politics to the surface and precipitating a trial of strength between the pro-'self-determination' forces on the one hand and pro-India political parties, backed crucially by the military power of the security forces, on the other. Once the NC leadership capitulated to enormous pressure from powerful political and bureaucratic circles in Delhi and shed its inhibitions about participating, the entire pro-India spectrum of parties came alive once again with the petty factional struggles and personality conflicts that had animated it before 1990. Politics as usual seemed to be making a comeback none had believed possible. The Hurriyat Conference, on the other hand, announced a door-to-door campaign by its leaders and activists to persuade citizens to boycott the polling. Despite some intimidation and harassment by the renegade groups and the security forces, Hurriyat representatives were able to conduct a reasonably energetic boycott campaign throughout the Valley and to a lesser extent in Doda. Yasin Malik and Javed Mir, the JKLF's youthful leaders, were particularly active in this campaign. Shabbir Shah, who had been suspended from the Hurriyat's executive following disagreements over his independent style of functioning, meanwhile launched his own, parallel boycott campaign, which also drew a reasonably positive response from the public.

The Indian government's determination to go ahead with these elections had nonetheless placed the Hurriyat in a difficult position. The politics of boycott, which places its protagonists in a purely negative, reactive mode, suffers from certain inherent limitations. As it is, the pejorative appellation of 'hartal party' has to some extent stuck to the Hurriyat. Most Kashmiris are simply exhausted with the murderous stalemate that prevails in their land, and frequent strikes (the Hurriyat's speciality), while a perfectly legitimate form of protest, do not offer any way out of this destructive impasse. Moreover, the Hurriyat is but a makeshift coalition of disparate political groups, fundamentally incompatible ideological tendencies and rival personalities. Kashmiris, who typically have a high level of political awareness, are fully conscious of this fact.

Nonetheless, the Hurriyat's inability to take part in these elections was in some ways understandable. It was certainly predictable. Apart from the strong Pakistani influence on some elements of the Hurriyat, it is difficult to the point of impossible for a body dedicated to defending the right to 'self-determination' of Kashmir to do something tantamount to unconditional surrender to the Indian authorities, especially when there are no serious signs of moderation on the part of those authorities and little substantive improvement in their treatment of the civilian population. Furthermore, even if the Hurriyat were to decide to participate for purely tactical reasons, it would have to contend with the facts that truly free and fair balloting is at present virtually impossible in Kashmir and that there is a real risk that practically any kind of outcome can be engineered by the Indian administration and its various intelligence agencies and security forces.

However, the Hurriyat's boycott campaign had several factors working in its favour. First, several political groups that are undeniably important in Kashmir's politics are represented in this coalition, unwieldy as it may be. These are the JKLF, the People's League (founded by Shabbir Shah), the Awami Action Committee (led by the late Maulvi Farooq, whose son, Umer Farooq, is the Hurriyat's convenor), the People's Conference (headed by Abdul Ghani Lone and very popular in Kupwara) and the Jama'at-i-Islami (which has a formidable though presently severely beleaguered organisational network). Any political process in Kashmir that does not include these forces is incomplete to say the very least. Another factor, however, was even more influential. Whatever the coalition's problems and contradictions, those constituents and leaders of the Hurriyat Conference who have a relatively clean image and stand for the independentist line are the only political forces in Kashmir today that can remotely lay claim to representing *Kashmiri* pride, identity and political aspirations (as distinguished from those politicians whose prospects are critically dependent on the

Indian state's power, or those who are Trojan horses for Pakistan's irredentist ambitions). Given the deep roots and continuing appeal of the *azaadi* ideology among Kashmir's people, it was assured that the boycott campaigns of figures like Yasin Malik and Shabbir Shah would receive a sympathetic and respectful hearing. Indeed, even those sceptical of the Hurriyat seemed to appreciate the reasons for the latter's stand. As a Srinagar businessman who intended to vote (for the NC) explained to me: 'There is no reason for the Hurriyat to participate in elections at this juncture and discredit itself needlessly. The National Conference is available for that purpose. The Hurriyat's role is different'.

The Hurriyat's peaceful efforts were supplemented by the distinctly non-peaceful endeavours of the guerrilla underground, which, to use a colloquial phrase, is down but definitely not out. While the level of violence had been relatively low in the first few months of 1996, there was a sharp upsurge in violence immediately after the completion of the parliamentary elections. Clashes between guerrillas and security forces increased and over 400 deaths (mostly civilians, as usual) were reported in June and July alone. On the day the NC announced its decision to contest the assembly polls (in the second week of August), 33 persons were officially reported killed in political violence; the next day, 41 persons were reported killed. On the day I arrived in Kashmir in the second half of August, 18 persons died; during my stay, a powerful bomb exploded next to a BSF post in Badshah Chowk in the heavily guarded centre of Srinagar. What passed for the election campaign was marked by sporadic but occasionally deadly attacks on canvassers and candidates. Some two dozen campaigners and activists affiliated to pro-India parties were murdered, NC supporters being the major victims. Polling day in Srinagar, 21 September, was punctuated by sporadic gunfire, rocket attacks and grenade explosions. Hundreds of gunmen assigned to protect Farooq Abdullah were unable to prevent two abortive attempts on his life—the first in Pulwama, in the southern part of the Valley, the second in Kishtwar, in the mountainous reaches of Doda district. As one correspondent who accompanied the NC president on the campaign trail observed, 'travelling with Abdullah...is like travelling in a military column passing through enemy territory', and noted that his typical audience consisted of 'about 150 villagers and close to 500 soldiers'.[14] The militants were obviously serving notice that while their armed struggle could be weakened, it could not be totally destroyed.

The eventual consequence of this tug-of-war between various contending forces and factors was that polling in the Valley was relatively low. Turnout was high—75 per cent on average—in most of the Jammu districts and in Ladakh, once again underscoring the great variations in the political contexts and circumstances of the different regions of Jammu & Kashmir. But it was clear from the outset that the crucial contest between pro-election and anti-election forces would be in the Valley, the focal point of the Kashmir problem, and that the worth of the entire process hinged critically on what happened in Kashmir proper.

Polling was, as I had anticipated from my pre-election survey, somewhat uneven in the Valley. In a number of constituencies, including the Shia-dominated zones of Pattan in Baramulla district and Magam in Badgam district or the Gujjar-populated zones of Uri, where people had an opportunity to vote for fairly popular local politicians, it was quite brisk. But in many other areas, the electorate turned out in disappointingly low numbers. Polling was particularly poor—only about 20 per cent—in Srinagar city, the focal point of the tussle for prestige and credibility between pro-India and pro-boycott forces. The *official* turnout figures for Srinagar and Anantnag districts were thus only about 25 per cent. The typical scene in Srinagar (largely replicated in Baramulla and Anantnag towns as well) was that 'most polling booths were deserted' and the areas around them 'filled with security forces and vehicles'.[15] Indeed, 'in some polling stations, no votes were cast till late evening'.[16]

There were reports of army and paramilitary units threatening and beating citizens and forcing them to vote in some areas, ranging from Soura on the outskirts of Srinagar to Trehgam in the remote Lolab valley of Kupwara. But, by and large, incidents of overt coercion remained sporadic and localised compared to the large-scale, systematic coercion employed in the parliamentary elections. For the most part, the security forces restricted themselves to exhorting unresponsive citizens to vote over public address systems. The high rates of participation in Jammu and Ladakh, and the moderate turnout in some areas of the Valley as well as in the predominantly Kashmiri Muslim zones of Doda, enabled government officials to cumulate statistics and claim an overall turnout, for the whole state, of approximately 50 to 55 per cent. But it was clear that despite the serious decline in numbers, firepower and popular support of the armed insurgency, the boycott call of the *azaadi* movement had still had a significant impact in the heartland of the struggle over Jammu & Kashmir's future.[17]

Prior to the elections, the NC had been widely expected to emerge as the single largest party in the new legislature at the very least, and probably as the winner of a narrow majority of the 87 seats (46 in the Valley, 37 in Jammu and 4 in Ladakh) at stake. But the scale of the NC's victory turned out to be simply overwhelming. The party's candidates won 55 of the 87 constituencies—together with its allies, the NC government commands 61 seats (a comfortable two-thirds majority) in the new assembly. This tally far surpasses even the party's impressive performances in 1977 (when it won 39 of the then 76 seats) and 1983 (when it secured 47 of 76 constituencies). In an ironic, indeed bizarre, twist of fate and circumstances, the party that had completely discredited itself with its mass base did better in the elections of 1996 than it ever had. While a truly remarkable turn of events, the victory was nevertheless tainted by several factors, including the totally abnormal conditions in which the elections took place and the scattered reports of coercion and fraud. Above all, however, it was unmistakably a triumph by default, since the main political forces with which the NC would have had to compete for the votes which made its victory possible had absented themselves from the contest.

The most predictable part of the results was that the NC swept the Valley of Kashmir, winning 40 of its 46 seats in the house. The outcome in the Valley amounted to an overwhelming rejection of all-India parties—the Congress obtained two seats here, the Janata Dal one—and revealed that the base of 'Indian' parties (as the Valley's residents tend to call them) remains pathetically weak and shallow in the Kashmiri heartland. That portion of the Valley's electorate which had cast votes had obviously reverted to habit and instinct—in which local loyalties play the defining role—inside the polling booth.

The less predictable and more interesting results were, however, the returns from the other two regions—Jammu and Ladakh. The NC, the party of quintessentially 'Kashmiri' lineage, did better in these two predominantly non-Kashmiri regions than ever before. The NC won 12 of the Jammu region's 37 seats on its own, while its ally, the Bahujan Samaj Party (BSP), which has a small but compact base among the lower-caste Hindu electorate in some of the region's districts, won another four. The combined NC–BSP tally in Jammu (16) was equal to that of the three major 'Indian' parties—BJP, Janata Dal and Congress—put together. The BJP, which had nurtured high hopes of emerging as the dominant party in Jammu, won only eight seats from the region, while the Congress faced near-annihilation with only four wins (the Janata Dal secured another four). In Ladakh, the Congress, the traditionally dominant force, was severely defeated. The party could hold on to only a single seat (Leh), while the other three went to the NC.

The NC's emergence, in these flawed elections, at least as the dominant party in Ladakh and as the single largest party in Jammu, was made possible by a conjunction of several factors. In Jammu, these are, in order of importance: first, division of non-NC votes among several contending all-India parties like the Congress, the BJP and the Janata Dal; second, consolidation of Muslim votes in Jammu (a third of Jammu's total electorate is Muslim) behind the NC; and third, transfer of a small but crucial chunk of low-caste Hindu support in some seats to the NC because of its alliance with the BSP (the BSP in turn benefited from reciprocal transfer of pro-NC votes). In a similar pattern in Ladakh, the Muslim elector-ate appears to have voted *en bloc* for the NC, enabling the party to easily win not only both seats in Shia-dominated Kargil district but also to snatch a third in Leh district, which has a Buddhist majority (suggesting that at least some Buddhist voters preferred the NC to competitors like the Congress and BJP).

Thus, most of the NC's victories in Jammu were clustered in the three districts which have predominantly Muslim populations: Poonch, Doda and Rajouri. In Poonch, which is 90 per cent Muslim but where most of the Muslims are Gujjars, Pahadis and Rajputs (i.e., not ethnically and linguistically Kashmiri), NC candidates won all three seats at stake. In Doda, which is particularly fasci-nating because of its roughly equal population balance between a slender Kashmiri Muslim majority (many of them pro-*azaadi*) and a sizeable Hindu minority (a large number of whom are pro-BJP), this phenomenon of communal polarisation was most apparent. In the parliamentary elections, the victorious BJP candidate from Udhampur had led in most areas of Doda district because of a combination of ballot fraud, a significant boycott by the Muslim population and a committed pro-BJP vote among local Hindus. This time, however, local Kashmiri Muslims turned out to vote in some strength, and as a result the NC emerged as the leading party in the district, winning three of its six seats (revealingly, the BJP was able to retain the Hindu-majority Ramban seat from this district). The NC also did well in Rajouri, which has a solid Muslim majority but where, like Poonch, most of the Muslims are not Kashmiris. And the NC's sole win in Kathua district (in southern Jammu), which has an overall Hindu majority of over 80 per cent, was in the district's one Muslim-dominated constituency.

Despite the flaws and exclusions of the election process, the results in Jammu and Ladakh have potentially significant implications for the state's politics. In particular, they seem to illuminate two, partly contradictory, tendencies that are emerging in Jammu & Kashmir's politics—a strong element of communal polarisation in voting patterns, and equally strong hints of the potential for a partial cross-regional consensus on autonomy for the state. It is not possible to say for certain yet why the Muslim vote in Jammu got largely consolidated behind the NC in this election, in spite of the ethnic, linguistic, regional and political differences between the NC's traditional core following in the Valley and the Jammu region's predominantly non-Kashmiri Muslims. But one possible explanation could be that this was a manifestation of the under- current of sympathy that runs among Jammu's Muslim communi- ties for their suffering compatriots in the Valley. Strong support among the Jammu Muslims for the NC can then be interpreted, perhaps, as a qualified endorsement of the yearning for self-rule that animates the Valley's population, but in the form of autonomy (as proposed by the NC leadership) rather than outright inde- pendence from India (such more immediate factors as the influen- tial Gujjar leader Mian Bashir leaving the Congress to join the NC just before the elections may also have had an effect in certain constituencies). The same explanation could perhaps at least par- tially account for the NC's strong showing in most areas of Ladakh except for the Buddhist stronghold of Leh (where sentiments favouring separation from 'Muslim' Kashmir are rampant), though I stress that politics in Jammu & Kashmir is presently in a situation of such uncertainty and fluidity that my inference must remain a tentative one at this stage.

On 9 October 1996, Farooq Abdullah was formally sworn in as the head of a new state government of Indian-administered Jammu & Kashmir.

After the Elections: Prospects for the Future

Does the installation of the provincial government led by Farooq Abdullah signify that the wheel has come full circle in Kashmir? Has that tortured land, defying all odds and predictions, simply reverted to the pre-uprising *status quo ante*? Superficially perhaps, in some ways. Yet surface appearances have always been rather deceptive in Kashmir's politics and an illusion of normalcy cannot substitute for very long for the real thing, which can only be achieved through a substantive solution to the Kashmir problem. That problem, in fact, remains grave and volatile, though the precise configuration of ground realities and forces has altered significantly in the tumultous years since 1990. Yet, it is an easy temptation to either deny that a major problem in fact still exists or to reduce its complicated dimensions to a simplistic caricature. It is therefore essential to develop an informed understanding of the essence of the Kashmir problem as it exists today, an understanding which transcends the partial and partisan perspectives promoted by ideologues of the official Indian and Pakistani positions as well as by those of the independentist movement. It is a truism, after all, that only an accurate and nuanced diagnosis can possibly lead to an effective cure.

Cosmetic surgery or instant fixes that seek to restore the *status quo ante* in all but name are likely to prove unstable in the longer run. Whatever the flaws and failures of the *azaadi* insurrection, it has fundamentally and permanently transformed Kashmir's political landscape. The politics of corruption and chicanery that plunged Jammu & Kashmir into this crisis will find it difficult to re-implant itself in this changed landscape. Kashmir's political metamorphosis is manifested mòst vividly in the thousands of 'martyrs' graves' that dot practically every town and innumerable villages in the Valley and in Doda. To most Kashmiris, these are not dehumanised 'Pak-trained terrorists' who richly deserve their fate, but sons, brothers, husbands, intimate friends and lifelong neighbours. A major reason for the relative success of the Hurriyat Conference's boycott campaign, despite the coalition's implausibly hotch-potch composition and the serious corruption allegations against some of its leading figures, was the campaign's emotive appeal. Hurriyat leaders tried to convince their audiences that a willing vote would be a betrayal of the *qurbani* ('sacrifice') of the tens of thousands who have given their lives for Kashmir since 1989 (estimated at at least 50,000 by Farooq Abdullah in October 1996). This is a theme that strikes a resonant chord with even the most jaded Kashmiri and continues to motivate the still not inconsiderable numbers of youth who believe that the gun is still the best guarantee that those deaths will not have been totally in vain.

Pacification without a serious, sustained attempt at a substantive political solution is likely to prove precarious for more mundane reasons as well. The Farooq Abdullah administration may be crippled due to the very circumstances of its birth. These congenital birth defects will probably mean that, belying the hopes of a segment of the population, substantial improvements in the day-to-day lives of ordinary people may not materialise in the immediate future. It will be difficult for what is, despite appearances, a weak government of dubious representative credentials to act as an effective check on the policies and conduct of forces under the control of the central government, the Army in particular. Large sections of these forces are permeated with an attitude that sees every Kashmiri Muslim as a fifth columnist for Pakistan. This, together with the unpleasant reality that low-intensity insurgent activity supported from across the border is likely to persist (and may even pick up with the possible onset of a fresh spell of frustration among the public), suggests that the relationship between the huge state-security apparatus and the people will probably continue to resemble one between occupier and occupied for the foreseeable future. As it is, the Indian forces continue to be deeply detested by the citizenry. Contrary to inaccurate reports that have been appearing in some sections of the Indian mass media, the security situation in the state remains quite volatile and major crackdowns, deeply humiliating experiences in the course of which citizens are routinely beaten brutally and abused in unspeakable language, are still occurring in various areas of the Valley and in

Doda. As my Kashmiri taxi driver, an elderly man of exceptionally 'moderate' views (he was planning to vote for the Congress in the assembly elections) told me in some disgust in September 1996: 'These soldiers' attitude is so bad. They will never change for the better, I think. I would not say this to anyone but you for fear of being misunderstood, but many of them are simply anti-Muslim'.

There is thus a real danger that the Abdullah government may come to be perceived (if it is not already) by much of the population as essentially a facade for a repressive military administration. At present, the first and most formidable barrier to any genuine, lasting normalisation in Kashmir is the pervasive presence and crushing weight of the security forces. But as Abdullah himself recognises, his personal and political survival is contingent upon these very forces. As he candidly put it even before being installed as chief minister, 'the presence of the paramilitary and the army will have to be beefed up if normalcy is to return to the state'.[18] It is also questionable whether the new government has either the authority or the inclination to put a decisive end to the activities of marauding renegade gangs. Abdullah, who had demanded in June 1996 that the renegades be disarmed, was by August complimenting them for their contributions to the 'restoration of democracy' in the state, indicating perhaps that he sees at least some of these elements more as inevitable partners and allies rather than as intolerable threats to a decent society.[19] Indeed, he has echoed sentiments expressed by some of these pro-Pakistan turned pro-India gunmen in threatening, in rhetoric reminiscent of his disastrous tenure as chief minister during 1987–89, to expel all Kashmiri leaders advocating 'self-determination' to Pakistan.[20] In any case, the renegades' mentors in the officer corps of the army and paramilitary forces are adamantly opposed to any major action against their favourites.

The pall of fear that hangs as heavily over Kashmir as the mists of its mountains is therefore unlikely to lift in the immediate future. And without some genuine progress towards a normalcy that is not simply the silence of the graveyard, it is premature to even broach such weighty subjects as 'maximum autonomy' for Jammu & Kashmir.

The National Conference government's predicament is however merely symptomatic of some profound changes that have taken place in Kashmir's political fabric over the last decade as a result of the independence movement and the violence and repression that have accompanied it. Despite the presence of a few principled leaders like Abdul Rahim Rather and Mohammed Shafi Uri and its impressive victory by default in the 1996 assembly elections, today's NC is ideologically and organisationally a pale shadow of what it once was. From being a mass-based party backed by a disciplined cadre, the NC has been reduced largely to a cabal of self-seeking politicians for whom elections held under the shadow of hundreds of thousands of cocked weapons constitute a lifeline to survival. The mass base and cadre strength that once constituted the backbone of this party are now largely substituted by the military might of the Indian state. Might it be possible to resuscitate the old NC? There are powerful factors that militate against that possibility.

One of the factors that made the NC the premier political force in Kashmir in Sheikh Abdullah's heyday was its capacity to attract the cream of Kashmir's youth. But the youth in Kashmir today are members of a very different political generation—the *azaadi* generation. Their lives have been defined by the movement for independence, and their convictions forged in the crucible of a brutal war in which they have witnessed thousands of their compatriots being killed, tortured and humiliated by those claiming to represent India's right to Kashmir. What made the NC (and subsequently the Plebiscite Front once Sheikh Abdullah was ousted and the official NC turned into a forum for New Delhi's minions) so attractive to the bygone and older generations in Kashmir was that it was the main vehicle for the expression and defence of Kashmiri pride, identity and political aspirations—above all the suppressed but never extinguished aspiration to 'self-determination' (which can, but need not necessarily, imply independent statehood). The people of Kashmir were prepared to overlook Sheikh Abdullah's dictatorial propensities and remain loyal to him in adversity as long as he was the personification of Kashmiri patriotism—the essence of *Kashmiriyat*, by which I mean a political identity with a cultural base. They were prepared to reward him for the suffering he had endured on their behalf with an electoral mandate (in 1977), even after he had reached a compromise with New Delhi (in 1975) that many Kashmiris regarded as unjust and humiliating to their pride and interests. They were even prepared to tolerate his *dilettante* son, just so long as he would speak up for *Kashmiriyat* too.

It is important to note that there was no necessary contradiction between Kashmiri patriotism and a sense of loyalty to the Indian Union—the two identifications could well have developed in harmony and coexisted in happy complementarity. The 'identity of democratic and secular aspirations' between Kashmir and India that Sheikh Abdullah cited in 1952 as the moral basis for that coexistence and co-development turned out in time, however, to be a cruel mirage. Consequently, while Kashmiri patriotism has become stronger and more radical since 1990 than ever before, it has also become totally estranged from, and vehemently opposed to, the state-sponsored ideology of Indian nationalism. Thus, any credible representative of *Kashmiriyat* today has to be, virtually by definition, a certified opponent of the Indian state and its Kashmir policy. That is why it is possible that the time when the NC—basically a grouping of tainted politicians beholden to and sponsored by New Delhi—could be credibly projected as the representative of *Kashmiriyat* has passed, perhaps forever.

The Question of 'Self-Determination': What Does It Mean Today and How Might It Be Resolved?

In principle, it is beyond question that ensuring genuine popular representation through democratically constituted institutions (such as freely elected legislatures) and thereby guaranteeing account-able, responsible government must form an integral part of any enduring resolution to the Kashmir question. In fact, this book has argued that the denial of democratic rights and subversion of democratic representation by the Indian state in Jammu & Kashmir, almost continuously since 1947, eventually led to the outbreak of a popular-based movement for separation from India. As Sheikh Abdullah put it in 1968 during one of his brief spells out of Indian prisons:

The fact remains that Indian democracy stops short at Pathankot [the last major town in eastern Punjab before one enters Jammu]. Between Pathankot and the Banihal [Pass, connecting Jammu with the Valley] you may have some measure of democracy, but after Banihal there is none. What we have in Kashmir bears some of the worst characteristics of colonial rule.[21]

Though this statement is somewhat ironic coming from a person who had, with Nehru's connivance, suppressed all political opposition when he was Kashmir's all-powerful leader between 1948 and 1953, it is nonetheless absolutely accurate, and these words remain as relevant in 1996 as they were in 1968. Even then, of course, there was an 'elected' (Congress) government in the state, headed in fact by some of the Sheikh's one-time comrades like G. M. Sadiq and Mir Qasim, who unlike faithful Abdullahites like Mirza Afzal Beg had proved unable to resist the lure of power and pelf that the Indian state has always offered to those who are prepared to play New Delhi's game in Kashmir. Yet the illusion of democratic government in Kashmir has usually been manufactured not only through the destruction of some of the basic principles of democracy (the government in office in 1968, for example, had come to power an year earlier in 'elections' in which no contest had been allowed in 39 of the 75 legislative assembly seats, including a majority of the Valley seats), but also by wantonly violating the fundamental rights and freedoms guaranteed in the Indian Constitution. As Sheikh Abdullah put it in a message on the occasion of India's Republic Day on 26 January 1968:

Respect for the rule of law, the independence of the judiciary, the integrity of the electoral process...are all sought to be guaranteed [by the Indian Republic]. It is not surprising that many other countries have drawn upon this constitution [of India], particularly the chapter on fundamental rights. Yet it must at all times be remembered that the Constitution provides the framework and it is for the men who work it to give it life and meaning. In many ways the provisions of the constitution have been flagrantly violated in recent years and the ideals it enshrines completely forgotten [with respect to Kashmir]. Forces have arisen which threaten to carry this saddening and destructive process further still.[22]

It is equally important to remember that this was happening at a time when there were no 'terrorists' and 'fundamentalists' in Kashmir to provide even a figleaf of an alibi for these policies. In short, the Indian state has never lacked for surrogates who, driven by petty greed and ambition, have been prepared to do its bidding in Kashmir. Usually, these surrogates—from Bakshi Ghulam Mohammed in 1963 to Ghulam Mohammed Shah in 1986—were simply discarded once they had served their time. Ultimately, however, none have been able to put the Kashmir question to rest for their masters.

The challenge of finding a democratic resolution to the Kashmir problem is a great deal more complex than simply reactivating some semblance of electoral processes. That is because there is another very important dimension to the Kashmir question—whether one chooses to call it the issue of 'self-determination' or prefers some more innocuous, less contentious term is really immaterial—whose existence and importance cannot be denied or downplayed if an abiding solution is to be found to the Kashmir question. Indian Jammu & Kashmir desperately needs institutionalised guarantees of popular representation and democratic government. But it will be difficult to stabilise and legitimise such a democratic polity without taking some substantive measures to address the other dimension of the problem—that of 'self-determination'.

The resilience of the urge for self-rule in Kashmir's popular consciousness is remarkable. The autonomist claim has been treated virtually as a form of criminal political behaviour by the Indian state since 1953, and constantly demonised as an expression of pro-Pakistan chauvinism (even when it was manifestly not, as in the case of Sheikh Abdullah's Plebiscite Front in the fifties and sixties and the JKLF's movement for *azaadi* in the eighties and nineties). Stigmatised and outlawed, its proponents jailed and persecuted, the autonomist spirit nonetheless lived on. It has a long and distinguished lineage, and deep roots in Kashmir's political culture going back to the popular movement against the tinpot despotism of the Dogra dynasty during the 1930s and 1940s. It is often forgotten that except for the last seven years (1975–82) of his long life, Sheikh Mohammad Abdullah was a crusader for Kashmir's right to 'self-determination' and that this is what won him the love and devotion of the people of Kashmir. It is equally easy for professional rewriters of history to gloss over the fact that the word 'national' in the National Conference's name refers to the territory and population of Jammu & Kashmir. Sheikh Abdullah's speech to his handpicked Jammu & Kashmir Constituent Assembly in August 1952, in the course of which he reported on the substance of the informal 'Delhi Agreement' reached between representatives of his administration and those of the Indian government, contained three explicit references to Jammu & Kashmir as 'our country'[23] (in the same speech, Abdullah made it clear that accession to India was final and complete and the issues at stake concerned the *terms* of membership in, and association with, the Indian union).

Even when, in the mid-seventies, the Sheikh finally abandoned his struggle for what he called in 1952 'maximum autonomy for the local organs of state power...while discharging obligations as an unit of the [Indian] federation',[24] the spirit of autonomism refused to die. Instead, it demonstrated an uncanny ability to find other agents to articulate its agenda. Sheikh Abdullah's admission of defeat in 1975 spurred a young Kashmiri named Shabbir Shah to form a new organisation—the People's League—to keep the quest for 'self-determination' alive. Like Abdullah, Shah paid the inevitable price—years on end in Indian jails. But as frustration with the Indian state's increasingly egregious authoritarianism in Kashmir mounted through the eighties, more and more Kashmiris became convinced that *Kashmiriyat* could only be safeguarded in an independent state. Not only did the appeal of 'freedom' become widespread, but its advocates, subjected to unlawful harassment and persecution by Abdullah's son and his patrons in Delhi for their peaceful dissident activities, gradually became radicalised. Founded in the mid-sixties in Pakistani Kashmir, the Jammu & Kashmir Liberation Front (JKLF) had never enjoyed much support in the Valley—indeed, it could not, as long as the pro-*azaadi* political space was occupied by Sheikh Abdullah's deeply rooted indigenous movement. Between 1988 and 1990, however, the JKLF emerged as the spearhead of a mass uprising, and a new generation of Kashmiri youth took up the gun in a desperate attempt to wrest the rights their fathers and grandfathers had been unable to obtain through peaceful means.

Even though that armed struggle has been on the wane since 1994 and Kashmir's people are severely demoralised by endless violence and relentless repression, the spirit that ignited the revolt still simmers in the popular consciousness. Kashmiris can indeed be quite crafty and reticent in revealing their actual political views and preferences, as wonderfully illustrated by Bakshi Ghulam

Mohammed's joke about the population simultaneously supporting him, Sheikh Abdullah and G. M. Sadiq during the 1950s. In the blood-spattered nineties, such reticence is even more vital, for it can make the difference between life and death. Yet Kashmiris do have ways of demonstrating their most deeply felt affections from time to time. In March 1968, for instance, Sheikh Abdullah arrived in the Valley after having spent the previous three years in prison under the Defence of India Rules. 'Almost the entire population of Srinagar turned out to greet him', reported the *Times of India*, adding in some trepidation that the crowds were shouting 'Sher-i-Kashmir zindabad, our demand plebiscite' (in his recently published memoirs, Syed Mir Qasim has acknowledged that the Plebiscite Front was by far the most popular force in Kashmir from the fifties through the seventies). In the very recent past, that sort of welcome, with hundreds of thousands of emotional people lining the route from Srinagar airport to Lal Chowk in the city centre, has occurred only twice—once in June 1994 when the JKLF's Yasin Malik was released from prison and arrived back in Kashmir; and then again in October 1994, when Shabbir Shah was freed from prolonged incarceration. Like Sheikh Abdullah, they had, in popular perception, stood up for Kashmir and suffered in consequence.

In an attempt to gauge the current level of appeal of the 'self-determination' idea, I travelled in the autumn of 1996 to, among many other places, a remote village called Soibugh in the Valley's Badgam district. In spite of only being a village, Soibugh is a household name throughout Kashmir. It happens to be the home village of Sheikh Salahuddin, commander-in-chief of the Hizbul Mujahideen (HM) insurgents; Ashraf Dar, another top HM commander who was killed in action in 1993; and Shabbir Siddiqui, a senior JKLF leader who was killed by the security forces outside Srinagar's Hazratbal shrine in March 1996. Even though the HM's fighters have recently been forced out of the immediate area by the Indian army, the village and its environs are still classified as a so-called 'red zone' by the security forces and a large army camp has been established just outside the village. Most recently, Soibugh hit the headlines during the parliamentary elections of May 1996 when it registered an impressively high turnout of voters, the redoubtable Salahuddin's brother among them. The news was prominently featured by India's state-controlled television network and by sections of its unofficial press as evidence both that the insurgency had been decisively defeated and that misguided Kashmiris had finally recovered their senses.

As we drove into the village, we encountered the slain Shabbir Siddiqui's elder brother. Though extremely courteous in a manner typical of Kashmir's superbly hospitable society,[25] he regretfully expressed his inability to have a discussion with me about the local situation. Apparently, there were informers in the village, the army was right next door, and he did not relish the prospect of a midnight visit from soldiers and renegades enquiring why he had spoken to an outsider and what he had disclosed to him. Slightly disappointed, we retraced our steps to the teashop on the main street, where we were met with suspicious stares. Upon enquiring what the *awaam* ('people') really desired in their hearts, I was informed by those present that 'there will be 100 per cent turnout here next month [in the assembly elections]'. The tune changed, however, once the villagers were reassured, after much effort, by my Kashmiri companions that I was neither an army officer in plainclothes nor an Intelligence Bureau (IB) agent (the IB is the Indian central government's main domestic intelligence agency and functions under the control of the Union Home Ministry). 'We want *azaadi*', the gathering chorused in unison, happily clarifying in response to another question that they wanted *khudmukhtari* ('self-rule'), not Pakistan.

Soibugh is fairly representative of two things that dominate life in Kashmir today—abject fear and the latent desire for self-rule. The intersection where the Srinagar–Baramulla road branches off towards Tangmarg and the famous resort of Gulmarg is festooned with a massive billboard which informs visitors that 'this road leads to the Switzerland of India'. Under the shadow of this proclamation, I struck up a conversation, pretending to be a naïve camera-waving tourist, with a group of roadside vendors, dressed in tattered clothes and selling fruits and vegetables. Were the troubles over, I enquired, and how did they feel about the present situation? 'For the moment, we just want the military to stop terrorising us', I was told, 'and as for the future, we have no respect for any politicians, including the Hurriyat Conference people. But we all want *azaadi*'.

Clearly, the 'self-determination' dimension cannot be ignored or bypassed if a serious solution to the challenge in Kashmir is to be found. The vital question, then, is whether there are any ways of addressing this aspect of the problem that are at once feasible and substantive.

To someone possessed of a truly democratic mentality, the territorial integrity of any state, actual or potential, cannot be an ultimate value in itself. To the true democrat, that value is *instrumental*—it stems from certain benefits and advantages, such as democracy, economic well-being and so on, that a state can offer its citizens.

The point of view frequently articulated in India that there is no problem in Kashmir—not much anyway—beyond that created by Pakistan and its agents flies in the face not only of all historical fact and evidence but also of current ground realities in Kashmir. The reason this rather unreal position, reflecting a typically ultra-nationalist obsession with 'national unity' and 'territorial integrity', is promoted so assiduously by certain circles in India is that it provides a convenient pretext for avoiding any admission of the Indian state's culpability in causing this crisis. The uncomfortable fact, however, is that there is a grave problem in Kashmir—including an issue of 'self-determination', though I reiterate that one can use a less controversial term to describe this dimension of the problem if one prefers. Contrary to a widely held belief, however, the Kashmir question as its exists today arises far less from the tangled events of 1947 (which are amenable to multiple interpretations) than from the quite unambiguously miserable treatment Jammu & Kashmir has received as a member of the Indian union *since* 1947. Specifically, the present crisis is the ultimate consequence of the consistent denial of democracy and autonomy to Kashmir by a state which by its own constitution is bound to guarantee those rights and freedoms to all its citizens and constituent regions (disregarding for the moment the particular commitments made to Kashmir that were not honoured). In short, the present generations of Kashmiris have ended up paying for the sins and follies, accumulated over a half-century by others, with their own blood.

The official Pakistani stance on Kashmir is, ironically enough, the mirror-image of its Indian counterpart. It is born of the same narrow nationalist obsession with sovereignty and territory. Pakistan's obsessive interest in Kashmir is not motivated by any concern for the aspirations of Kashmiris to a dignified existence and a democratic political life. Instead, Pakistan's national project is seen as being incomplete unless and until 'Muslim' Kashmir is brought into the fold. This is not only a dogmatically irredentist position, but it is permeated with a virulently communal content. Lip-service to the democratic and human rights of Kashmiris merely provides a handy stick with which to beat the Indians, who are indeed violators of those rights.

Meanwhile, elections in 'Azad Kashmir' continue to be a manipulated farce. In the most recent ones, held in June 1996, pro-independence political parties were again barred from participating because their candidates refused to compromise their principles by signing affidavits certifying their allegiance to Pakistan, a legal requirement for filing valid nominations. Even the partial contest that did take place, limited to an assortment of Pakistani parties and pro-Pakistan groups, was severely tainted by rampant irregularities and fraud. Fortunately, it does appear that valley Kashmiris have seen through the real nature of Pakistan's agenda *vis-à-vis* Kashmir. In the late 1980s, popular identification with Pakistan was widespread in Indian Kashmir, more as a result of utter disillusionment with India than anything else. The eruption of the *azaadi* uprising, with the staunchly independentist JKLF as its driving force, changed that equation by firmly implanting the idea of independence in the mass consciousness. Though the JKLF proved unable to sustain its initially dominant position in the insurgency—the cumulative effect of Indian repression, Pakistani sabotage and the organisation's own limitations and weaknesses[26]—its ideology has proved impressively resilient at the popular level. Pakistan's crude attempts to hijack the *azaadi* movement through its agents in Indian-administered Kashmir, who have not hesitated to physically eliminate fellow-Kashmiris (including many independence advocates) who disagreed, has gradually fostered something of a major backlash against Pakistan among Kashmiris. In 1995, I got the impression from extensive travelling in the heartland of the Kashmir conflict, i.e., the Valley and Doda, that while a decisive majority in this region of the state favoured the independence idea, the second largest group (albeit a very distant second) supported Pakistan. A year later, in 1996, independence supporters were still by far the largest category in this region, but this time I got the distinct impression that the pro-India segment of public opinion had advanced to second position, leaving Pakistan's partisans to bring up the rear.

During the run-up to the assembly elections in Indian Kashmir, Pakistani leader Benazir Bhutto expressed the hope that substantive talks between India and Pakistan on Kashmir would commence once these elections were 'out of the way'. As the election results were being declared in early October, she dismissed them as a 'sham' and urged the United Nations to convene a multilateral conference (involving, in addition to India and Pakistan, all five Security Council members and, for some reason, Germany and Japan as well) to resolve the Kashmir dispute and establish a regional security system in South Asia. This seemed to be a desperate attempt to put the Kashmir question back on the world body's agenda, though probably intended more for rhetorical effect than anything else. The element of desperation is however understandable, especially in light of the realities in Indian Kashmir—Pakistan's 'covert war' strategy is failing and Pakistan's credibility among the population there is currently extremely low, restricted largely to a small minority of diehard supporters (there has always been, and will always be, a hardcore of Pakistan enthusiasts in the Valley, a fact Indians will have to learn to live with).

A *modus vivendi* between India and Pakistan on the Kashmir conflict remains desirable in the interests of both a permanent settlement to that dispute and of the subcontinent as a whole. The need for an operational security system in a nuclearised region is equally apparent. Yet, because the two states' perceptions of the Kashmir issue remain not just distant but thoroughly contradictory and mutually incompatible, the question does arise: Is there any serious possibility of such an agreement or even perhaps a lasting understanding on Kashmir? The compulsions of Pakistan's domestic politics will probably not allow any party or leader in that country to openly endorse any solution that leaves current territorial jurisdictions unchanged. At the same time, India is equally determined that any alteration of existing borders is a non-option and constraints in India's domestic politics do not permit any serious contemplation of such changes in that country. So the complicated reality seems to be that while it will be difficult to fortify the painfully emerging peace in Indian Kashmir without

Pakistan, it will also be difficult to make any progress towards a much-needed compromise solution to the present crisis in Indian Kashmir *with* Pakistan—unless of course Pakistan's state-sponsored nationalism radically revises its communally charged, irredentist and thoroughly unrealistic ambitions in Kashmir. Is that likely?

Most ironically, however, the standard pro-independence position also suffers from a variant of the 'territorial integrity' syndrome. As I have discussed at length in Chapter 5, advocates of this position make an unwarranted presumption in projecting the entire territory of the pre-1947 princely state of Jammu & Kashmir as some sort of timeless, sacred geography and the sole legitimate political unit for the exercise of the 'right to self-determination'. This stance not only disregards the contingency of *all* territorial units and borders, but also the inescapable fact that the erstwhile princely state ceased to exist in 1947 and that its disparate territories have been divided between two hostile states for the last fifty years. But most importantly, as I have underscored throughout this book, even Indian-administered Jammu & Kashmir, the crux of the contemporary Kashmir problem, is composed of three distinct regions—Kashmir Valley, Jammu and Ladakh—each with very different political conditions and circumstances. This injects a level of complexity into the question of 'self-determination' for Jammu & Kashmir that the standard independentist line is simply not equipped to cope with. As the prominent Kashmiri independentist leader Shabbir Shah frankly admitted to me in the autumn of 1996, the reality is that 'the question of reopening the issue of the state's accession to India is not acceptable' to the majority of inhabitants in the Jammu and Ladakh regions.

One conceivable solution to this conundrum would be to limit the question of 'self-determination' to Kashmir proper, where pro-independence sentiment is undoubtedly strong and widespread. But as I have pointed out in Chapter 5, this option is fraught with a host of problems and dangers of its own. Moreover, the entire political spectrum in Kashmir is united in its opposition to any suggestion of dividing Jammu & Kashmir on *de facto* communal lines (and it is by no means clear how much popular support the 'trifurcation' concept enjoys even in the Jammu region). When, in an interview to the BBC in late August 1996, India's Home Minister Indrajit Gupta reportedly mentioned the possibility of delinking Ladakh from the state and making it an Union Territory (i.e., bringing it under Delhi's direct jurisdiction), and allegedly implied some sort of similar arrangement for Jammu as well,[27] I happened to be in Kashmir. I was struck by the visceral reaction Gupta's purported statement aroused among people of all shades of political opinion in Kashmir. Shabbir Shah dramatically charged the minister with 'reviving the two-nation theory', but Gupta was sharply criticised even by some pro-India politicians. In a way, this commitment to coexistence among Jammu & Kashmir's various regional, religious, linguistic and ethnic groups, in spite of their political differences, is really admirable. If Kashmiri independentists restricted their claim to 'self-determination' to Kashmir proper, their demand would in a certain sense become more coherent, though it would also take on overtly communal overtones. But their refusal to countenance truncation as the price of 'self-determination' effectively forecloses the path of partition. It also makes the question of 'self-determination' for Jammu & Kashmir very complicated indeed.

Moreover, as I have argued in Chapter 5, the mechanism by which independence advocates propose to actualise the right to 'self-determination' (the plebiscite decided by simple majority) has serious flaws and risks of its own. First of all, there is the question of feasibility. India's implacable opposition to any notion of plebiscite, and Pakistan's manifest lack of interest in the idea except for propaganda purposes, makes the likelihood of any such exercise extraordinarily remote. As Shabbir Shah told me in autumn 1996, 'the demand for plebiscite has become impractical in today's circumstances'. Additionally, as I have shown in Chapter 5 with illustrations drawn from experiences in Quebec and Bosnia, a plebiscite is hardly an appropriate instrument for resolving highly sensitive and complex questions of 'self-determination'. In fact, it has been said that 'because they cannot measure intensities of belief or work things out through discussion...referendums are bound to be dangerous...to minority rights'.[28] Indeed, a problem as sensitive and complex as that in Kashmir requires an approach that emphasises tools of surgical precision, not the blunt instrument of plebiscitary majoritarianism.

Apart from the irrelevance and inappropriateness of the plebiscite demand and the doubtful political viability of an independent Jammu & Kashmir even if it were to ever come into existence, there is another factor that those interested in a substantive settlement to the Kashmir question must come to terms with. As Ved Bhasin, editor-in-chief of *Kashmir Times* and one of the most respected public figures in Jammu & Kashmir, put it to me in autumn 1996: 'People in the Valley are emotionally by and large still for independence. But they now realise that no solution outside the Indian framework is possible for the time being'. In 1989–90, the (predominantly JKLF) pioneers of the independence movement as well as their mass following naively believed that 'freedom' would come sooner or later, especially given their commitment to the cause and willingness to make sacrifices for the sake of the struggle. After all, they reasoned, India is a vast country incredibly rich in numerous regional and local traditions, of which Kashmir is only one example. Why then should India hold on indefinitely to Kashmir by force against the wishes of its people?

That was a grievous miscalculation on their part. It is tragically ironic that Kashmiris themselves simply did not realise how crucially important their land is to the founding myth and *raison d'être* of the Indian state born amidst the bloodbath of partition in 1947—the creed of 'secular nationalism'. Because they failed to appreciate this elementary fact, they profoundly underestimated the lengths to which the Indian state was, and is, prepared to go to crush their movement. A mere six years after hundreds of thousands flooded the streets of Srinagar in massive pro-independence demonstrations, it has been proven beyond reasonable doubt that the democratic Indian state is incomparably more tenacious and ruthless than Kashmir's Kalashnikov-wielding militants. Freedom can either be granted or it can be taken by force. India will not—it cannot—voluntarily relinquish Jammu & Kashmir or any portion thereof, and it is clear, in retrospect at least, that a few thousand youth armed with AK-47s and grenades could never have been realistically expected to get the better of hundreds of thousands of soldiers employed by one of the world's most formidable military establishments. There is thus a fundamentally futile quality to the maximalist, all-or-nothing rhetoric that continues to dominate the discourse of Kashmir's pro-*azaadi* political forces.

Is there, then, any way at all of tackling the essence of the contemporary Kashmir problem that is both feasible and substantive?

The negotiation and permanent institutionalisation of any substantive autonomy for Jammu & Kashmir, maximum or otherwise, would be a monumentally challenging and complex task. It would require a kind of intelligence, ability and vision that Indian politicians (leave alone the bureaucrats and security officials effectively responsible for Kashmir policy) are not renowned for, and a kind of competence, honesty and popularity that their favoured Kashmiri politicians clearly lack. It will also be extremely difficult to make any substantial progress (as distinguished from bombastic rhetoric and publicity stunts) towards realising such an autonomous status because of adverse ground conditions prevailing in the state, not to mention the rather confused and uncertain situation in India's national-level politics. Even as assembly elections were being completed during September 1996, the BJP, which is the largest single party and principal opposition in India's Parliament, announced its intention of opposing any post-poll moves to institutionalise autonomy for Jammu & Kashmir. Because of all these daunting factors, it is difficult to be optimistic that magical word 'autonomy' will actually come to mean something more than just fine words.

In Kashmir itself, I have already noted, people are currently still much too preoccupied with the day-to-day survival of their families and society at large to bother about entirely vague and indeterminate talk of autonomy. They are also understandably cynical about the prospect of ever receiving anything of positive worth and substance from India's leaders. Nonetheless, I enquired in autumn 1996 of Shabbir Shah, perhaps the most pragmatic of Kashmir's pro-*azaadi* leaders, whether significant autonomy within the Indian union might be acceptable to the population of the pro-independence region of the state in light of objective realities and the balance of power. He replied in the following vein:

You will understand that it is very difficult for me or anyone else to go to a people who have sacrificed and suffered so much and persuade them to be content with 'autonomy', whatever that means. At the same time, I also feel that there is no scope for any rigid positions or closed minds on the matter, on any side. But any discussions on this subject must be as open and inclusive as possible. It should include my colleagues like Yasin Malik, Umer Farooq, Abdul Ghani Lone and Syed Ali Shah Geelani. I have personally been approached already by emissaries of the Indian government, but I have made it clear to them that I will not be a party to backroom deals worked out with particular individuals through clandestine channels. That will not solve the Kashmir question.

I would like to conclude this postscript by elaborating on a few points which I feel would be extremely important to any, as yet hypothetical, process to (re)institutionalise autonomy for Jammu & Kashmir within the territorial framework of the Indian union.

It would seem that any process leading to an effective negotiation and implementation of autonomy for Jammu & Kashmir needs to involve, as key participants, persons and forces who are credible representatives of Kashmiri patriotism and its autonomist spirit—*Kashmiriyat*—and of what I have earlier called the *azaadi* generation. It is a commonsensical conclusion that those activists and organisations who are not crucially dependent on the power of the Indian state for their political existence, but instead have an autonomous base and appeal in the pro-*azaadi* areas of Jammu & Kashmir, are favourably placed to achieve two goals. First, they are more likely to have the independent mentality and clout essential for bargaining effectively and securing a truly substantive and hence enduring political settlement. Second, only the participation of those leaders who have personally suffered and seen comrades die in the cause of *azaadi* will give any autonomy process the credibility it needs in order to be accepted by the large pro-independence section of Jammu & Kashmir's population.

There is an additional, related reason why this is singularly important. The participation of those political forces who credibly represent the core value of *Kashmiriyat*—a fiercely assertive spirit of autonomy from New Delhi—in institutions of popular representation in Jammu & Kashmir (such as the state government and its legislature) would help ensure that any autonomous status for the state proves both real and lasting and does not turn out to be a cipher like Article 370. Those political personalities and organisations who are capable of asserting a political line independent of New Delhi's agenda of the moment (a capability demonstrated by a record of principled, perhaps even militant, opposition to New Delhi's policies of denial, repression and manipulation in Kashmir) are most favourably placed to defend and safeguard the autonomy of an autonomous Jammu & Kashmir.

Kashmir's political history stands as mute yet compelling testimony to this fact. Sheikh Abdullah *had* to be removed from office in 1953 in order to pave the way for the methodical destruction of Jammu & Kashmir's autonomy; for the Sheikh, despite his authoritarian ways, was a leader with a mind of his own, who enjoyed a mass base and was backed by a well-knit organisation. In short, he was simply too powerful and popular to be tolerated. It was imperative to oust him from power, divide his organisation and install a succession of pliable, spineless clients in his place (periodically 'legitimated' through bogus 'elections', a practice snidely referred to by three generations of effectively disenfranchised Kashmiris as 'selections') before the policy designed to effectively revoke Jammu & Kashmir's autonomy could be initiated and carried through to conclusion. Article 370 categorically stipulated that the central government could legislate even on the three categories of central subjects specified in the Instrument of Accession—defence, external affairs and communications—only 'in consultation with the Government of Jammu & Kashmir State', and on all other subjects only with 'the final concurrence of the Jammu & Kashmir [State] Assembly'. The kind of 'consultation' and 'concurrence' New Delhi needed in order to erode and destroy the substance of Article 370 would only be forthcoming from a puppet government and assembly, and logically necessitated that the only Kashmiri leader with a popular following be deposed and cast into prison. The agenda of killing Kashmir's autonomy could only be achieved, therefore, through the cynical subversion of all democratic rights, procedures and institutions in Kashmir, and by totally denying the mass aspiration to self-rule, which nonetheless continued to simmer and eventually erupted in an explosive form after many other egregious provocations.

The challenge of a just peace in Kashmir today thus involves two inseparably interconnected and mutually dependent elements—ensuring representation of the broadest possible spectrum of political ideologies and interests in democratically constituted governmental and legislative institutions, and reaching an honourable *rapprochement* with the autonomist urge that can be suppressed by force and fraud but, as history eloquently demonstrates, cannot be extinguished. Indeed, the configuration of the contemporary Kashmir problem is such that the consolidation of meaningful, popularly entrenched and legitimated democracy is not possible without wideranging autonomy, and the realisation of substantive autonomy is not possible without extending the sphere and deepening the meaning of democratic politics. Those leaders and forces who articulate the autonomist agenda as a matter of principle today—as distinguished from an essentially opportunist exploitation of the autonomy slogan by some other politicians in an effort to recover lost credibility—cannot easily enter the democratic process until the question of self-rule is admitted as a central element in the search for a just peace in Kashmir.

The possibility of some elements of known 'militant' background and 'secessionist' proclivities playing an important role in Kashmir's government and legal politics in the not too distant future would no doubt be alarming to those who view the Kashmir crisis strictly from the angle of 'national security' in India. Such alarm would be understandable, especially since I know very well that Kashmir contains several million people antagonistic towards the Indian state's authority in a deep, fundamental sense unknown even in other Indian regions that have seen separatist movements in recent years, like Punjab and the North-east.

But for a lasting solution to be found to this conflict, India's political elite will have to recognise and accommodate the existence of something called Kashmiri patriotism, deeply rooted in *Kashmiriyat*, that proud but not fanatic autonomist political identity arising from an unique cultural base of syncretist, eclectic Sufi Islam. It will also have to be realistically acknowledged that patriotism has, for no fault of its own, become deeply alienated from any sense of voluntary allegiance to the Indian union. If the challenge in Kashmir is not to prove completely insurmountable, those who win fair, inclusive elections in the future must be allowed to run the government of an autonomous Jammu & Kashmir regardless of their political backgrounds and affiliations, despite the real and imaginary risks to the 'national interest'. Those who lóse elections overall but demonstrate significant popular support must, in another departure from established practice in Indian Jammu & Kashmir, have the right to function as a viable, institutionally sanctioned opposition within democratic institutions like the legislature, again regardless of what their backgrounds and convictions may be.

My argument should not be misunderstood—'pro-India' voices in the Valley and Doda must have as much of a right to be heard and to be represented as any other strand of political opinion. What I *am* suggesting, though, is that it will be extraordinarily unhelpful at this critical juncture to view the Kashmir conflict through the myopic lens of pernicious dichotomies, such as the one frequently made between 'pro-India' (hence 'legitimate') and 'anti-India' (therefore 'illegitimate') political groups. Kashmir's bleeding society sorely needs a healing touch (to use a well-worn cliche) and its fractured political scene needs an approach that is as consensually oriented and inclusive as possible. While it is clearly unrealistic to expect an overnight emergence of 'consensus' on issues as divisive as the legitimacy of the Indian state's jurisdiction over Jammu & Kashmir, a coercive and exclusive approach, recent history once again tells us, is virtually guaranteed to aggravate the problem and produce destructive consequences. Nor will it help to pretend that the Kashmir question is nothing more serious than the dilemmas of federalism faced elsewhere in India. While any strengthening of India's federal structure is to be welcomed, there is no certainty that Kashmir—always condemned to be an unhappy exception in India's democratic and federal polity—will benefit from any such restructuring. Besides, Kashmir is hardly West Bengal or Tamil Nadu, and cannot quite be bracketed even with such troublespots as Punjab or Assam. The concept of 'asymmetric federalism'—whereby one or more constituent regions of a federation enjoys greater autonomy than other units by virtue of an unique historical, cultural or political context—may have much to commend it in any search for an abiding solution to the problem in Jammu & Kashmir.

The other salient issue that any autonomy process will have to confront and resolve concerns the major social and political variations between the three distinct regions of (Indian-administered) Jammu & Kashmir.

Among some segments of the populations of Jammu and Ladakh, especially but not only among those of Hindu and Buddhist faith, there is a fear of 'Kashmiri domination', which is in a certain way understandable. After all, the *azaadi* agitation has had no major impact in the Jammu region outside of Doda district and almost none in Ladakh. Most of the citizens of Jammu and Ladakh have no wish to be dragged along in the wake of a movement in which they have no part and which many of them fundamentally disagree with. And there is a strain in the secularist discourse of *Kashmiriyat* which tends in the direction of something of an imperial attitude towards the predominantly non-Kashmiri regions of Jammu & Kashmir. Taken together, however, these rather disparate non-Kashmiri areas of Jammu and Ladakh account for as much as 40 per cent of the 87 seats in the provincial legislature.

As I have repeatedly stressed throughout this book, especially in Chapters 4 and 5[29] and this postscript, these divergences between the political contexts and aspirations of the three regions must be factored into any democratic approach to resolving the Kashmir problem and are especially relevant to any process designed to reinstate Jammu & Kashmir's lost autonomy. Dividing Jammu & Kashmir into regional compartments is, however, highly inadvisable because it risks legitimating the communal principle, and in any case infeasible, since regional boundaries are not congruent with patterns of demographic settlement of religious groups—three of 'Hindu-majority' Jammu's six districts have Muslim majorities, and one of 'Buddhist-majority' Ladakh's two districts, Kargil, has a Shia Muslim majority of over 80 per cent. Additionally, as I have argued, religion is but one basis of social identity and political affiliation in Jammu & Kashmir and there are numerous cross-cutting cleavages based on region, ethnicity, language, caste and political ideology which make any straightforward division between communal groups impossible. This is especially true of the Jammu region, which is a patchwork mosaic of a multitude of religious, ethnic and linguistic communities. In other words, it is absurd to talk in terms of monolithic 'Hindu' and 'Muslim' blocks in Jammu & Kashmir; there is simply too much diversity *within* communities professing the same broad religious faith.

Innovative yet workable proposals made over the years to set up a multi-tiered, decentralised institutional framework in Jammu & Kashmir guaranteeing each of the constituent regions a measure of autonomous administration and legislative authority within an autonomous institutional structure for the state as a whole can potentially reconcile the differences between the regions within an overarching common framework. The specific contents and recommendations of some of these proposals have been discussed in Chapter 5.[30] Any process intended to reinstitutionalise Jammu & Kashmir's autonomy must ensure equitable sharing of political power, natural resources, and economic revenues and budgetary allocations between the regions, particularly between Kashmir and Jammu, the two major regions (Ladakh, despite its large land area, has a very tiny population). A conscious effort has to be made to pre-empt and assuage perceptions of regional inequality and discrimination if any such solution is to prove stable and successful. *Ad hoc* treatment of inter-regional problems as they arise, on an issue-by-issue basis, will not suffice. Institutional mechanisms must be created to accommodate the fact of regional diversity within the structures of Jammu & Kashmir's autonomous government such that any and all differences can be mediated within the context of an institutional framework specifically geared to their resolution through dialogue and negotiation. In short, an institutionalised *modus vivendi* between the regions, particularly the two major regions, will be essential in legitimising any autonomy formula for Jammu & Kashmir throughout the state.

At the same time, a very sharp distinction needs to be drawn between the justified and necessary imperative of equality and equity between the regions and mischievous attempts to exaggerate and inflame inter-regional differences, manipulate them to stoke communal antagonism between Hindus and Muslims as well as Buddhists and Muslims, and exploit regional grievances, particularly in Jammu but also in Ladakh, towards the destructive end of sabotaging a democratic resolution to the Kashmir question. The BJP, the self-proclaimed spokesperson of a non-existent monolithic 'Hindu' region of Jammu, has for example a deliberate strategy of presenting the variations between Kashmir and Jammu as a communal contradiction between Hindus and Muslims. This demagogic stance has helped the BJP widen its electoral support in the Jammu region to some extent. But its mischievous opportunism is revealed by the fact that the party has adopted a self-contradictory posture of demanding autonomous government for the Jammu region but opposing autonomy for Jammu & Kashmir as a whole. The latter, the party claims, would amount to 'appeasement'. Yet, the reality is that any autonomous status would be conferred not on any particular religious, regional or cultural group but on the state as a whole, and would potentially—if regional diversities are taken into account in the process of institutionalisation of the autonomous regime—benefit all the constituent regions and all sectors of the population. Jammu has been politically marginalised and economically neglected for a long time, but the root cause of this neglect has been the absence of democratically mandated, accountable and responsible government in Jammu & Kashmir as a whole. Kashmiri Muslims, who have suffered the most from the denial of democracy and autonomy, cannot be held accountable for this. The culpability lies ultimately in New Delhi.

Yet, the temptation to encourage communal and sectarian expressions of various regional discontents, as part of a deliberate 'divide-and-rule' strategy intended to make the Kashmir problem more manageable, can be a very strong one indeed for those who make a habit of manipulating Jammu & Kashmir's politics from New Delhi. Ladakh, a region much more marginalised and neglected than even Jammu, has seen an agitation since 1989 demanding that the area be detached from Jammu & Kashmir and made a Union Territory. It is incontrovertible that the region needs better representation of its interests at the state level, as well as local autonomy and a more equitable share of development funds. But the agitation, which was openly supported by the BJP and in which the Congress party figures in Leh district played a leading role, turned explicitly sectarian and communal instead of organising itself as a broad-based movement for regional rights. The Ladakh Buddhist Association (LBA), which led the movement, equated 'Ladakhi' identity solely with the Buddhist community. Anger at Srinagar's neglect and insensitivity was expressed in the form of a violent campaign against Leh district's Muslim minority, regardless of the fact that Srinagar governments have been for the most part unrepresentative of Kashmir's Muslim population (most recently, Farooq Abdullah's 1987–89 government was considered illegitimate by most Kashmiri Muslims and since then Kashmir has been effectively under military rule). As two field researchers report on the little-known developments in Ladakh's politics over the past several years:

A social boycott of the local Muslims was ordained by the Buddhist leadership. Beginning in 1989, it lasted for three full years. It was the first time that this traditional Ladakhi tool for dispute settlement was applied to an entire community.... Many Muslim families who had to flee their villages in 1989 and 1990 have yet to return.[31]

The demand for Union Territory status was subsequently formally downgraded to that of a hill development council, and the coordination committee established to negotiate with the Indian government on its constitution and responsibilities came to include a few Muslims. Yet, when the autonomous council was formally instituted in August 1995—the governor of Jammu & Kashmir, a retired general, being a vocal enthusiast of the concept—not only was it limited to the predominantly Buddhist district of Leh, thereby excluding Muslim-majority Kargil, but its membership was virtually monopolised by LBA activists. These LBA activists now announced that they were joining the Congress(I), whose then government in Delhi had conceded the council, and in elections to the council LBA members turned Congressmen were 'elected unopposed' to 22 of the 26 seats at stake.

Like Jammu, Ladakh illustrates the complexities of institution-alising self-rule for Jammu & Kashmir. It is clear that given the heterogeneity of Jammu & Kashmir, decision-making should not be centralised in Srinagar. In the case of Ladakh, 'the hill council formula is an improvement over centralised rule from the state and national capitals, where there is little sympathy and less under-standing for marginal areas and populations'.[32] But it is equally clear that exploiting inter-regional variations and group differences in an insidious game of 'divide-and-rule' is in the interest of neither the constituent regions nor the urgent imperative of devising a viable solution to the Kashmir problem. Such policies can only encourage a proliferation of communal sectarianisms and the deep-ening of differences not only between the regions but also between communities *within* each region. The net result is likely to be that Jammu & Kashmir will become more chaotic and ungovernable, not less. By empowering only the most vocal advocates of one particular group, the Leh Autonomous Council runs the risk of further aggravating communal tensions within Ladakh and of mak-ing the entire concept of regional and local autonomy within Jammu & Kashmir suspect in the eyes of Valley Kashmiris who would otherwise appreciate both the need for and the efficacy of such autonomy. Nor will the council experiment necessarily benefit all sections of the Buddhist community or solve Ladakh's chronic problem of development. Even apparently successful group mobi-lisation along communal lines cannot permanently evade the reality that 'the nomadic herdsman in Changthang does not have much in common with the hotel owner in Leh or the peasant in Sham, and rifts are bound to float to the surface as soon as the hill council is activated'.[33] In sum, a clear line must be drawn between satisfying legitimate aspirations to regional and local self-government in Jammu and Ladakh, and pandering to communal sectarianisms in a way harmful to coexistence and cooperation among Jammu & Kashmir's diverse social groups, a pre-requisite for meeting the challenge of democracy, self-determination and a just peace.

Notes

1. I am once again grateful to Ved Bhasin and Imtiaz Sofi for their help in making this trip productive.
2. Coverage of these elections in some sections of the Indian press exhibited a peculiar schizophrenic trait. While most eyewitness reports filed by correspondents depicted the process as a farce, editorials appearing in some of the same papers within days extolled the 'restoration of democracy' in Jammu & Kashmir. A possible explanation for this anomaly was related to me in confidence by a senior editorial staffer at one such paper, a major English daily published from Delhi. His testimony ran as follows. The spot report detailing massive coercion arrived by fax very late at night from Srinagar. In consequence, it was not vetted by any of the senior editors, all of whom had gone home, and was run without alteration in the following day's edition. That morning, the paper was swamped with calls from officials in the Ministry of Home Affairs and the Prime Minister's Office protesting against the publication of articles damaging to the 'national interest' and demanding remedial action. The journalist who had filed the report was immediately recalled from Srinagar and subsequently made to write a byline contradicting the substance of the original story. Moreover, the senior editors were summoned to an emergency meeting with the owner of the paper, a wealthy businessman, where a decision was taken to publish an editorial applauding the conduct of the polls and abusing anyone who dared criticise the exercise. This 'written to order' editorial (as my informant put it) duly appeared a few days later.
3. For a sampling, see Baweja (1996b); Burns (1996); Nag (1996a and b); Ahmad (1996a and b).
4. See Ahmad (1996a).
5. See Burns (1996).
6. See Baweja (1996b) p. 48.
7. The pro-'self-determination' Hurriyat Conference coalition also, predictably, called for a boycott.
8. See Mojumdar (1996b); Krishnan (1996). In the event, none of the renegade candidates succeeded in getting elected, though all polled sizeable numbers of votes according to official statistics. Enraged at their defeat, which they construed as betrayal by their mentors, some of these thugs then went on rampage in Srinagar and Anantnag, stoning shops and vehicles and assaulting passers-by in an attempt to enforce a general strike.

9. I repeat that the return and rehabilitation of the Pandit migrants must form an integral part of any serious solution to the Kashmir question. Indeed, some migrant families have begun to trickle back to the Valley (though mostly at the moment to Srinagar and other towns like Baramulla), rejoining the thousands of Pandits who either never left the Valley at all or moved out only temporarily. See Chapter 4, especially pp. 77–80, for testimonies gleaned from my interviews with Pandits conducted in mid-1995 who continued living in the Valley all through the difficult years since 1989–90. It is very curious that the media, particularly in India, chose to almost completely overlook the sizeable number of Pandits who continued living in the Valley even after 1990, and instead focused almost exclusively on the Pandits who migrated. Wakhloo and Wakhloo (1993) in a rambling and melodramatic but nonetheless gripping and moving narrative of their time as hostages of a Kashmiri guerrilla group, relate a fascinating account of the interactions between the women of one such rural Pandit family still residing in the Valley (in whose house the Wakhloos were put up briefly during their captivity) and the armed Muslim militants escorting the hostage couple. This was in September 1991, at the height of the insurgency.

The returning Pandits have almost invariably been greeted with great affection by their Muslim cohorts. There is still, however, a strong undercurrent of resentment towards Pandits among Kashmiri Muslims. As one Muslim civilian (of deeply secular convictions) in the town of Handwara in northern Kashmir said to me in August 1996: 'After all, at least 40,000 people have died here in the last few years. I do not personally know of a single Pandit who has raised his voice in protest against the atrocities committed against fellow-Kashmiris'. Indeed, when I toured Pandit migrant camps in Jammu district in mid-1995 and also spoke with middle-class Pandits living in private accommodations in Jammu city, I found it impossible to get a single one of them to even admit the possibility that inhuman atrocities have been committed against innocent Kashmiri Muslim civilians.

10. This might explain why a relatively small proportion of the ballots had been spoiled outright in the troubled constituencies. With 'supervision' by non-Kashmiri polling officers and gun-wielding soldiers making a mockery of the principle of secret ballot, it is probable that many Kashmiris, who have if nothing else developed a keen survival instinct over the past several years, would be reluctant to take the potentially grave risk of actually spoiling their papers.

11. The UF government's principal adviser on Kashmir policy is reportedly Harkishan Singh Surjeet, an elderly official of the Communist Party of India (Marxist). Surjeet has not long ago expressed views on the crisis in Kashmir which reek of Indian national-chauvinism (see Note 25 to Chapter 3, pp. 53–54). The CPI(M) is a small party in an all-India context and it has no base in any part of Jammu & Kashmir.

12. See Mushtaq (1996).

13. See Thakur (1996a).

14. See Thakur (1996b).

15. See Naqvi (1996).

16. See Ahmad (1996b).

17. For what I fear will turn out to be a prematurely over-enthusiastic endorsement of the assembly elections and an over-optimistic assessment of their potential contribution to the 'normalisation' of Kashmir, see cover story in *India Today* (1996). It is noteworthy that the magazine, which has several examples of fine journalism on the Kashmir crisis to its credit, declared the elections a grand success and the Hurriyat's boycott campaign an ignoble failure merely on the basis of the first phase, held on 7 September, of the four-phase election, which only concluded at the end of September. Of the troubled areas, only Baramulla and Kupwara districts had gone to the polls on 7 September and the turnout in those districts had been uneven and mixed, ranging from fairly brisk in some areas to almost nil in others. Anantnag, Badgam, Pulwama and Doda districts as well as Srinagar had not even voted when the magazine's story was finalised and went to press.

18. Interview to *Asian Age*, reported by UPI (New Delhi), 14 September 1996.

19. Renegade chieftain Koka Parray was declared elected to the state assembly from his home turf of Sonawari, not far from Srinagar. He will be the only 'pro-India militant' gracing the assembly; all of the dozens of other renegade candidates lost. Strong rumours were circulating in Kashmir prior to the elections that Parray had been 'guaranteed' this seat by the Indian security apparatus, possibly with the NC's tacit approval, as a sort of consolation prize to the renegades for their contribution to the 'restoration of democracy'.

20. Interview to *Asian Age*, reported by UPI (New Delhi), 14 September 1996.

21. See Plebiscite Front (1968), vol. 2, p. 13.

22. See Plebiscite Front (1968), vol. 1, pp. 15–16.

23. The full text of the speech can be found in Soz (1995), pp. 121–39.

24. Ibid., p. 128.

25. In late August 1996, a major tragedy occurred during the annual Hindu pilgrimage to the Amarnath caves, situated in the mountainous heights above Pahalgam in the southern region of the Kashmir Valley. A sudden blast of severe blizzards and arctic temperatures hit the area just as the pilgrims were nearing their destination and almost 250 of them, mostly the elderly, died. The crisis was compounded by the inefficiency of the government and its local administrative machinery. However, there was a silver lining to the disaster. To cite one report: 'If it were not for the Muslims of Anantnag [district], the toll would have been much higher. The locals threw open their houses for the starving, shivering and dying pilgrims and offered them everything they could. After the State Government's apathy towards the pilgrims and its helplessness in dealing with the crisis, Anantnag's residents turned out to be angels for them...though these pilgrims are sad at not being able to make it to Amarnath, they are also carrying sweet memories of the hospitality bestowed on them by Kashmiri Muslims in their hour of need' (*The Pioneer*, 28 August 1996, p. 1). Incidentally, many of the pilgrims who owe their lives to local Kashmiri Muslims belong to far-right communal political groups such as the Bajrang Dal, a militant youth affiliate of the RSS and BJP. These groups, based primarily in northern India, were particularly active in organising large delegations of Amarnath pilgrims from amongst their followers, more as a symbolic means of asserting Indian sovereignty over Kashmir than of fulfilling religious beliefs.

26. Pakistani agencies involved in formulating and running Pakistan's Kashmir strategy worked hard not just to build up the HM and other client groups but to actively undermine and weaken the JKLF. The HM also had an important advantage over JKLF within Kashmir. The HM is politically connected to the Jama'at-i-Islami, which has a well-organised, well-funded party apparatus in Jammu & Kashmir. Thus, the HM could rely on the Jama'at's infrastructure in Kashmir, while nothing comparable was available to the JKLF. Nonetheless, the HM never succeeded in winning the kind of spontaneous mass support the JKLF enjoyed in its prime. Once the security forces gradually gained the upper hand over the HM's insurgents, the limitations of the HM's 'gun power' were graphically revealed.

27. Gupta subsequently denied that he had suggested dividing the state. He claimed that he had merely asserted that during the process of conferring 'maximum autonomy' on Jammu & Kashmir, the distinct situations and interests of Jammu and Ladakh would be kept in mind. The BBC, however, stood by its original report.

28. See Butler and Ranney (1978), p. 36.

29. See especially pp. 88–95 (Chapter 4) and pp. 119–24 (Chapter 5).

30. See especially pp. 128–30.

31. See van Beek and Bertelsen (1995), pp. 7–15.

32. Ibid.

33. Ibid.

Appendix
Epitaph to a Human Rights Activist:
In Memory of Jalil Andrabi

As I put the finishing touches to this book, I received a poignant personal reminder of the continuing tragedy in Kashmir. On 27 March 1996, Jalil Andrabi, a prominent Kashmiri human rights attorney who was personally known to me, was found tortured and shot to death in Srinagar, after having gone 'missing' two and a half weeks earlier. According to his wife, who was with him at the time of his 'disappearance', Andrabi was summarily detained while driving home by soldiers from the Rashtriya Rifles or RR (a special counter-insurgency force raised from regular Indian Army units), who were accompanied by a group of 'renegade militants'. As chairman of the Kashmir Commission of Jurists, a local human rights body, and a practising advocate at the Jammu & Kashmir High Court, Srinagar, Andrabi had worked tirelessly during the last few years of his life in an uphill battle to obtain justice, through legal means, for the thousands of victims of summary arrest and incommunicado detention in Kashmir (and for the families of hundreds who 'disappeared' or perished after being taken into custody). In 1994, in response to a petition filed by him, the Jammu & Kashmir High Court issued a judicial order to all security agencies operating in Kashmir, directing that teams of doctors and lawyers be allowed to visit all detention and interrogation centres in the state (the order was almost entirely ignored, however). In 1995, as a result of another petition submitted by Andrabi, the Court ruled that political prisoners from the state should not be transferred to jails outside Jammu & Kashmir.

In his death, Andrabi joined a considerable and growing list of distinguished and politically committed members of the Kashmiri intelligentsia (including doctors, lawyers, professors and human rights activists) who have fallen in the past few years to the bullets of assassins. Unlike most Kashmiris, who die not just brutally but anonymously, his prominence ensured that the manner of his death sparked widespread international outrage and condemnation. The United Nations High Commissioner for Human Rights, the United States Department of State, Amnesty International and Human Rights Watch were among the many organisations which called strongly upon the Government of India to conduct a prompt and genuine investigation into the circumstances of his abduction, torture and murder, and ensure speedy and exemplary punishment for the killers. At the time of writing, no such inquiry has been instituted, and the Indian army has officially denied that any of its members was responsible for Andrabi's detention and/or his subsequent fate. The day after Andrabi's mutilated body was recovered from the Jhelum river, and as thousands demonstrated in the streets of Srinagar and marched in his funeral procession even as a protest strike crippled Kashmir, I contributed the following obituary and comment to Kashmir Times, *the major daily newspaper in Indian-administered Jammu & Kashmir:*

In a place where rule of law is non-existent, and any mention of human rights sounds like a bad joke, a human rights lawyer cannot normally be expected to have much success. It is a tribute to Jalil Ahmed Andrabi's dedication, tenacity and brilliance that he 'succeeded', even in such grim circumstances. Indeed, he was apparently so successful in his dangerous and difficult work that he had to be savagely silenced. In the end, it was his courage that proved to be his undoing—he was a fearless crusader for basic morality and human dignity in a situation where all morality has disappeared, human dignity is incessantly and wantonly violated, and fear is pervasive. Such individuals do not survive for very long in Kashmir, as the tragic fate of Dr Abdul Ahad Guru, Pandit Hriday Nath Wanchoo, and now, Jalil Andrabi (among others) clearly demonstrates.

I met Jalil for the first time in January 1995 in Calcutta, when he came from Srinagar to participate in a major international conference devoted to advancing the cause of peace, common security and regional cooperation in South Asia. He came as a leading member of a delegation from Kashmir, headed by Jammu & Kashmir Liberation Front (JKLF) chairman Mohammad Yasin Malik, which attended that conference. Participants at the conference were greatly impressed by Jalil's eloquence, his strength of conviction, and his eagerness to learn by interacting constantly with other delegates at the conference, who included a galaxy of prominent personalities from India, Pakistan and Bangladesh.

My last memories of Jalil date to just a few months ago, when he came to New York on human rights-related work. Sitting over a long and leisurely lunch in an Indian restaurant, he commended me for taking the trouble, and showing the guts, to travel extensively around the war-torn Kashmir Valley and Doda district (Jammu) during the previous summer [1995], to see and judge the situation for myself. 'Really, it is not safe!', he exclaimed, as he eagerly asked about my assessment of the situation, and predictions for the future. As he disappeared into one of New York's yellow taxis, we made plans to meet up again soon, probably in Srinagar. *Inshallah*, of course.

What I did not tell Jalil then was that he was seriously exaggerating my courage. Being an outsider, I could simply do my work and then conveniently flee the hell that Kashmir has been reduced to, after a few hectic weeks. But the irony is that Jalil Andrabi, despite being a son of Kashmir, probably also had that choice. For a man of his background and qualifications, it would have been easy to migrate to, say, Delhi, establish a flourishing legal practice there, and lead a safe, comfortable life. But Jalil did not want such a life. He made a conscious decision to stand with his people in their hour of crisis, and struggle tirelessly for their rights and dignity in whatever way he could.

He paid for that decision with his life. Thus it came about that the man who has probably done more than anyone else to publicise and campaign against illegal detentions, custodial torture and extrajudicial executions in Kashmir became a victim of precisely that kind of detention, torture and execution. If the manner of Jalil Andrabi's abduction was a violation of basic tenets of legality, the manner of his murder was a violation of the most fundamental norms of human civilisation. What makes this barbaric crime all the more obscene is that Jalil's methods of struggle had been entirely peaceable and lawful. While a strong believer in the idea of an independent Kashmir, Jalil sought to protect his people not through the gun, but by ceaselessly demanding that the Indian state abide by its constitutional obligation to respect the life, liberty and property of its Kashmiri citizens.

That was probably what made him an object of such hatred to those who carefully planned and perpetrated his assassination. It would not do to simply finish the man off with a bullet to the head; he would first have to be degraded and punished for his intolerable defiance. The grotesque spectacle of one of Srinagar's most prominent citizens showing up as a mutilated corpse in the Jhelum would also serve to send a useful message to a population already severely demoralised by years of repression. If such a well-known personality ends up in a burlap sack with his eyes gouged out, what can the typical nameless, faceless Kashmiri civilian expect? The message is crystal-clear—your struggle is futile; give it up and accept the reality. We are all-powerful—you are powerless. Eliminating Andrabi in such dramatic fashion would further be a richly deserved lesson for those troublesome meddlers, Amnesty International and Human Rights Watch, for whom he was an invaluable contact and resource person. So much for 'transparency' on the rights situation in Kashmir.

Jalil has now formally been enshrined in Kashmir's pantheon of 'martyrs' (his tombstone in Id Gah, Srinagar's 'martyrs' graveyard', bears the simple inscription: 'Jalil Andrabi, *Shaheed*'). As his tortured body is laid to rest, his bereaved family and friends can perhaps draw some solace from words once penned by Ali Sharia'ti, the revolutionary socialist thinker of Iran:

> A *shaheed* is the heart of history. The heart gives blood and life to the otherwise dead blood-vessels of the body. Like the heart, a *shaheed* sends his own blood into the half-dead body of the dying society ... which has accepted submission.... The greatest miracle of *shahadat* [martyrdom] is giving to a generation a renewed faith in itself. A *shaheed* is ever-present and everlasting.

Or, for that matter, from the words of Subhas Chandra Bose, the Indian nationalist and freedom fighter Jalil ardently admired:

> What greater solace can there be than the feeling that one has lived and died for a principle? What greater satisfaction can a man possess than the knowledge that his spirit will beget kindred spirits to carry on his unfinished task? What greater consummation can life attain than peaceful self-immolation at the altar of one's cause? ... Hence it is evident that nobody can lose through suffering and sacrifice. If he does lose anything of the earthy, he will gain much more in return by becoming the heir to a life immortal.

Jalil's memory deserves to be remembered and honoured not just by his fellow-Kashmiris, but by all in South Asia and beyond who believe that serious and complex political problems such as the Kashmir question cannot and should not be resolved through brutal violence. As a South Asian, a secularist and a democrat, I feel proud to have had this fellow-South Asian, fellow-secularist and fellow-democrat as my friend.

Bibliography

Abdullah, Farooq. 1985. *My Dismissal.* New Delhi: Vikas.

Ahmad, Mukhtar. 1996a. 'Kashmiris Say Army Forced Them To Vote', UPI (Anantnag), 23 May.,

————. 1996b. 'Kashmiris Go to Polls Amid Violence', UPI (Srinagar), 30 May.

————. 1996c. 'Violence, Terror Mark Kashmir Poll', UPI (Ganderbal), 21 September.

Aina (Srinagar), 1975, 31 May.

Akbar, M. J. 1985. *India, The Siege Within.* Harmondsworth: Penguin.

Alsafa (Srinagar). 1990, 18 October.

Amnesty International. 1992. *Country Report on India.* London (March).

————. 1995. *India: Torture and Deaths in Custody in Jammu & Kashmir* (January).

Anderson, Benedict. 1991 (2nd edn). *Imagined Communities: Reflections on the Origin and Spread of Nationalism.* London: Verso.

Anderson, Lisa. 1991. 'Obligation and Accountability: Islamic Politics in North Africa', *Daedalus* (summer).

Asia Watch. 1991. *Kashmir Under Siege.* New York (May).

Asia Watch—Physicians for Human Rights. 1993a. *Rape in Kashmir: A Crime of War.* New York (June).

————. 1993b. *The Human Rights Crisis in Kashmir: A Pattern of Impunity.* New York (June).

Bachrach, Peter and **Aryeh Botwinick.** 1992. *Power and Empowerment: A Radical Theory of Participatory Democracy.* Philadelphia: Temple University Press.

Barber, Benjamin. 1984. *Strong Democracy: Participatory Politics for a New Age.* Berkeley: University of California Press.

Baweja, Harinder. 1996a. 'Kashmir: A Risky Gamble', *India Today*, 31 May.

Bazaz, Premnath. 1987 (orig. edn 1941). *Inside Kashmir.* Mirpur: Verinag Publishers.

Bharucha, Rustom. 1994. 'On the Border of Fascism: Manufacture of Consent in Roja', *Economic and Political Weekly* (4 June), pp. 1389–95.

Booth, Ken. 1991. 'Security and Emancipation', *Review of International Studies* 17, 4 (October).

Bose, Sumantra. 1995. 'State Crises and Nationalities Conflict in Sri Lanka and Yugoslavia', *Comparative Political Studies* 28, 1 (April), pp. 87–116.

——————. 1996. '"Hindu Nationalism" and the Crisis of the Indian State: A Theoretical Perspective', in Sugata Bose and Ayesha Jalal (eds), *Nationalism, Democracy and Development: State and Politics in India*. Delhi: Oxford University Press.

Bose, Tapan, Dinesh Mohan, Gautam Navlakha and **Sumanta Banerjee.** 1990. *India's Kashmir War.* Committee for Initiative on Kashmir. Delhi.

——————. 1991. *India's Kashmir War.* Reprinted as Appendix II, pp. 224–70, in Asghar Ali Engineer (ed.), *Secular Crown on Fire: The Kashmir Problem.* Delhi: Ajanta Publishers.

BPHRG (British Parliamentary Human Rights Group). 1992. *Kashmir: Heaven on Fire.* London.

Breuilly, John. 1993 (2nd edn). *Nationalism and the State.* Manchester: Manchester University Press.

Bruce, C. G. (Hon. Mrs). 1911. *Kashmir.* London: Adams and Charles Black.

Brussels. 1994. *Round Table Discussion on Kashmir.* European Parliament (February).

Buchanan, Allen. 1991. *Secession: The Morality of Political Divorce from Fort Sumter to Lithuania and Quebec.* Boulder and Oxford: Westview Press.

——————. 1992. 'Self-Determination and the Right to Secede', *Journal of International Affairs* 45, 2 (winter), pp. 347–65.

Burns, John F. 1996. 'India Sends in Troops to Make Sure Kashmiris Cast Votes', *New York Times* (Baramulla), 24 May.

Burton, John. 1984. *Global Conflict: The Domestic Sources of International Crisis.* Brighton: Harvester Wheatsheaf.

Butler, David and Austin Ranney. 1978. 'Theory', in David Butler and Austin Ranney (eds), *Referendums: A Comparative Study of Practice and Theory.* Washington, DC: American Enterprise Institute.

Chopra, Pran. 1994. *India, Pakistan and the Kashmir Tangle.* Delhi: Harper Collins India.

Cohen, Lenard. 1995 (2nd edn). *Broken Bonds: Yugoslavia's Disintegration and Balkan Politics in Transition.* Boulder and Oxford: Westview Press.

Committee for Initiative on Kashmir. 1991. *Kashmir: A Land Ruled by the Gun.* Delhi (December).

Connor, Walker. 1990. 'When is a Nation', *Ethnic and Racial Studies* 13, 1 (January), pp. 92–103.

Dahl, Robert. 1971. *Polyarchy: Participation and Opposition.* New Haven: Yale University Press.

——————. 1982. *Dilemmas of Pluralist Democracy.* New Haven: Yale University Press.

——————. 1989. *Democracy and Its Critics.* New Haven and London: Yale University Press.

——————. 1991. 'Democracy, Majority Rule and Gorbachev's Referendum', *Dissent* (fall), pp. 491–96.

Dasgupta, J. B. 1968. *Jammu and Kashmir.* The Hague: Martinus Nijhoff.

Desmond, Edward. 1995. 'The Insurgency in Kashmir, 1989–91', *Contemporary South Asia* 4, 1 (March).

Engineer, Asghar Ali (ed.). 1991. *Secular Crown on Fire: The Kashmir Problem.* Delhi: Ajanta Publishers.

Fanon, Frantz. 1963. *The Wretched of the Earth.* New York: Grove Press.

Fernandes, George. 1992. 'India's Policies in Kashmir: An Assessment and Discourse', in Raju Thomas (ed.), *Perspectives on Kashmir.* Boulder: Westview Press.

Foucault, Michel. 1986. 'Disciplinary Power and Subjection', in Steven Lukes (ed.), *Power.* New York: New York University Press.

Fox, Richard. 1989. *Gandhian Utopia: Experiments with Culture.* Boston: Beacon Press.

Frontline (Madras). 1990. 'The Fleeing Pandits', 29 September.

Gellner, Ernest. 1983. *Nations and Nationalism.* Oxford: Basil Blackwell.

Giddens, Anthony. 1985. *The Nation-State and Violence: Part Two of a Contemporary Critique of Historical Materialism.* Berkeley: University of California Press.

GOI (Government of India). 1981. Census of 1981.

Golwalkar, Madhav Sadashiv. 1968. *Bunch of Thoughts.* Bangalore: Vikram Prakashan.

Gopal, Sarvapalli. 1979. *Jawaharlal Nehru, Vol. 2, 1947–56.* Oxford: Oxford University Press.

Gottlieb, Gidon. 1993. *Nation Against State: A New Approach to Ethnic Conflict and the Decline of Sovereignty.* New York: Council on Foreign Relations Press.

Gutmann, Amy (ed.). 1994. *Multiculturalism: Examining the Politics of Recognition.* Princeton: Princeton University Press.

Hasan, Saqina, Primila Lewis, Nandita Haksar and **Suhasini Mulay.** 1990. *Kashmir Imprisoned.* Delhi (July).

Hayes, L. D. 1971. *The Impact of U.S. Foreign Policy on the Kashmir Conflict.* Tucson: University of Arizona Press.

HT (*Hindustan Times*, New Delhi). 1990, 2 March.

Huntington, Samuel. 1993. 'The Clash of Civilisations?', *Foreign Affairs* (summer), pp. 22–49.

IA (*India Abroad*, New York). 1994a, 25 February.

————. 1994b, 18 March.

————. 1994c, 22 April.

IKS (Institute of Kashmir Studies). 1993. *Catch and Kill.* Srinagar.

ISF (*In Search of Freedom, Vol. 5*). 1992. Muzaffarabad: Press and Publications Department, Prime Minister's Secretariat.

IT (*India Today*). 1986a, 15 November.

————. 1986b, 30 November.

————. 1987a, 31 March.

————. 1987b, 15 April.

————. 1989, 'Kashmir: Valley of Tears', 31 May.

————. 1990a, 31 January.

————. 1990b, 'The Other Kashmir', 31 March.

————. 1990c, 30 April.

————. 1991, 15 September.

————. 1992a, 29 February.

————. 1992b, 15 March.

IT (*India Today*). 1993a, 28 February.

——————. 1993b, 31 May.

——————. 1994, 15 February.

——————. 1995, 15 October.

——————. 1996, 'Kashmir: A New Beginning', 30 September.

IW (*India Week*, Delhi). 1990, 24 August.

IWI (*The Illustrated Weekly of India*), 1992, 10–16 October.

Jackson, Robert and Carl Rosberg. 1982. 'Why Africa's Weak States Persist: The Juridical and Empirical in Statehood', *World Politics* (October), pp. 1–24.

Jackson, Robert. 1990. *Quasi-States: Sovereignty, International Relations and the Third World.* Cambridge: Cambridge University Press.

Jain, R. K. (ed.). 1979. *Soviet–South Asian Relations 1947–78, Vol. 1.* Atlantic Highlands: Humanities Press.

Jan, Tarik and Ghulam Sarwar (eds). 1990. *Kashmir Problem: Challenge and Response.* Islamabad: Institute of Policy Studies.

Jung, Courtney and Ian Shapiro. 1995. 'South Africa's Negotiated Transition: Democracy, Opposition and the New Constitutional Order', *Politics and Society* 23, 3 (September).

Kadian, Rajesh 1992. *The Kashmir Tangle: Issues and Options.* New Delhi and Bombay: Vision Books.

Kagal, Ayesha. 1990. 'Accidental Terrorists', *The Times of India*, 29 April.

Kaldor, Mary 1990. *The Imaginary War: Understanding the East–West Conflict.* Oxford: Basil Blackwell.

Kannabiran, K. G. 1991. 'Abuses of Article 370', in Asghar Ali Engineer (ed.), *Secular Crown on Fire: The Kashmir Problem.* Delhi: Ajanta Publications.

KT (*Kashmir Times*, Jammu). 1990. 1 March.

——————. 1993, 19 May.

Kateb, George. 1984. 'On the Legitimation Crisis', in William Connolly (ed.), *Legitimacy and the State.* New York: New York University Press.

Kaul, Gwashanath. 1968 (8th edn, first pub. 1924). *Kashmir Then and Now.* Cited in M. J. Akbar. 1985. *India, The Siege Within: Challenges to a Nation's Unity.* Harmondsworth: Penguin.

Kaul K. L. and M. K. Teng. 1992. 'Human Rights Violations of Kashmiri Hindus', in Raju Thomas (ed.), *Perspectives on Kashmir.* Boulder: Westview Press.

Khan, Amanullah. 1970. *Free Kashmir.* Karachi: Central Printing Press.

——————. 1991. 'India v/s India'. Muzaffarabad, Srinagar and Rawalpindi: JKLF.

Khan, Muhammad Ishaq. 1989. 'The Hazratbal Shrine', in Christian Troll (ed.), *Muslim Shrines in India.* Delhi: Oxford University Press.

——————. 1994. *Kashmir's Transition to Islam: The Role of Muslim Rishis.* Delhi: Manohar.

Kishwar, Madhu. 1994. 'Voices from Kashmir', *Manushi* 83 (July–August), pp. 6–21.

Krishnan, Murali. 1996. 'Pro-Pakistan Militants Somersault into Government's Lap', *The Telegraph* (Calcutta), 22 May.

Kymlicka, Will. 1989. *Liberalism, Community and Culture.* Oxford: Oxford University Press.

Kymlicka, Will. 1995a. *Multicultural Citizenship: A Liberal Theory of Minority Rights*. Oxford: Oxford University Press.
————. 1995b. (ed.). *The Rights of Minority Cultures*. Oxford: Oxford University Press.
Kymlicka, Will and Wayne Norman. 1995. 'The Return of the Citizen: A Survey of Recent Work on Citizenship Theory', in Ronald Beiner (ed.), *Theorising Citizenship*. Albany: State University of New York Press.
Ladjensky, Wolf. 1977. 'Land Reform: Observations in Kashmir', in L. J. Walinsky (ed.), *Agrarian Reforms as Unfinished Business*. Oxford: Oxford University Press.
Lamb, Alastair. 1966. *Crisis in Kashmir, 1947 to 1966*. London: Routledge and Kegan Paul.
Lapidoth, Ruth. 1992. 'Sovereignty in Transition', *Journal of International Affairs* 45, 2 (winter), pp. 325–46.
Lenin, V. I. 1970. 'The Right of Nations to Self-Determination', in *Questions of National Policy and Proletarian Internationalism*. Moscow: Progress Publishers.
Linz, Juan. 1978. *The Breakdown of Democratic Regimes: Crisis, Breakdown and Reequilibration*. Baltimore and London: Johns Hopkins University Press.
Madan T. N. 1993. 'Whither Indian Secularism?' *Modern Asian Studies* 27, 3 (July).
Malik, Gauri Bazaz. 1991. 'Democracy and Kashmir Problem', in Asghar Ali Engineer (ed.), *Secular Crown on Fire: The Kashmir Problem*. Delhi: Ajanta Publishers.
Margalit, Avishai and Joseph Raz 1990. 'National Self-Determination', *Journal of Philosophy* (September), pp. 439–61.
Minhas A. R. and Mustahsan Aqil. 1991. *Kashmir: Cry Freedom*. Mirpur: Kashmir Record and Research Cell.
Mojumdar, Aunohita. 1996a. 'Kashmir's Version of War and Peace: White Terror Strikes Pampore, Baramulla Returns to Normal', *The Statesman*, 16 March.
————. 1996b. 'One Gun Too Many for the Valley's Voters', *The Statesman*, 19 May.
Morgenthau, Hans. 1985 (6th edn). *Politics Among Nations: The Struggle for Power and Peace*. New York: Knopf.
Mostov, Julie. 1994. 'Democracy and the Politics of National Identity', *Studies in East European Thought* 46: 1, 2 (June), pp. 9–31.
Mushtaq, Sheikh. 1996. 'Hope Meets Cynicism as Kashmiris Vote for Peace', Reuters (Banihal), 30 September.
Nag, Arindam. 1996a. 'Police Break Up Anti-Election Crowds in Kashmir', Reuters (Srinagar), 23 May.
————. 1996b. 'At least 30 injured in Kashmir Election Violence', Reuters (Srinagar), 30 May.
Naqvi, Javed. 1996. 'Kashmir Poll Violence Kills One, Twenty-Four Wounded', Reuters (Srinagar), 21 September.
Narayan, Jayaprakash. 1964. 'Our Great Opportunity in Kashmir', *The Hindustan Times*, 20 April. Reprinted as Appendix IV in A. G. Noorani. 1964. *The Kashmir Question*. Bombay: Manaktalas.

Newberg, Paula, R. 1995. *Double Betrayal: Repression and Insurgency in Kashmir.* Washington D.C.: Carnegie Endowment for International Peace.

Niranjana, Tejaswini. 1994. 'Integrating Whose Nation? Tourists and Terrorists in Roja', *Economic and Political Weekly* (15 January), pp. 79–82.

Noorani, A. G. 1964. *The Kashmir Question.* Bombay: Manaktalas.

—————. 1992. 'The Betrayal of Kashmir: Pakistan's Duplicity and India's Complicity', in Raju Thomas (ed.), *Perspectives on Kashmir.* Boulder: Westview Press.

—————. 1994. 'The Tortured and the Damned: Human Rights in Kashmir', *Frontline*, 28 January, pp. 44–48.

O' Molley. 1941. *Modern India and the West.* Cited in Balraj Puri. 1995.

Pasha, Mustafa Kamal. 1992. 'Beyond the Two-Nation Divide: Kashmir and Resurgent Islam', in Raju Thomas (ed.), *Perspectives on Kashmir,* pp. 369–87. Boulder: Westview Press.

Phillips, Anne. 1993. *Democracy and Difference.* University Park: Pennsylvania State University Press.

Plebiscite Front. 1968. *Speeches and Interviews of Sher-i-Kashmir Sheikh Mohammad Abdullah, Vols. 1 and 2.* Srinagar: Plebiscite Front.

PUCL (People's Union for Civil Liberties). 1991. *Report on the Kashmir Situation.* 1990. Reproduced in Asghar Ali Engineer (ed.), *Secular Crown on Fire: The Kashmir Problem.* Delhi: Ajanta Publishers.

—————. 1993. Report of May 1993.

PUDR (People's Union for Democratic Rights). 1993. *Lawless Roads: A Report on TADA, 1985–93.* Delhi (September).

Puri, Balraj. 1981. *Jammu & Kashmir: Triumph and Tragedy of Indian Federalisation.* Delhi: Sterling Publishers.

—————. 1983. *Simmering Volcano: Study of Jammu's Relations with Kashmir.* Delhi: Sterling Publishers.

—————. 1993. *Kashmir: Towards Insurgency (Tracts for the Times 4).* Delhi: Orient Longman.

—————. 1995. '*Kashmiriyat*: The Vitality of Kashmiri Identity', *Contemporary South Asia* 4, 1 (March).

Przeworski, Adam, et al. 1995. *Sustainable Democracy.* Cambridge: Cambridge University Press.

Qasim, Syed Mir. 1992. *My Life and Times.* Delhi: Allied Publishers.

Rettie, John and **Ghulam Nabi Khayal.** 1994. 'Kashmiris Round on Pro-Pakistan Groups', *The Guardian* (London), 22 June, p. 11.

Reus-Smit, Christian. 1992. 'Realist and Resistance Utopias: Community, Security and Political Action in the New Europe', *Millennium: Journal of International Studies* 21, 1.

Rizvi, Gowher. 1993. *South Asia in a Changing International Order.* New Delhi: Sage.

Rose, Leo. 1992. 'The Politics of Azad Kashmir', in Raju Thomas (ed.), *Perspectives on Kashmir.* Boulder: Westview Press.

RSS (Rashtriya Swayamsevak Sangh). 1991. *Genocide of Hindus in Kashmir.* Delhi: Suruchi Prakashan.

Said, Edward. 1981. *Covering Islam: How the Media and Experts Determine How We See the Rest of the World.* New York: Pantheon Books.

Said, Edward. 1988. 'The Essential Terrorist', in Edward Said and Christopher Hitchens (eds), *Blaming the Victims: Spurious Scholarship and the Palestinian Question*. London.

Samad, Yunas. 1995. 'Kashmir and the Imagining of Pakistan', *Contemporary South Asia* 4, 1 (March), pp. 65–77.

Savarkar, Vinayak Damodar. 1984. *Hindu Rashtra Darshan*. Bombay: Veer Savarkar Prakashan.

Schmitter, Philippe and **Terry Karl.** 1993. 'What Democracy Is... and Is Not', in L. Diamond and M. Plattnet (eds), *The Global Resurgence of Democracy*. Baltimore and London: Johns Hopkins University Press.

Schumpeter, Joseph. 1950 (3rd edn). *Capitalism, Socialism and Democracy*. New York: Harper and Row.

Shah, Mehtab Ali. 1995. 'The Kashmir Problem: A View From the Four Provinces of Pakistan', *Contemporary South Asia* 4, 1 (March), pp. 103–12.

Sharia'ti, Ali. 1982. 'Return to the Self', in J. Donohue and J. Esposito (eds), *Islam in Transition: Muslim Perspectives*. New York and Oxford: Oxford University Press.

Singh, Tavleen. 1995. *Kashmir: A Tragedy of Errors*. Delhi: Viking.

Singh, V. B. 1994. *Data Handbook on Lok Sabha Elections: Vol. 2*. New Delhi, Thousand Oaks and London: Sage Publications.

Soz, Saifuddin (ed.). 1995. *Why Autonomy in Kashmir?* New Delhi: Indian Centre for Asian Studies.

Stein M. A. (ed. and trans.). 1991 (orig. edn 1900). *Kalhana's Rajatarangini: A Chronicle of the Kings of Kashmir*. Mirpur: Verinag Publishers.

Spruyt, Hendrik. 1994. *The Sovereign State and its Competitors*. Princeton: Princeton University Press.

Sufi, G. M. D. *Kashmir*. 1974 edn, p. 696. Cited in Balraj Puri. 1995. 'Kashmiriyat: The Vitality of Kashmiri Identity', *Contemporary South Asia* 4, 1 (March), p. 61.

Sunday (Calcutta). 1994, 23–29 January, pp. 70–74.

Tahir, Afzal Khan. 1993. 'Human Rights Violations in Pakistan-Occupied Kashmir'. A Memorandum of JKPNP (15 September), p. 2.

Tamir, Yael. 1993. *Liberal Nationalism*. Princeton: Princeton University Press.

Taylor, Charles. 1991. 'Shared and Divergent Values', in R. Watts and D. Brown (eds), *Options for a New Canada*, pp. 53–76. Toronto: University of Toronto Press.

————. 1992. *Multiculturism and the Politics of Recognition*. Princeton: Princeton University Press.

TH (The Hindu, Madras). 1990, 2 October.

TH (The Hindu, international edn). 1993, 20 November.

Thakur, Sankarshan. 1996a. 'Kashmir at the Crossroads: Government Feeds Fear in Valley', *The Telegraph*, 16 September.

————. 1996b. 'Kashmir at the Crossroads: Only Guns, No Roses in Bloom Yet', *The Telegraph*, 15 September.

Thorner, Daniel. 1976 (2nd edn). *The Agrarian Prospect in India: Five Lectures Delivered in 1955 at the Delhi School of Economics*. Bombay: Allied Publishers.

Tilly, Charles. 1985. 'War-Making and State-Making as Organised Crime', in Evans, Rueschemeyer and Skocpol (eds), *Bringing the State Back In.* Cambridge: Cambridge University Press.

―――――. 1994. 'States and Nationalism in Europe, 1492–1992', *Theory and Society* 23, 1 (February).

TOI (The Times of India) 1990a, 23 April.

―――――. 1990b, 6 May.

Tremblay, Reeta C. 1992. 'Jammu: Autonomy Within Autonomous Kashmir?', in Raju Thomas (ed.), *Perspectives on Kashmir.* Boulder: Westview Press.

TS (The Statesman, Calcutta). 1991, 18 July.

―――――. 1994, 5–6 April.

―――――. 1995a, 23 January.

―――――. 1995b, 4 March.

―――――. 1996, 16 March.

TT (The Telegraph, Calcutta). 1990. 'Long Road From Home', 1 April.

―――――. 1996a, 16 March.

―――――. 1996b, 22 May.

USDS (United States Department of State). 1992. *Country Report on Human Rights Conditions in India.* Washington, DC.

―――――. 1993. *Country Report on Human Rights Conditions in India.* Washington, DC.

Vanaik, Achin. 1990a. *The Painful Transition: Bourgeois Democracy in India.* London: Verso.

―――――. 1990b. 'The Kashmir Problem', *The Times of India*, 18 April.

Van Beek, Martijn and Kristoffer Brix Bertelsen. 1995. 'Ladakh: "Independence" is not Enough', *HIMAL* 8, 2, pp. 7–15.

Varadarajan, Patanjali. 1993. *Kashmir: A People Terrorised.* Federation Internationale des Ligues des Droits de L'Homme. Paris: La FIDH (August).

Wakhloo, Khemlata. 1992. *Kashmir: Behind the White Curtain, 1972–91.* Delhi: Konark Publishers.

Wakhloo, Khemlata and O. N. Wakhloo. 1993. *Kidnapped: 45 Days with Militants in Kashmir.* Delhi: Konark Publishers.

Whelan, Frederick. 1983. 'Prologue: Democratic Theory and the Boundary Problem', in J. Roland Pennock and John Chapman (eds), *Liberal Democracy: NOMOS* XXV, pp. 13–47. New York and London: New York University Press.

Wirsing, Robert 1994. *India, Pakistan and the Kashmir Dispute: On Regional Conflict and its Resolution.* New York: St. Martin's Press.

Woodward, Susan. 1995. *Balkan Tragedy: Chaos and Dissolution After the Cold War.* Washington, DC: Brookings Institution.

Yasmeen, Samina. 1992. 'The China Factor in the Kashmir Issue', in Raju Thomas (ed.), *Perspectives on Kashmir.* Boulder: Westview Press.

Young, Crawford. 1992. 'National and Colonial Questions and Marxism', in Alexander Motyl (ed.), *Thinking Theoretically About Soviet Nationalities: History and Comparison in the Study of the USSR.* New York: Columbia University Press.

Young, Iris Marion. 1989. 'Polity and Group Difference: A Critique of the Ideal of Universal Citizenship', *Ethics* 99 (January), pp. 250–74.

―――――. 1990. *Justice and the Politics of Difference.* Princeton: Princeton University Press.

Index